Handgun Bullet Stopping Power

Beyond the Hyperbole of Cartridge Advocacy

by
George B. Bredsten

CCB Publishing
British Columbia, Canada

Handgun Bullet Stopping Power: Beyond the Hyperbole of Cartridge Advocacy

Copyright ©2008 by George B. Bredsten
ISBN-13   978-1-926585-03-1
First Edition

Library and Archives Canada Cataloguing in Publication

Bredsten, George B., 1935-
Handgun Bullet Stopping Power: Beyond the hyperbole of cartridge advocacy /
written by George B. Bredsten.
Includes bibliographical references.
ISBN 978-1-926585-03-1
1. Pistols. 2. Ballistics. 3. Bullets. 4. Cartridges. I. Title.
TS538.B74 2008   623'.51   C2008-906124-1

United States Copyright Office Registration #TXu 1-304-389

Extreme care has been taken to ensure that all information presented in this book is accurate and up to date at the time of publishing. Neither the author nor the publisher can be held responsible for any errors or omissions. Additionally, neither is any liability assumed for damages resulting from the use of the information contained herein.

All rights reserved. No part of this publication may be reproduced, stored in a retrieval system or transmitted in any form or by any means, electronic, mechanical, photocopying, recording or otherwise without the express written permission of the publisher. Printed in the United States of America and the United Kingdom.

Publisher: CCB Publishing
             British Columbia, Canada
             www.ccbpublishing.com

This book is dedicated to those Law Enforcement officers who put their life on the line to protect and preserve society.

Contents

Acknowledgments 1

Exordium 3

Chapter I: *Effective Stopping Power (ESP)* 12

Chapter II: *Physiological Response* 19

Chapter III: *Psychological Response* 27

Chapter IV: *Time-Frame Parameter* 42

Chapter V: *Bullet Efficacy* 49

Chapter VI: *Bullet Performance Characteristics* 63

Chapter VII: *Stopping Power Concepts/Formulae* 75

Chapter VIII: *Concepts/Formulae Comparison Graphs* 131

Chapter IX: *Recapitulation/Conclusion* 150

Appendix A: *Penetration Potential* 157

Appendix B to F: *Incapacitation Due to Hemorrhage (Blood Loss)* 163

Appendix G: *Hatcher's Relative Stopping Power Values (Various Handgun Loads)* 183

Bibliography 191

About the Author 205

ACKNOWLEDGMENTS

This opuscule is a product of avocational/vocational experience, interest and knowledge plus the extremely important input (comments, criticism, remarks and suggestions) of many persons. These included local, state and federal law enforcement officers, law enforcement firearms instructors, ballistics consultants/engineers/technicians, medical personnel (physicians, nurses, emergency medical technicians and paramedics) and employees/staff of both small and large ammunition companies.

Also considered was the input of literally hundreds of law enforcement students attending the Federal Law Enforcement Training Center/Firearms Division (FLETC/FAD). The experiences of these students varied from none to extensive, as would be reflected by students who ranged from new recruits, journeymen officers attending in-service training, officers receiving advanced training (e.g., Law Enforcement Rifle Program or the Precision Rifle and Observer Program), as well as officers who made or were in the process of making an occupation change from one law enforcement agency to another.

While name recognition of all individuals (who gave of their time to participate in surveys, discuss [pro and con] bullet-stopping power in general and effective bullet-stopping power in particular) is prohibited by space constraints – to all who were involved, you have my sincere appreciation and thanks.

However, there are those who participated/assisted to a degree that printed name recognition is warranted. Their participation (whether input was in agreement or disagreement) helped the author maintain an objective approach that may not have otherwise occurred. With the person's name is the employing agency, company or in the case of Kelly Bredsten, the author's editor – at or during the time of the various discussions (vocal and/or written). Since that time, some individuals have been promoted, some have made and others are considering making an occupation change, a few have retired and most regrettably two persons have passed away. The failure to include the name or names of other individuals who are in this group would have been inadvertent and you have my apology for any omissions.

NAME and AGENCY/COMPANY
Kelly BREDSTEN – Editor
Kevin BROPHY – BOP
Charlie BROWN – BOP
Steve BRYANT – USMS Armorer
Bob BURNETT – FLETC/FAD
Raymond BUSKEY – USBP

Warren BUTTLER –	FLETC/FAD
Wayne CHAPPEL –	FLETC/FAD
Harvey COOPER –	*FLETC/FAD*
James COPULOS –	USCS, Canine Enforcement
Bob DINNDORF –	USCP
Tim DOBBS –	USCS
Martin FACKLER, M.D. –	Col. US Army (Ret.)
Dan FAIR –	USMS
Tim FISCHER –	USBP
Mark FRITTS –	FLETC/FAD
Wayne GOTKE –	USCS
Barry HAIGHT –	Fairbanks, AK FD/EMT (Ret)
John HILLEGASS –	FLETC/FAD
John HUGGINS –	BOP
John G. JACOBS –	*USBP*
Bill JONES –	FLETC/FAD
Ivan KALISTER –	BATF (Ret.)
Michael McINNIS –	Winchester LE Rep
Larry McINTOSH –	FLETC/FAD
Donald PERRYMAN –	USCS
Wade PLUCKER –	Federal LE Rep
Dale OTTERBACHER –	NCIS
Jack RINNIER –	FLETC/FAD
Gary ROCKLAGE –	NPS
Billie SAVELL –	FLETC/FAD Armorer
Dona SHOWALTER –	FLETC/FAD
Andy SMOTZER –	FLETC/FAD
Darrell (Ranger) WALKER –	FLETC/FAD

To Charles NESTER, Jr. – Senior Instructor FLETC/FAD and Bob ROGERS – Senior Agent USBP (now ICE) – both of whom have the inexplicable talent to cogently discuss what first appears to be ineffable subjects and to do so in a manner that is readily understood – your involvement in various ballistics endeavors was/is invaluable and will continue to be sought. A very special thanks and appreciation are extended to James LANIER, Chief FLETC/FAD, Jim DISKIN, Branch Chief FLECT/FAD and Bill McDONALD, Branch Chief FLETC/FAD who were extremely helpful to the author by authorizing the acquisition and use of essential equipment together with the necessary time to conduct numerous ballistics tests.

EXORDIUM

OVERVIEW

The study of Effective Stopping Power (ESP) and how it can be best achieved is both an interesting and intriguing subject. As is the case with other controversial subjects, there can be augmenting, complimenting, conflicting and diametric views regarding the methods and the technologies to use in achieving the most consistent ESP. Depending upon the method of study, ESP can be defined and described using esoteric and/or layman language but in general, there are three basic methods that can be used to study and evaluate ESP.

The first method is based on *theoretics* and involves the theorist who is primarily concerned with reasoned speculation. An example of reasoned speculation is found in the statement: "In scientific terms, the stopping power of a bullet is the amount of kinetic energy the impacting bullet transfers to the target."[1] To some, this may appear to be a statement of fact, but as it pertains to stopping a lethal threat action, it is actually a hypothesis and for a number of reasons cannot be scientifically proven. One important reason is the complete lack of any experimental proof as is required before it can be even tentatively accepted as scientifically valid:

> All branches of science, pure and applied, agree in demanding experimental proof and test and, where possible, quantitative measurements must replace qualitative observations.[2]

Another important reason the statement remains a hypothesis is that no currently available method exists that can isolate and then evaluate (test) some of the other factors that affect the type (effective or ineffective) of achieved stopping power. For example, not considered are the possible differences and/or the degree of differences in the psychological mindset of the shootee.

The second method is based on *pragmatism* and involves the pragmatist who is primarily interested in achieved results. Whenever a person has been involved in or believes he will soon become involved in a lethal threat action, the pragmatic choice (whenever possible) is usually selected in favor of what a theoretical consideration might have otherwise indicated.

For example, during the so-called Philippine Insurrection, in an official report dated 22 October 1902 Captain M. W. Rowell (stationed at Garona, Tarlac, the Philippine Islands), wrote:

> During the recent campaign (savage warfare) in Samar I carried whenever in the brush with a detachment a single action Colt .45, this through preference to either the Luger automatic or the Colt double action .38, although each of the latter were available. This because it fits the hand and because I had greater confidence in its being safe, sure and a **hard hitter** [emphasis added] at close range while I believed it sufficiently rapid and to carry enough cartridges for all practical purposes in case the boloman arose from the ground and tried a rush.[3]

A relatively recent example of pragmatic decisions occurred in Afghanistan:

> Its ball round (9mm Luger) has proven to be worse than the 38 Colt pistol slug used by the U.S. Army in the Philippines until it was retired almost a century ago in favor of the 45 ACP M1911 – fielded to stop Moros, who ironically were also Islamic fanatics . . . but the only Rangers who use the Beretta – even as backup – are those who can't afford to buy their own firearms, and they and the rest of these elite fighters unanimously agree that they can't trust this fragile, unreliable sidearm. . . .[4]

Both the semiautomatic pistol (30 Luger) and the double action revolver (38 Colt) were considered to be technological improvements over the single action revolver (45 Colt). This may or may not have been true, but regarding stopping power, there were few then and even fewer now who would opine the 30 Luger, the 38 Colt or the 9mm Luger to be as effective a fight stopper as the 45 Colt.

Stated somewhat differently: ". . . battle-wise veterans . . . were not interested in proving or disproving abstract theories, nor were they interested in developing a cult of personality. They were interested in what worked."[5]

The third method uses a meld of pragmatism and theoretics, and is called (to-coin-two-words) "pragtheoretics" and involves the "pragtheorist" whose primary task is to attempt to objectively reconcile and/or resolve differences (perceived or real) of opinions maintained by pragmatists and theorists. The author uses the third method (pragtheoretics) because, in general a more inclusive abstract study, analysis and evaluation can be made while, at the same time an adequate number of factual specifics pertaining to the premise under consideration can be included.

The use of this method also helps prevent or at least reduce the possibility of a misunderstanding due to what some readers might otherwise consider to be ambiguous or equivocated wording.

EFFECTIVE STOPPING POWER (ESP)

Because there is not one particular definition of ESP that is generally recognized and accepted as *the* standard definition, there can be more than one acceptable definition. But to be acceptable and valid, a definition should be lucid and unambiguous. As a result, a definition should NOT include, as a component of the definition, any extraneous stipulations.

Examples of extraneous stipulations include nonsensical shootee responses, an arbitrary number of foot pounds of energy deposit/transfer, an exaggerated importance of the temporary wound cavitation caused by a handgun bullet and the alleged significance of distant (remote) neural shock. Some of these extraneous stipulations may, at first, appear to be relevant or at least innocuous, but are actually fallacious and inane expostulations. When extraneous stipulations are included as part of a definition, the consequences can be erroneous evaluations and insipient conclusions. If extraneous stipulations ALSO include the use of ambiguous words and/or terms, the risk of duplicity exacerbates and already exasperating situation. A definition of ESP, unencumbered by extraneous stipulations, is also much more difficult to misconstrue.

Because extraneous stipulations almost invariably include qualifying modifiers that tend to be absurd, confusing, ludicrous and/or vague, some of the problems resulting from the use of extraneous stipulations are addressed and analyzed in detail in chapter one.

In an effort to be lucid, unambiguous and to avoid the use of extraneous stipulations, Effective Stopping Power (ESP) is defined:

> THE ABILITY OF A BULLET TO IMMEDIATELY STOP A LETHAL THREAT ACTION THAT, IF NOT IMMEDIATELY STOPPED, <u>COULD</u> RESULT IN THE DEATH OR SERIOUS BODILY INJURY TO THE PERSON AT RISK.[6]

The word "could" is underlined because it is important to understand even if a lethal threat action is completed; the results may vary from being unsuccessful to successful – ranging from no physical injury, minor bodily injury, serious bodily injury to the death of the person at risk.

There are four core factors that contribute to the reality of any "stopping" phenomenon within the term ESP. These are the Physiological Response, the Psychological Response, the Time-Frame Parameter and the Bullet Efficacy.

PHYSIOLOGICAL RESPONSE

This refers to anatomical damage or dysfunction and the shootee's ability or inability to physically commit a lethal threat action after receiving a nonfatal or a fatal gunshot wound. When the variations of the physiological responses and the deadly force options are considered, there are four categories of possible behavior. These are:

1. The **Nonfatal** gunshot wound and the **Inability** to commit deadly force.
2. The **Fatal** gunshot wound and the **Inability** to commit deadly force.
3. The **Nonfatal** gunshot wound and the **Ability** to commit deadly force.
4. The **Fatal** gunshot wound and the **Ability** to commit deadly force.

PSYCHOLOGICAL RESPONSE

This refers to the mental condition or mindset of the individual at the instant of bullet impact. When the psychological options are considered, there are three basic categories of mental condition or mindset. These are:

1. **Neutral** – Unaware/unconcerned/unprepared.
2. **Angry** (enraged) – Rational destructive violence.
3. **Berserk** (maniacal/stoical) – Irrational destructive violence.

When these three mindset options are considered with the physiological response options that include the ability to commit deadly force, there are six categories of possible behavior. These are:

1. **Nonfatal** gunshot wound/**Ability** to commit deadly force – **Neutral**.
2. **Nonfatal** gunshot wound/**Ability** to commit deadly force – **Angry**.
3. **Nonfatal** gunshot wound/**Ability** to commit deadly force – **Berserk**.
4. **Fatal** gunshot wound/**Ability** to commit deadly force – **Neutral**.
5. **Fatal** gunshot wound/**Ability** to commit deadly force – **Angry**.
6. **Fatal** gunshot wound/**Ability** to commit deadly force – **Berserk**.

TIME-FRAME PARAMETER

The time-frame parameter is the period of time that begins the instant deadly force action is begun and stops the instant deadly force action ceases. While other factors (e.g., visibility and movement of the combatants) might be included by some as part of the components of the time-frame parameter, they are more appropriately considered to be subjects of strategy or tactics. Whereas, <u>duration</u>, <u>increased risk</u> and <u>reduced bullet efficacy</u> have a direct bearing on the time-frame as defined above.

BULLET EFFICACY

This refers to how and to what degree the bullet from a particular cartridge (calibre, design, impact velocity and weight) can be expected to cause or bring about ESP. As with ESP, there can be more than one acceptable definition of Bullet Efficacy. The following definition of Bullet Efficacy is to be applied/understood whenever it is mentioned or referred to within this text:

> A numerical value indicating the relative position of a bullet's effectiveness when compared with other bullets as it pertains to the **probability** of achieving ESP.

"Probability" is in bold because it emphasizes that all such numerical values are and can only be based on reasoned speculation. This is true regardless of who is the source. Consequently, it is only through the application of "Informal Logic" that unbiased conclusions can be determined as to which values are more reliable indicators of probable ESP.

DETERMINANTS

While there can be minor differences in the wording, any acceptable definition of bullet efficacy will make reference to a grading or ranking of handgun cartridges relative to their *probability* of achieving ESP. However, there are significant differences of opinions regarding just how bullet efficacy can be best determined. These differences of opinions seldom are about which determinants should be included or how they should be defined. Instead, and quite often there is a divergence of opinions about the significance and the comparative or relative importance of each determinant as it affects stopping power.

The primary determinants of bullet efficacy are Calibre (Diameter), Cross Sectional Area, Design, Meplat, Penetration, Shape, Velocity and Weight. What then are the individual as well as the combined affects of these determinants relative to ESP? The answer depends upon how and by whom the comparative importance of each determinant is established and then how each of the determinants is described (quantified). Consequently, it is the manner and the extent of the application of each determinant that affects the actual achieved ESP. The variables in the manner and the extent of these applications are what make it virtually impossible to categorically claim one cartridge (load) can be relied upon to produce results always better OR always worse than another cartridge (load).

These determinants are addressed in detail in chapter five and then are subsequently described, analyzed and evaluated as to their importance or significance in each of the considered stopping power concepts and/or formulae.

BULLET PERFORMANCE CHARACTERISTIC(s)

The application (utilization) of the determinants can be best explained by identifying, describing and quantifying by example(s) specific bullet performance characteristics (BPC). These BPC include, but are not necessarily limited to Energy, Momentum, Anatomical Disruption, Hemorrhage and Neural Dysfunction. Each BPC is described as if it exists independently. Then using each determinant and BPC, an explanation is given regarding the interrelationship and interaction of these determinants as they influence the specifics of the various stopping power concepts and/or formulae.

STOPPING POWER CONCEPTS/FORMULAE

There are numerous concepts and/or formulae that purport to correctly explain and then predict the relative killing, **stopping** and/or wounding power of various cartridges (loads). In this work, the subjects of killing and wounding power are ancillary to the main subject of stopping power. If or when appropriate, both killing and wounding power considerations may be included in order to have an elucidatory affect regarding the relationship of bullet efficacy as it pertains to achieving Effective Stopping Power. A detailed description of a number of concepts and/or formulae is given (most of which contain several examples), with comments that elaborate upon the merits of each concept and/or formula. In chapter nine a recapitulation is presented followed by the author's conclusions regarding these concepts/formulae.

Some of the stopping power concepts and/or formulae described and evaluated are: Jeff Cooper's Short Form Relative Stopping Power, Vincent J.M. DiMaio's Energy Loss, Steven Fuller's Fuller Index Technique, Julian S. Hatcher's Relative Stopping Power, Elmer Keith's Pounds Feet, Ed Matunas' Power Index Ratio, Carroll Peters' Impulse Ratio, Veral Smith's Terminal Sectional Density and Terminal Displacement Velocity, Chuck Taylor's Modified Short Form Relative Stopping Power, John Taylor's Knock Out, The United States Department of Justice's Relative Incapacitation Index and John Wootters' Lethality.

A serious effort was made to include as many relevant concepts and/or formulae as was practicable. However, in the author's opinion, there are some concepts and/or formulae that are enigmatic and/or incredulous to the degree that their use should be limited to works of science fiction or other types of fantasy writings. Others are so esoteric in nature that only persons who understand and use advanced mathematics can appreciate the technical details that are involved, e.g., Duncan MacPherson's "Wound Trauma Incapacitation."[7] Still other concepts and/or formulae are nothing more and nothing less than poorly concealed attempts to promote what "at-the-time" are considered to be politically correct – with little if any regard for the negative affect it may have on the survivability of the law enforcement officer or civilian who is required to use such illogically mandated ammunition. These kinds of concepts and/or formulae have been intentionally omitted.

READER CATEGORY

Regarding these and perhaps other not included or not considered concepts/formulae, it can be stated that most, if not all, readers of this work can be classified as belonging to one of the following categories and they will respond accordingly.

Category One

These individuals maintain and will continue to maintain erroneous and implacable opinions regarding the efficacy of bullets and ESP. Whether favorable or not, they are rarely if ever influenced by facts. These individuals tend to live in an illusory world similar to Hollywood or television make-believe, i.e., whatever their opinions, the reality of biology and physics is of no concern. For example, one member of a military special operations group should have known otherwise and perhaps does, but nonetheless incorrectly wrote:

> . . . with the stainless S&W 357 Magnum pistol, or . . . with the Beretta . . . we used heavy loads that **would knock terrorists down no matter where we hit them** [emphasis added]. Head, chest, arm, leg, it didn't matter.[8]

Because of ignorance, obduracy or an intent to exaggerate into fantasy (wishful thinking), such individuals refuse to acknowledge and even deny the existence of demonstrable and irrefutable proof (facts) and choose to remain in the nethermost realm of knowledge and understanding.

Category Two

These are the individuals who also maintain and will continue to maintain obdurate opinions regarding bullet efficacy and ESP, but whatever the opinions, they are supported by arbitrarily selected facts. These facts can be of either a pro or con nature, but they will always be in harmony with the particular opinions espoused by these individuals. Although many of these individuals will acknowledge there may be other facts that can support contrary opinions, the significance of such facts is ignored, glossed over or illogically disputed and then unilaterally dismissed from additional consideration.

Category Three

Here are the individuals who have definite opinions regarding bullet efficacy and ESP, but these opinions are based on evidence and known facts pertaining to biology, physics and other recognized and relevant sciences. These individuals are willing to and continuously do objectively consider and then evaluate all forthcoming relevant factual data. These individuals will then make objective decisions regarding the significance of this data and its subsequent affect on ESP concepts and/or formulae. This might result in a particular concept and/or formula being held in abeyance until more relevant data is obtained. It could also result in either major or minor modifications that result in the continued acceptance OR the rejection of a particular concept and/or formula used to determine probable ESP values.

It is for readers of this last category that this book has been written. However, it is not intended to be nor should it be inferred to be a reference source of exactitude. Instead, it has been written to provide factual information that will enable the reader to establish a basis or foundation upon which additional research, study and analysis can be undertaken. It is also intended that this material will enable the reader to obtain a more comprehensive understanding of the application and interrelationship of those factors that determine the actual degree of achieved stopping power effectiveness. Finally, it is intended that the contents of this book may serve as a guide for the interested reader from which an informed and appropriate decision can be made as to which concept and/or formula appears to be more consistent with logic and reality. Whether or not this has been achieved is for the reader to decide.

EXORDIUM ENDNOTES

[1] Vincent J.M. DiMaio, M.D., *Gunshot Wounds* (New York, New York: Elsevier Science Publishing Company, 1985), pp. 310-311.

[2] W. L. Baillie, "Averages, Means and the Theory of Errors," *Lefax Leaf + Facts* (Philadelphia, Pennsylvania: Lefax Publishing Company, a division of Smith-Edwards Co., Order No. 14-120, Dewey 519, undated), p. 1.

[3] Michael Reese II, *1900 Luger U.S. Test Trials*, rev. ed. (Union City, Tennessee: Pioneer Press, 1976), pp. 38-39.

[4] David H. Hackworth (Col. USA Ret.), "Sound Off," Soldier of Fortune, Volume 27, No. 11 (November 2002), p.82.

[5] William L. Cassidy, *Quick or Dead* (Boulder, Colorado: Paladin Press, 1978), p. 104.

[6] George Bredsten, John Hillegass and Ron Dempsey, Semiautomatic Pistol Ammunition and Ballistics, Lesson Plan 6093.02, rev. ed. (Glynco, Georgia: Federal Law Enforcement Training Center/Firearms Division, 1994), p. 6.

[7] Duncan MacPherson, *Bullet Penetration: Modeling the Dynamics and the Incapacitation Resulting from Wound Trauma* (El Segundo, California: Ballistic Publications 1994), pp. 86-148.

[8] Richard Marcinko and John Weisman, *Rogue Warrior* (New York: Pocket Books, a Division of Simon & Schuster, Inc., 1992), p. 19.

CHAPTER ONE

EFFECTIVE STOPPING POWER (ESP)

OVERVIEW

From about the first decade of the 1900s to the present time, serious and organized efforts were made and continue to be made to define, describe and understand ESP. Often ESP is defined and/or described as the one-shot stop, and there is no dearth of opinions as to how it can be best defined and achieved. Some definitions are both concise and precise, e.g., ". . . stopping power, that is, the ability to put an adversary out of the fight instantly, even though the blow may not be in a vital spot."[1] Such definitions do not contain extraneous stipulations.

In contradistinction to the foregoing luculent definition are the definitions that appear to be inane or vacuous and include criteria that are both illogical and unreasonable, e.g.:

1. Only torso hits were used. It is unrealistic to include incidents where a person was hit in a nonvital area and then use that incident to criticize the load as ineffective.
2. Multiple hits were also discarded. Again we did not think it would be fair if we included an incident where an offender took multiple hits and collapsed.
3. We have defined a stop as follows: If the person shot was assaulting someone when hit, the aggressor must collapse without being able to fire another round or strike another blow. If he or she was fleeing, they collapse within 10 feet.[2]

Criteria containing extraneous stipulations permit subjective decisions to be made regarding what shooting incidents will or will not be included in the database and then additional subjective decisions can be made as to what is and what is not considered to be ESP. The following is not to be construed as being either an animadversion or a diatribe regarding the foregoing three part example, but is instead presented as constructive criticism in order to emphasize why extraneous stipulations should NOT be used.

Consider Number 1:

"Only torso hits were used. . . ." A significant omission in an effort to evaluate bullet stopping power is the failure to distinguish between the effect of one bullet wound in or through one anatomical location with the effect of another bullet wound

in or through a different anatomical location. If, for example, in one shooting incident, a bullet penetrates front to back the right clavicle and in another shooting incident a bullet penetrates the second thoracic vertebra and severs the spinal cord, is it reasonable to expect each bullet wound will produce the same physiological debilitating effect? Remember the above criterion does NOT take into consideration what body part(s) the bullet penetrates and/or perforates – only that the bullet must penetrate somewhere in the torso.

This failure to compare "apples with apples" was tacitly acknowledged when the authors of the above criterion described in detail how – during the *alleged* "Strasbourg Tests" – the goats were carefully positioned so that each animal would be shot from the same angle and each bullet would penetrate the same internal body parts. Yet in their most recent work – which includes a reference to the *alleged* "Strasbourg Tests" – the vague "only torso hits" criterion was not changed.[3] Why not? Was this dissimulation? If not, then the use of the vague "only torso hits" criterion is apt to result in analyses that have fallible and irrelevant conclusions.

Consider Number 2:

"Multiple hits were also discarded. . . ." To discard (exclude) shooting incidents where multiple hits occurred is a sophism. To objectively determine the ESP of a bullet (specific cartridge and load) requires that all information (known/obtained by the writer/researcher) involving the use of that specific cartridge (load) must be included in the database. For example, a shooting incident occurs where multiple hits were made. Without additional facts, an argument can be made that only one hit was needed to stop a lethal threat action, even though two or more hits were made. An argument can also be made that more than one hit was required because two or more hits were made before the lethal threat action ceased.

Unless and until additional evidence is obtained that negates the argument that more than one hit was required, the irrefutable fact remains that multiple hits were made. Any incidents involving more than one hit MUST be included as part of the database that is used to evaluate a cartridge's stopping power. To exclude these incidents can result in erroneous conclusions – consider the following hypothetical example:

Cartridge Number	% **Claimed** One-Shot Stops	Total Incidents	% **NOT** One-Shot Stops	% **ACTUAL** One-Shot Stops
1	94/108 = 87 %	176	82/176 = 46.6%	94/176 = **53.4%**
2	88/110 = 80 %	147	59/147 = 40.1%	88/147 = **59.9%**

The reader may point out there were only 147 hypothetical incidents for cartridge number two compared with the 176 hypothetical incidents for cartridge number one. This is true, but it is of no import. The reason is it would be extremely fortuitous if the researcher could locate the same quantity of shooting incidents for each and every cartridge being evaluated. While the quantities of shooting incidents might/can/will vary; if the study is to have any meaningful relevance, the collected data for each cartridge (load) must also provide answers for the same set of statistical questions. That consideration aside, from the numbers in the above example, the second cartridge produced a higher percentage of one-shot stops. The question is: Why would any author(s) pretend the incidents involving more than one hit did not occur OR were not considered fair? One possible answer is subreption. To conceal, distort or ignore the statistical significance of multiple hits because of possible author predilection is sufficient cause to suspect and possibly impugn the credibility of the method, study, evaluation and conclusion of these authors.

Consider Number 3:

"We have defined a stop as follows, if the person shot was assaulting someone when hit, the aggressor must collapse without being able to fire another round or strike another blow. If he or she was fleeing, they collapse within 10 feet." Is it necessary for the shootee to collapse? Is it relevant whether or not the shootee, attempting to flee, moves less than or more than 10 feet? The answer for each question is NO. If the shootee staggers ten feet, one inch (10' 1") but is unable to attempt or resume a lethal threat action – is this a failure to stop? If a shootee flees a distance of nine feet, eleven inches (9' 11") and then while collapsing turns and shoots the shooter – is this a one-shot stop? Again, the answer for these questions is NO.

What degree of precision were the measurements of ten feet? Were the ten feet estimated? Were the measurements made to the nearest quarter of an inch – to the nearest tenth of an inch – perhaps to the nearest one hundredth of an inch? When a fleeing shootee collapsed and his feet/legs were less than ten feet away but his torso was more than ten feet, was this or was this not a one-shot stop? Who knows? Whether no or yes, it will be a subjective decision. Remember the criterion of ten feet was <u>categorical</u>. The use of extraneous stipulations makes it possible for there to be a "spin" zone complete with "smoke and mirrors."

However, even extraneous stipulations cannot completely account for the display of convoluted and disjointed logic that considers the following example to be a failure to stop:

> He reached in the bag and wrapped his hand around the gun. He started to pull it but the man stabbed him before he completed the draw. Gasping, he pulled the gun and opened fire.[4]

How can any firearm/cartridge combination be expected to stop a lethal threat action IF NO SHOTS ARE FIRED UNTIL **AFTER** THE LETHAL THREAT ACTION HAS BEEN (in this case successfully) COMPLETED? Extraneous stipulations aside, this is unmitigated sophistry. In addition, this example was included in those authors' database to calculate the percentages of alleged failures to stop. The use of the foregoing example might have been due to an oversight, i.e., originally intended to describe another aspect of stopping power and unintentionally included as a failure to stop? Perhaps, but the following raises serious doubts because it too is another example of convoluted and disjointed logic:

> He approached the machine and was engrossed in using it when he was struck from behind. Falling to his knees, he felt a man grab his wallet and start to run. He pulled his snub and emptied it at his attacker.[5]

Once more the question: How can any firearm/cartridge combination be expected to stop a lethal threat action IF NO SHOTS ARE FIRED UNITL **AFTER** THE LETHAL THREAT ACTION HAS BEEN COMPLETED? In this case, the lethal threat action had stopped and the assailant was already running AWAY before the victim began shooting.

Be that as it may, the subject of extraneous stipulations is considered to have been addressed in sufficient detail to permit each reader to decide whether or not the criticism was appropriate, objective and free from author bias.

EFFECTIVE STOPPING POWER (ESP)

Effective Stopping Power has been redefined:

THE ABILITY OF A BULLET TO IMMEDIATELY STOP A LETHAL THREAT ACTION THAT, IF NOT IMMEDIATELY STOPPED, COULD RESULT IN THE DEATH OR GRIEVOUS BODILY INJURY TO THE PERSON AT RISK.[6]

The word "serious" in the definition of ESP as given in the exordium of this book has been replaced with the word "grievous" and was done because grievous is to be understood to mean a body injury can be permanent disablement/paralysis or the injury can be such that partial or complete amputation of a body part becomes necessary, e.g., a hand or arm. Whereas, serious is understood to mean the bodily injury can result in hospitalization and surgery, BUT eventually the individual is expected (barring complications) to make a complete recovery.

Apparently there are some people who have only a vague idea of what "immediately stop" means. For those people, "immediately stop" is defined and is to be understood to mean the instantaneous and permanent cessation of a lethal threat action OR the shooter is provided with sufficient time to take and maintain physical control of the shootee before any further attempt can be made by the shootee to commit a lethal threat action.

In the first instance, that is, "the instantaneous and permanent cessation of a lethal threat action," it is irrelevant whether or not the shootee crawls, staggers, walks, trots, dances to a Strauss Waltz or runs a marathon. The only relevant fact to determine is did lethal threat action _instantaneously_ and _permanently_ cease? If the answer is yes, then ESP did occur – period. If the answer is no, then ESP did not occur – period.

In the second instance, i.e., "the shooter is provided with sufficient time to take and maintain physical control of the shootee before any further attempt can be made by the shootee to commit a lethal threat action," that sufficient time can vary from a few seconds to perhaps several minutes. An example of a short but sufficient time occurred (May 1916) during "World War One" where sappers (similar but not identical to the "Tunnel Rats" in the Viet Nam War) often had only a few seconds to act, e.g.:

> At that, Westacott switched on his electric torch, shone it into the officer's eyes from just a few feet away and pulled the trigger on his 455-inch Webley revolver, shooting the other man in the stomach. Acutely aware that his back presented the best target for his own men, he flung himself to the tunnel's floor, and seconds later both heard and felt the roar of Sergeant Brown's revolver as he fired on the next man in the German party, and then stepped on his officer in his haste to get to the German NCO, kick the pistol out of his hand and administer a _coup de grâce_.[7]

An example of significantly longer sufficient time was reported by John Farnam and occurred (date not indicated) during a law enforcement lethal threat confrontation:

> The chin shot was the final one: It put the suspect down. The bullet (40 S&W) entered on the point of the chin and traveled around the contour of the lower mandible, exiting on the side of his face. The suspect lay motionless for several minutes. Just after the fire department folks examined him and pronounced him 'dead,' he sat up! He had merely been knocked out. . . .[8]

It is also irrelevant whether or not the shootee dies or later makes a complete recovery. The only relevant fact to determine is did the shootee regain the ability and then attempt a lethal threat action? If the answer is no, then ESP did occur – period. If the answer is yes, then ESP did not occur – period.

The foregoing expanded explanation of ESP is given in order to minimize intentional or unintentional misinterpretation. The author does not claim this definition of Effective (Bullet) Stopping Power as given is either the best or the only definition. However, with the author's definition in mind, the main subject of this work (Bullet Efficacy Relative to Effective Stopping Power) can now be addressed.

CHAPTER ONE ENDNOTES

[1] Julian S. Hatcher, *Textbook of Pistols and Revolvers* (Plantersville, South Carolina: Small Arms Technical Publishing Company, 1935 – Reprinted Prescott, Arizona: Wolfe Publishing Company, Inc., 1985.), p. 401.

[2] Evan P. Marshall and Edwin J. Sanow, *Stopping Power: A Practical Analysis of the Latest Handgun Ammunition* (Boulder, Colorado: Paladin Press, 2001), p. viii.

[3] Ibid. pp. 13-14.

[4] Ibid. p. 289.

[5] Ibid. p. 291.

[6] George Bredsten, et al., Test Report Number: HG/DEP/1999-FLETC/FAD (Glynco, Georgia: Federal Law Enforcement Training Center/Firearms Division, 1999), p. 154.

[7] Roger Ford and Tim Ripley, *The Whites of Their Eyes: Close-Quarter Combat* (Dulles, Virginia: Brassey's Inc., 2001), p. 21.

[8] John Farnam, "Combat Weaponcraft" Soldier of Fortune (August 2004), p. 20.

CHAPTER TWO

PHYSIOLOGICAL RESPONSE

OVERVIEW

While military organizations and terrorist groups generally issue carbines, rifles, shotguns and/or submachine guns as the primary firearms to be used by the individual combatant, within the United States of America the vast majority of law enforcement officers are apt to rely on a handgun as their primary firearm. This is because a handgun is usually the only type of firearm immediately available when most armed confrontations occur, and it is considered to be a firearm of opportunity and NOT a firearm of first choice. The same is true, to a somewhat lesser extent, regarding the typical civilian and the type of firearm available to use in a life threatening situation. Consequently, this disquisition will be primarily concerned with the ESP of handgun ammunition and secondarily with the ESP of either rifle or shotgun ammunition.

Among the general population, there are many myths and other misinformation about what a bullet or bullets can or cannot do to the human body. One common myth is "if a man is still standing after being shot with a 45 Colt, you need to walk behind that man to see what is holding him upright."[1] Even though this and other bullet performance myths are contrary to the currently known facts pertaining to biology and physics, many people continue to believe such myths to be true. Other sources of unfounded/unsubstantiated information usually contain little if any data that might prove helpful in acquiring a more realistic understanding of ESP.

Within this book, there is a conscientious endeavor to exclude the use of unfounded information, be it conjecture, guesswork, hypothesis (unless so stated), supposition or theory. Instead, evidence and facts dealing with pertinent and relevant information are systematically described. Any conclusions presented are based on an analysis of the available evidence and facts regarding the subject or subjects under consideration.

Because there does not appear to be a more practical way to adequately describe the physiological response to handgun bullet wounds, it may appear to some readers that this chapter contains an unnecessary quantity of anatomical and medical terms. However, medical professionals (doctors, nurses, emergency medical technicians and paramedics) are apt to consider the material to be sophomoric. Since the author is not a member of the medical profession, a degree of forbearance is expected for any medical word/term incompletely or incorrectly expressed.

ANATOMICAL DAMAGE VERSUS ANATOMICAL DYSFUNCTION

At the onset, it is necessary to differentiate between anatomical damage and anatomical dysfunction. Anatomical damage is physical injury that usually involves discomfort, some degree of pain and limited or somewhat restricted functioning of the affected body part. By extension, anatomical dysfunction can be construed to be but an extreme type of anatomical damage. However, as it applies to bullet wounds, there is a significant difference between anatomical damage and anatomical dysfunction. Anatomical damage DOES NOT immediately disable or incapacitate the affected body part(s), whereas anatomical dysfunction DOES immediately disable or incapacitate the affected body part(s).

Thus a person who receives a gunshot wound that causes anatomical damage still has the capability to initiate, continue or resume physical activity – including life-threatening action, while a person who receives a gunshot wound that results in anatomical dysfunction is unable to continue physical activity with the injured body part because it has been disabled.

When the variations of the physiological responses and the deadly force options are considered, there are four categories of possible behavior:

1. The **Nonfatal** gunshot wound and the **Inability** to commit deadly force.
2. The **Fatal** gunshot wound and the **Inability** to commit deadly force.
3. The **Nonfatal** gunshot wound and the **Ability** to commit deadly force.
4. The **Fatal** gunshot wound and the **Ability** to commit deadly force.

Category 1: The **Nonfatal** gunshot wound and the **Inability** to commit deadly force.

This kind of gunshot wound typically affects:

1. Ligaments and/or tendons within a muscle or muscle group.
2. Essential skeletal part(s).
3. Local or specific nerves, nervous system or the central nervous system (CNS).
4. Wounds involving a combination of 1 through 3.

It would be unusual for a gunshot wound to be inflicted where only ligaments or tendons are affected. Concurrent damage to adjacent bone and/or muscle is much more typical. An example of muscle(s) dysfunction caused by a bullet wound occurred (October 1993) in Mogadishu, Somalia:

> In the same back room was Errico, a machine gunner who had been wounded in both biceps manning his gun, and Neathery, who'd been wounded in the upper arm when he took over for Errico. Neathery

was distressed. The bullet had damaged both bicep and tricep and he couldn't make his right arm work at all.[2]

Whenever possible and practical, a seriously wounded man would be replaced by an unwounded or less seriously wounded soldier. Because of this, it is unknown whether or not the wounds to Errico's biceps had rendered his arms dysfunctional. However, no such doubt exists regarding the effect of the bullet wound to Neathery's bicep and tricep.

An example of <u>skeletal</u> dysfunction caused by a bullet wound occurred (February 1887) in Fort Worth, Texas. This gunfight between "Long Haired" Jim Courtright and Luke Short is one where a generally acknowledged "deadlier" gunfighter lost because of his inability to continue (timely) an act of deadly force after suffering a nonfatal wound. Even with the disadvantage of added reaction time, Courtright was almost able to draw and fire his shot with Short's. However, the bullet from Short's wild shot smashed the thumb of Courtright's gunhand. This prevented Courtright from cocking and firing his single action revolver. Before Courtright could shift the revolver to his other hand or fan-cock the revolver with his other hand, Short ended the gunfight by firing three more shots (bullets) into Courtright's chest.[3]

Another example of <u>skeletal</u> dysfunction caused by a bullet wound occurred (September 1895) in Elgin, Kansas. During a shootout with peace officer Bill Tilghman, the outlaw William Raidler was shot in the wrist. The bullet broke Raidler's wrist and the injury was such that he could no longer maintain a grip on his pistol. He then attempted to escape.[4]

The third gunshot wound of this type causes either temporary or permanent <u>paralysis</u> by making dysfunctional a specific motor nerve plexus or the CNS. This is called synapsis (neuron) dysfunction and is in effect a short circuit within the affected nerve system that prevents the mental impulse (command) from reaching the body part(s) needed to commit a physical act of deadly force.[5] This is a gunshot wound that, for instance, results in either partial or total paralysis of the arm, hand or finger(s) needed to complete an act of deadly force. Gunshot wounds of this type often involve some degree of long lasting (if not permanent) associated damage to the spinal column/cord.

An example of this type of gunshot wound occurred (August 1985) in or near Duluth, Minnesota. While two prisoners were being transported from one prison to another, one of the prisoners was able to free himself of the waist chain and handcuffs. Then during a scuffle with the victim deputy's partner the prisoner obtained his 357 Magnum revolver. During the struggle, the revolver was tossed into the back seat where the other prisoner took the revolver and fired four shots. One bullet hit the victim officer in the chest resulting in <u>paralysis</u> from the chest down.[6]

Category 2: The **Fatal** gunshot wound and the **Inability** to commit deadly force.

This type of gunshot wound also precludes any behavioral response involving the ability to use deadly force. A wound in this category often, but not always, results in the dysfunction of vital organs; the debilitating effect of such a wound is instantaneous and complete. Impacted, penetrated and/or perforated body parts that result in a fatality and the inability to commit deadly force include gunshot wounds to the central nervous system, major skeletal structure(s) with concurrent damage to vital organs and/or major blood vessels.

An example of this type of lethal wound occurred (December 1883) in Caldwell, Kansas where a bullet first perforated an arm and then penetrated into the thorax. Town marshal Henry Brown attempted to stop Newt Boyce, who had recently made threats against Brown. When Boyce reached inside his coat (weapon?), Brown fired two shots from his rifle. One bullet went through Boyce's right arm and then penetrated into his side. Boyce staggered into Phillip's saloon and collapsed. Later about 3:00 AM, Boyce died.[7] In this incident, the rifle bullet accomplished two things. It appeared to have incapacitated while it perforated the arm, and then the bullet penetrated into Boyce's side to inflict the fatal wound.

Another example involving this type of physiological response occurred (April 1896) in Carlsbad, New Mexico. Sheriff Les Dow had just come from the post office when Dave Kemp stepped forward and fired a shot into Dow's face, shattering his jaw. As he staggered back, Dow pulled his gun, but collapsed before he could fire. Dow died later that night.[8]

A final example of this type of gunshot wound occurred (November 1896) in Pawnee, Oklahoma where lawman Frank Canton confronted fugitive Bull Dunn. As Dunn said, "I've got it in for you," Canton drew a 45 and shot Dunn in the forehead. Dunn fell on his back, his unfired gun dropped from his hand, the dying man's trigger finger twitched convulsively for several moments.[9]

In these examples, the affect of the gunshot wound immediately prevents the shootee from committing deadly force – even though death may not occur until several hours later. The physical reactions of the shootee to this type of gunshot wound are often reported to be a combination of staggering and/or collapsing/falling.

Category 3: The **Nonfatal** gunshot wound and the **Ability** to commit deadly force.

This type of gunshot wound typically involves penetration or perforation of a muscle or a muscle group. Where such a gunshot wound results in muscle dysfunction (e.g., sartorius), the location of the wound is such that the dysfunctional muscle is uninvolved/unnecessary for there to be an attempted act of deadly force. Where the gunshot wound does involve a muscle or muscle group needed by the shootee to commit an act of deadly force, the degree of muscle damage is insufficient to prevent the physical movements needed to complete an act of deadly force. In the latter situation, there remain sufficient functional voluntary striated muscle fibre and motor nerves to continue, resume and/or begin an act of deadly force. An example would be bullet damage to the brachio-radialis or brachial plexus of the arm holding the weapon. A common characteristic associated with this type of gunshot wound is the shootee is the recipient of two or more bullets – none of which are able to immediately stop the lethal threat action.

A classic example of the general ineffectiveness of this type of gunshot wound(s) occurred (November 1875) in Bell County, Texas. During the initial phase of this gunfight, after Lew Sawyer fired what apparently was the first shot; W. P. (Wild Bill) Longley fired and hit Sawyer in the right shoulder. Sawyer was not only able to return fire; he later used a shotgun to drop the horse Longley was riding. Both men now afoot, this gunfight continued until Sawyer was killed with a bullet fired into his head. Sawyer took a total of twelve bullets and continued fighting until the thirteenth bullet hit him in his head.[10]

To the present era, the physiological response to this type of gunshot wound has not changed. Drug Enforcement Agency (DEA) special agents were involved in an undercover operation (February 1988) that quickly degenerated into a shooting confrontation. Two DEA special agents were killed, but a third DEA special agent (although wounded in both legs) was able to return fire.[11]

Category 4: The **Fatal** gunshot wound and the **Ability** to commit deadly force.

This type of gunshot wound often involves the penetration/perforation of a major blood vessel or vital organ(s), e.g., the brachiocephalic artery or the heart. "Depending upon which major blood vessel or vital organ is made dysfunctional, physical incapacitation may not occur for several minutes to more than one hour later."[12] An example of this type of gunshot wound occurred (August 1891) on a train near Waukomis, Oklahoma. Deputy U.S. Marshal Ed Short was taking Charles Bryant to the nearest federal court. The deputy left the handcuffed prisoner for a short time and during that time the prisoner was able to get possession of handgun. Returning to the passenger car, the deputy was immediately shot by Bryant. After being shot in the chest, Ed Short returned fire with his rifle and the bullet severed Bryant's spinal column. However, before dying Bryant continued shooting until the pistol was empty.[13]

These pyrrhic victories continue to the present, e.g., in Miami, Florida (11 April 1986) two FBI agents were killed and five other FBI agents were wounded by a criminal who had already been hit with a 9mm Luger hollow point bullet that perforated his arm and then penetrated into his thorax – cutting a major blood vessel. Even though this gunshot wound was latter alleged to have been non-survivable, the criminal remained alive and continued volitional lethal threat actions for a period of time estimated to be more than four minutes. It was within this time frame that the criminal was able to kill and wound the FBI agents.[14,15,16]

Another example involved a Fullerton, California policeman working an undercover assignment (June 1990). This officer was hit five times from a Browning Hi-Power 9mm, but was able to return fire and kill the suspect before he died.[17]

Yet another example involved a Santa Clara County, California deputy sheriff (September 1990) who, in a struggle to take a 38 calibre handgun away from an assailant, was shot three times in the chest. Although mortally wounded, the deputy was able to fire six shots, killing his assailant.[18]

A final example occurred in Deming, New Mexico (July 2002), where, after being shot through the left lung and heart with a bullet from a 25 Auto, the shootee was able to shoot his opponent in the head with a 357 Magnum. Both persons died and were found about five feet from each other.[19]

From the aforementioned examples, it would not be unreasonable to expect a typical law enforcement handgun cartridge (bullet) may and occasional will fail to achieve ESP – even when a bullet is fired into the heart. However, very few persons would believe a bullet in the heart from a "high power" rifle cartridge would ever fail to achieve ESP.

An example that should dispel such a view was given by Charles Askins who, while a member of the U.S. Border Patrol, reported: That first shot (from a 351 WSL) must have torn his heart to pieces. . . . he kept on shooting, firing at least two rounds from the old single action after his heart was torn to shreds.[20]

It is important to recognize and understand the following truism: The maximum physiological response to a bullet wound CANNOT exceed the potential maximum anatomical physical effort available in or to the affected body part.

To insert a brief bit of levity that emphasizes an important point, ponder the following: A _given_ physiological response is NOT always a _given_. If the meaning of this terse sentence has been comprehended, then the essence of this chapter has been effectively communicated to the reader.

CHAPTER TWO ENDNOTES

[1] J. Henry FitzGerald, *Shooting* (Hartford, Connecticut: G. F. Book Company, 1930), p. 248.

[2] Mark Bowden, *Black Hawk Down* (New York, New York: Signet, a Division of Penguin Putnam, Inc., 2001), p. 294.

[3] Eugene Cunningham, *Triggernometry, A Gallery of Gunfighters* (Caldwell, Idaho: Caxton Printers, Ltd., 1941 – 6th printing 1952), pp. 216-217.

[4] Bill O'Neal, *Encyclopedia of Western Gun-Fighters* (Norman, Oklahoma: University of Oklahoma Press, 1979 – 3rd printing 1983), p. 259

[5] F. R. Winton, M.D., D.S. and L. E. Bayliss, PhD., *Human Physiology* (Boston, Massachusetts: Little Brown and Company, 5th edition, 1962), pp. 377-389.

[6] U.S. Department of Justice, Federal Bureau of Investigation, *Uniform Crime Reports – Law Enforcement Officers Killed and Assaulted, 1991*, p. 42.

[7] O'Neal, op. cit. p. 52.

[8] Ibid. p. 175.

[9] Ibid. pp. 153, 154.

[10] Ibid. p. 194.

[11] U.S Department of Justice, Federal Bureau of Investigation, *Uniform Crime Reports – Law Enforcement Officers Killed and Assaulted, 1988*, p. 25.

[12] V. J. M. DiMaio, *Gunshot Wounds* (New York: Elsevier Science, 1985), p. 25.

[13] O'Neal, op. cit. p. 53.

[14] David Rivers, *Shooting Incident Homicide Case Number: 153261-G* (Miami, Florida: Metro Dade Police Department – unpublished).

[15] U.S. Department of Justice, Federal Bureau of Investigation, *Uniform Crime Reports – Law Enforcement Officers Killed and Assaulted, 1986*, p. 27.

Handgun Bullet Stopping Power

[16] W. French Anderson, M.D., *Forensic Analysis of the April 11, 1986 FBI Firefight* (Los Angeles, California: University of Southern California School of Medicine, 1996 – 2nd printing 1997), p. 3.

[17] U.S. Department of Justice, Federal Bureau of Investigation, *Uniform Crime Reports – Law Enforcement Officers Killed and Assaulted, 1990*, p. 23.

[18] Ibid.

[19] Associated Press, "Deming Man, teen-ager kill each other" Silver City Daily Press (Silver City, New Mexico), 17 July 2002, pp. 1, 9.

[20] Charles Askins, *The Pistol Shooter's Book* (Harrisburg, Pennsylvania: The Telegraph Press, 1951 – 2nd printing 1957), p. 291.

CHAPTER THREE

PSYCHOLOGICAL RESPONSE

OVERVIEW

Psychology can be considered to be the systematic study of mental processes and the subsequent physiological behavior. What are some of the mental processes a person can use to decide what the physiological reaction to a gunshot could be? While the professional psychologist will view, perhaps with dismay, and conclude the simplistic approach and classification methods utilized in presenting this material have been incompletely or even incorrectly developed; it is not the intent of the author to delve in the technical terminology or theory which defines and explains the possible affects and effects of various contributory psychological factors.

Erich Fromm opined: "man seeks for drama and excitement, when he cannot get satisfaction on a higher level, he creates for himself the drama of destruction."[1] If this is true, a person's perspectives, priorities and behavior patterns can be affected by one or more of many factors. The affect of these factors can vary in degree and intensity according to the particulars of the occasion, but the behavior pattern of primary interest is that which ultimately is manifested as some type of aggression:

> Aggression is considered to be all acts that cause, and are intended to cause damage to another person . . . the most fundamental distinction among all kinds of impulses subsumed under the category of aggression is that between biologically adaptive, life-serving, benign aggression and biologically nonadaptive malignant aggression.[2]

There isn't any need to differentiate between benign and malignant aggression. Also at this juncture, there is neither a need to establish whether or not there is a psychological or a neurophysiological basis for the aggression, nor is there a need to establish whether or not the aggression may have been activated by a psychedelic influence. Whatever the underlying psychological reason(s), the primary interest is the mental condition or the mindset of the shootee at the moment of bullet impact.

When psychological options are considered, there are three basic categories of mental condition or mindset:

1. **Neutral** – Unaware/unconcerned/unprepared.
2. **Angry (enraged)** – Rational destructive violence.
3. **Berserk (maniac/stoic)** – Irrational destructive violence.

Handgun Bullet Stopping Power

When these three mindset options are considered with the two physiological response options, that include the ability to commit deadly force, there are six categories of possible behavior:

1. **Nonfatal** gunshot wound – **Ability** to commit deadly force – **Neutral** mindset.
2. **Nonfatal** gunshot wound – **Ability** to commit deadly force – **Angry** mindset.
3. **Nonfatal** gunshot wound – **Ability** to commit deadly force – **Berserk** mindset.
4. **Fatal** gunshot wound – **Ability** to commit deadly force – **Neutral** mindset.
5. **Fatal** gunshot wound – **Ability** to commit deadly force – **Angry** mindset.
6. **Fatal** gunshot wound – **Ability** to commit deadly force – **Berserk** mindset.

It is important to realize the "<u>ability</u>" to commit deadly force does not necessarily mean an attempt will be made to commit deadly force. Even if an attempt is made, the attempt may prove to be unsuccessful. However, even if the attempt is successful, the inflicted gunshot or other type of wound may be a so-called minor flesh wound of a non-serious nature, it may be a serious wound but NOT life threatening, the wound may in be life threatening or it may even cause death.

Category 1:
Nonfatal gunshot wound – **Ability** to commit deadly force – **Neutral** mindset.

The neutral mindset is referred to by Jeff Cooper as being in condition white.[3] Even though the debilitating physical effect of a bullet wound is minor, the mindset of the shootee is such that a major psychological barrier exists which effectively precludes the implementation of any aggressive and/or retaliatory behavior. A neutral mindset is more often than not "self" oriented, and from a philosophical viewpoint, the "self" orientation is almost egocentric. Thus, the shootee's reaction to a nonfatal and relatively minor bullet wound is to perhaps think: "This isn't real." – "I've been shot." – "I'm hurt." – "I might die." – "I'm going to die." or "I'm dying." The Shootee then <u>collapses</u> or <u>flees</u>.

The following example illustrates one type of behavior response (collapse) of a shootee with a neutral mindset to a nonfatal gunshot wound. General Julian S. Hatcher observed (date not indicated) the results of an attempted suicide and said the person had used the smallest and least powerful centerfire cartridge (.32 revolver) available, and the bullet did NOT reach a vital spot, but the person <u>dropped</u> like a log at the shot and lay there prostrated until he was wheeled off to the hospital to recover in a few days.[4] In this case, the after being shot behavior can be considered to be a predetermined physical response to the shootee's mindset at the moment of the attempted suicide. His <u>collapse</u> was a result of a mindset that denied the reality of the actual effectiveness of the gunshot wound, and instead his body response was consistent with what he thought should happen.

Contrast the above with the effect of an unintentional self-inflicted gunshot wound that happened to the well-known archaeologist Roy Chapman Andrews (May 1928) while on an exploration trip into the Gobi region of Mongolia:

> Andrews' finger slipped and a round was fired (Colt 38 Army Special) through the holster and into his left leg. The bullet entered his thigh and exited below the knee, in the process ***chipping the end of the femur*** [emphasis added]. It was a terrible wound and according to Andrews, "The heavy bullet struck me such a terrific blow that I went down as though felled by a sledge."[5]

"Chipping the end of the femur" has been emphasized by this author to point out that Andrews may have sincerely believed he fell down due to a perceived "terrific blow" but in reality his falling was more likely caused by either a possible combination of his psychological reaction to being shot and the physiological damage to the end of the femur OR perhaps just to the physiological damage to the end of the femur (bone).

Another different behavior response associated with a neutral mindset has the shootee immediately making an attempt to escape, flee, hide or otherwise disassociate himself from the location where the shooting occurred. This can be considered to be the shootee's choice of the flight response of the so-called "fight or flight" syndrome. An example of this type of response (flee) occurred (December 1881) in Tombstone, Arizona:

> . . . as the United States Deputy Marshal (Virgil Earp) was crossing Fifth Street, between the Oriental saloon and Eagle brewery, and when in the middle of the street, he was fired upon with double barreled shotguns, loaded with buckshot, by three men. . . . Marshal Earp was wounded in the left arm just above the elbow, producing a longitudinal fracture of the bone. One shot (buckshot pellet) struck him above the groin, coming out near the spine. . . . Parsons reported that Virgil did not fall after being hit and that he recrossed the street to the Oriental.[6-7]

There is also the combinations of the two types of responses, i.e., flee and collapse, as the following example shows. "After being shot in the face just below the right eye with a 44 Magnum, the man turned and crawled (fled) about a half city block and collapsed."[8]

In each of the examples, whether self-inflicted or shot by another person and whether or not armed, the physical response of the shootee was to <u>collapse</u> and/or turn and <u>flee</u>. This physical response (flee) can also be due to an overriding concern of the shootee to preserve "self" and of the choice between "fight or flight" the shootee may believe flight will contribute more to "self" survival than will fight. Another possibility – because of the mental stress and the perception of physical pain caused by the gunshot wound – the shootee does not consciously evaluate the reasons for this pain but decides to move away from the source of the pain. Instead, the movement can be likened to a reflex action of the body. An analogy would be when a person inadvertently touches a hot frying pan on the stove. There is no conscious thought by the person to move his hand away from the hot pan. A reflex action moves the hand away before a conscious decision can be made to move the hand.

Category 2: **Nonfatal** gunshot wound – **Ability** to commit deadly Force – **Angry**.

Although the enervating effect of a gunshot wound may be relatively minor, the mindset of the individual is such that the psychological response involves a decision to utilize a behavior response that includes an act or acts of rational destructive violence. The person with an angry mindset is primarily "goal" oriented. This goal orientation is concerned primarily with determining who is responsible for causing the gunshot wound. As a consequence, the shootee may react by thinking: "I've been shot." – "You did this to me." – "I'll use violence to resolve this life threatening situation." The shootee then attempts some act or acts of rational destructive violence. If armed with a firearm, an attempt is made to shoot the shooter. If not armed with a firearm, an attempt is made to stop the shooter using another object as a weapon, e.g., a knife, a hammer, a screwdriver or if nothing else is available the hands and/or feet.

An example occurred (December 1875) in the town of Campo, California. Luman Gaskill was shot in his lung and <u>dropped</u> to the floor, apparently dead. . . . regaining consciousness, he picked up his shotgun and blasted one of the gang members that had shot the sheepherder. . . . another bandit came around the corner of the blacksmith shop and Luman dropped him. Luman Gaskill survived the gunshot wound to his lung.[9]

Another example occurred (April 1879) in Dodge City, Kansas between Frank Loving and Levi Richardson. These two individuals got into an argument which developed into a gunfight. Loving's gun misfired and Richardson missed. Richardson got off two more shots, but only wounded Loving in the hand. Loving then put three bullets into Richardson – arm, chest and side. Richardson <u>staggered</u> backwards, firing several more shots before he <u>dropped</u>. Loving, still enraged, had to be restrained from emptying his gun into the dying Richardson.[10]

A more recent example occurred (March 1993) and involved a NYPD detective and a drug dealer. Working undercover in a narcotics "buy and bust" operation and while attempting to make an arrest, the detective returned fire after the male who had delivered the marijuana began shooting at the detective. Each fired three shots and both men were hit. The detective suffered a fatal wound to the upper torso, while his assailant survived a gunshot wound to his hip.[11]

A final example occurred (October 1993) in Mogadishu and involved a Somali:

> He was loading (inserting) a new magazine in his rifle when Nelson fired about a dozen rounds at him. Nelson saw the rounds go right through the man, but the guy still got up, retrieved his weapon, and even got off a shot or two in Nelson's direction. Nelson was shocked. He fired another twelve rounds at the man, who was still able to crawl behind the tree. This time he didn't shoot back.[12]

Category 3: **Nonfatal** gunshot wound – **Ability** to commit deadly force – **Berserk**.

Even though the physical debilitating enervating effect of a gunshot wound is minor the mindset of the individual is such that the psychological decision is to utilize a behavior response that includes an act or acts of irrational destructive violence. The person with a berserk mindset is "goal exclusive" oriented. The primary difference between "angry" and "berserk" is found in the keyword "exclusive." The angry (enraged) mindset may be dissuaded from continuing the violent aggressive behavior by means other than violence, e.g., "vis-à-vis" oral exchanges. Whereas, only physical incapacitation will stop a person with a berserk mindset from completing the act of irrational destructive violence. An example of this type of mindset was reported (no date indicated) by General John J. Pershing:

> The captain had been surprised and attacked by a juramentado - a berserk Moro native armed with a bladed weapon. Whipping out his .38 calibre Colt service revolver, the officer quickly blasted his assailant six times. Hardly flinching, the Moro stormed right up to his astounded, khaki-clad target and cut him to pieces. The apparently bullet-proof apparition "started on his way rejoicing." According to Pershing's account, "when a guard finally finished him with a .45 calibre bullet.[13]

Although this report did not specifically indicate the Moro native had sustained non-fatal wounds, if the report was without hyperbole, a person would be unlikely to start on his way rejoicing if the six bullet wounds caused by the 38 bullets were severe/life threatening.

Another example is given by Colonel Louis A. LaGarde where a prisoner,

Handgun Bullet Stopping Power

attempting to escape (October 1905), in a hand-to-hand encounter was shot four times at close range by a 38 calibre Colt's revolver. One or both of the prisoner's lungs were penetrated by three of the four bullets, yet he did not stop fighting until struck on the forehead with the butt-end of a Springfield carbine. After about one month of treatment in a military hospital, the prisoner was turned over to civil authorities cured.[14]

A final example of this type of gunshot wound occurred (January 1995) in North Las Vegas, Nevada where a police officer was shot and later died (during surgery) while attempting to subdue a man who creating a disturbance:

> The officer radioed for backup before approaching the man who was standing in the middle of the street growling at the moon. Two minutes later, the victim officer again radioed police headquarters, this time requesting emergency medical assistance. When backup officers arrived at the scene, they found the victim officer had been shot in the upper back, the left forearm and the elbow. Before losing consciousness, the officer stated the man had shot him. Police pursued the alleged assailant for over two blocks, exchanging gunfire. **Under the influence of drugs** [emphasis added] at the time of the incident, the 41-year old man was shot by police numerous times before he committed suicide. The victim officer died during surgery later that day.[15]

Category 4:
Fatal gunshot wound – **Ability** to commit deadly force – **Neutral** mindset.

With the obvious difference of a resulting fatality, this category is otherwise similar to Category 1. Reaction to a fatal wound by a person with a neutral mindset can be equally bizarre. The shootee may respond to the gunshot wound as if nothing had happened (unaware), or perhaps may display what appears to be an almost total indifference to the effect of the bullet wound. The following incident has been used as the genesis for James (Wild Bill) B. Hickok's reputation as a deadly gunfighter. This was the infamous shooting that occurred (July 1861) at McCanles Rock Creek Station, Nebraska where Hickok:

> ... grabbed the rifle and fired through the curtain, hitting McCanles in the heart. McCanles's son, Monroe, was still there with his father and said later that his father fell backward out the door on his back, sat up and looked at him as if to say something then dropped back dead.[16]

Another example of a neutral mindset occurred (1895) in Telluride, Colorado:

> . . . a short time later a shot rang out as Clark stepped out of a beer joint. The ex-marshal jerked, then pulled himself together and wobbled across the street into a brothel, poor Jim mustn't have realized how bad he'd been hit, for he died in the joyhouse.[17]

The mindset of an individual involved in a lethal threat confrontation does not necessarily remain in a static state, and for various reasons there can be volitional change from one mindset to another; i.e., a mindset can change from neutral to either angry or berserk OR from angry to either neutral or berserk. However, the berserk mindset continues <u>unchanged</u> unless/until the "goal exclusive" act is achieved or the berserk individual's action is physically stopped.

An example of a mindset change – angry to neutral – occurred (January 1867) in Otoe County, Nebraska between Scott Keysinger and George Karness. As Keysinger passed through the saloon door, Karness struck him over the head with his gun. The blow did not knock Keysinger down, and he wheeled on Karness with a knife. He swung (knife) at his assailant, but did very little damage. Karness then fired point blank at Keysinger, the bullet hitting him in the back. The bullet did not hit the heart, but it did cut two arteries. Keysinger broke away and ran back into the saloon, yelling that he had been shot. Little could be done, as the severed arteries spurted blood until Keysinger died about forty minutes later.[18]

Another example of a mindset change – neutral to angry – occurred (September 1995) in Green County, Tennessee where a deputy sheriff, while in the process of taking pictures of a vehicle involved in a hit-and-run accident, was shot in his side. The deputy then turned to confront the suspect and was shot again. Up to and including the time of being shot the officer had a neutral mindset (unaware), but after being hit with the first bullet, the officer was able to transition into an angry mindset and shoot the suspect. Unfortunately, the deputy died later that evening during surgery.[19]

Category 5:
Fatal gunshot wound – **Ability** to commit deadly force – **Angry** mindset.

While anger/rage usually exists before deadly force is contemplated and used – this is NOT necessarily always the case. There are people who kill or murder without being angry or enraged. These are the individuals who "enjoy" killing, are "indifferent" to killing or have government authority to execute for the "State." Examples would include members of "Nazi" type execution squads, professional assassins (hit men) and government authorized executioners of court "sentenced to death" criminals. Whether or not these people would "enjoy" or be "indifferent" to being killed is another subject – best addressed by professional psychiatrists and/or psychologists.

Excluding these human aberrations, the usual precursor to an action and/or reaction involving the use of deadly force is anger/rage. One example occurred (July 1898) in Skagway, Alaska and involved an armed confrontation between Jeff "Soapy" Smith and Frank Reid:

> Soapy struck at Reid with his rifle barrel. Reid grabbed the barrel with his left hand and thrust it aside, at the same time reaching for the gun in his pocket. He pulled the trigger but the first cartridge missed fire [sic]. Soapy with both hands on the rifle, jerked it up against Reid and fired, the bullet striking Reid in the groin. Reid, however, fired a shot at the same instant and the slug tore into Soapy's heart. Both men fell to the planks, but in falling Reid fired another shot that struck Soapy eight inches above the knee. Reid lingered twelve days before he died.[20]

Another example occurred (July 1882) in Tombstone, Arizona where Deputy Sheriff Kiv Phillips attempted to arrest Filameno Orante. Orante raised his pistol and shot the deputy in cold blood. Though mortally wounded and with blood gushing from his mouth, Phillips drew his sixgun and fired four shots at Orante. Then he turned and walked through the saloon and out the back door, where he fell dead after walking thirty steps. Orante's bullet passed through the upper part of Phillip's right arm, between the ribs, through the lobe of the right lung, cutting the aorta and the windpipe, and then lodged in the left lung. Orante lived four days before he also died.[21]

Perhaps one of the most violent gunfight/knife fight incidents occurred (June 1873) in Medicine Lodge, Kansas between Hugh Anderson and Art McCluskie:

> The reason for this fight was Art McCluskie's vow to avenge his brother's death, who had been killed by Anderson and others in August 1871. These men agreed to fight to the death and in this duel (?) McCluskie drew blood first by putting a bullet into Anderson's arm causing him to fall, but Anderson was able to get to his knees and then put a bullet into McCluskie's jaw. Blind with rage, McCluskie lunged forward only to receive a bullet into his shoulder and another into his belly. From a downed position McCluskie then shot Anderson in the stomach. Wanting to make sure that Anderson was dead, McCluskie drew his knife and began dragging himself toward Anderson. When McCluskie got close and was within reach, Anderson rolled over and sunk the blade of his knife into McCluskie's neck. McCluskie in a

final dying effort, then drove his knife into Anderson's side.[22]

The above incident was one where the participants began with angry (enraged) mindsets, but then transitioned into berserk mindsets, i.e., from "goal" to "goal exclusive."

A more recent example of an angry mindset occurred (June 1992) while a sheriff was attempting to make an arrest:

> The sheriff grabbed both of the man's arms and a struggle ensued. In order to draw his service revolver, the sheriff apparently had to release one of the man's hands, enabling the assailant to shoot the sheriff in the stomach. Although fatally wounded, the sheriff was able to return fire, killing the assailant with a shot to the neck.[23]

Category 6:
Fatal gunshot wound – **Ability** to commit deadly force – **Berserk** mindset.

Unlike Category 3, where the effect of the gunshot wound can be minor, in Category 6, the gunshot wound is such that death is the final result – whether or not medical aid is given to the shootee. However, and before death occurs, the individual with a berserk mindset has the ability to and intends to commit irrational destructive violence. The public's general perception of a berserk person is usually that of a maniacal individual who gesticulates while screaming/yelling in an incoherent manner as he attacks a person or persons with murderous intent. Yet, also in this category is the stoical individual who is almost robotic (outwardly calm and very deliberate or methodical) in his physical movements and tone of voice as he attempts to murder a person or persons. It is also possible in the same individual that there could be a merging of the maniacal with the stoical behavior depending upon the specifics of a particular situation. Regardless, both the maniacal and the stoical berserker can be considered to have psychopathic (temporary or permanent) personalities.

One example involved a police officer and a farmer who had murdered young children (his own?) and was about to shoot his daughter. The police officer commanded the farmer to "freeze," but the farmer's response was to grin and then shoot his daughter. He then swung the shotgun toward the officer. The officer's response was to empty his revolver into the farmer. The farmer grunted, stumbled and fell to one knee. The officer moved into the next room in order to reload. The farmer followed him into the room, raised the shotgun, and yelling "goodbye cop," fired – hitting the officer in the right side. Then the farmer ran outside, got into a car and drove for several hours before being stopped and fatally shot while pointing his shotgun at a trooper. The autopsy found that **all six 38 hollowpoint bullets** [emphasis added] had hit their intended target, and all bullets had expanded without hitting bone.[24]

The next example involved two police officers and a person who most, if not all, would consider to be a psychopath. Entering the apartment, the officers observed bodies of children and adults. About this time, they heard a high-pitched laugh and were confronted by a knife-wielding father. The knife-wielder said: "Hello, my name is God. That gun is useless against an immortal being like myself. Why don't you lay it down and I'll free you like I did the rest." The officers ordered him to drop the knife, but were met with laughter and the father lunged toward them. The officers fired three times and the father <u>staggered</u> and <u>collapsed</u> – hit by only one bullet.[25]

This final example involved a bartender (moonlighting cop). Near closing time two men entered the bar; one man approached the bar and ordered a beer and the other man stood near the restroom door. When the beer was served, the man produced a sawed-off rifle and announced a holdup. The second man produced a pistol and ordered all the customers on the floor. The bartender turned to open the cash register and drew his revolver. As he turned he grabbed the rifle, deflecting its aim, and shot the wielder twice in the chest. Letting go of the rifle, he fired two shots at the second holdup man, who dropped his pistol and put up his hands. The off-duty officer was turning to check on the first holdup man when he was struck in the throat. He tried to bring his gun up, but he collapsed dead. His killer ran outside, where he collapsed and died.[26]

The author recognizes that initially the holdup man's mindset may not have been that of a berserker, but after being shot twice in the chest, he exhibited the tenacity and verve to become "goal exclusive." Consequently, the author considers the mindset of the holdup man to have transitioned (at the moment of bullet impact) to that of a berserker.

Excluding gunshot wounds that result in anatomical dysfunction can the anatomical location of a gunshot wound consistently (but not always) result in a specific psychological response to being shot? The answer appears to be a qualified "yes."

While it is unknown (to this author) who might have said it at an earlier time, it was reported that James B. Hickok told (before August 1876) Charles Gross:

> Charlie, I hope you never have to shoot any man, but if you do shoot him in the guts near the navel; you may not make a fatal shot, but he will get a shock that will paralyze his brain and arm so much that the fight is all over.[27]

One example of the effect of such a "gut" shot wound occurred (October 1881) in Tombstone, Arizona, where Frank McLaury was shot in the belly. He <u>staggered</u> off on the sidewalk....Frank McLaury was dead from a wound in the stomach, one inch left of the naval.[28]

Another example occurred (April 1886) in El Paso, Texas, where William Raynor received a gunshot wound in the stomach:

> At that moment Raynor burst into the room firing wildly. Rennick quickly knelt on the floor and, holding the gun in both hands, fired at his adversary, hitting him in the shoulder and stomach. Dazed, Raynor emptied his gun into a billiard table before he turned and <u>staggered</u> out to a streetcar and <u>collapsed</u> across one of the seats.[29]

A final and relatively recent example of the general effectiveness of this type of wound occurred in Georgia where:

> . . . Donald Benjamin, 34, was sentenced to 15 years in prison for injuring five people with a bat and a knife in the Peach County courthouse. He said he went off his medication for schizophrenia before the attack Sept. 18, 2003, that ended when an officer shot him once in the stomach.[30]

PHYSIOLOGICAL – PSYCHOLOGICAL INTERRELATIONSHIP

The interrelationship between the known (physiological) and the unknown (psychological) appears to present a dichotomy. On one side, physiological factors can be considered to be FINITE, i.e., the possible physical performance characteristics of anatomical parts are limited to the degree of development potential of the particular body part(s) being considered. Thus, no matter the kind or amount of chemicals, diet, exercise and training – body part(s) cannot be developed beyond a given limit. That this limit varies between individuals does not alter the fact that the extent of physical activity CANNOT exceed the potential maximum anatomical physical effort available in or to the affected body part. If relative comparisons were made based on physical strength alone, there would be a linear relationship between individuals, i.e., weakest to strongest.

On the other side, the psychological influence can be considered to be INFINITE, i.e., the psychological performance characteristics are non-linear and are only limited by the degree of mental thought involved. This degree of mental thought is randomly limitless, in that the mind can perceive of accomplishing anything. That can be understood to mean "there is always something more or something less that can be achieved."

Because of this "limitless" mental thought process, a linear relationship between individuals would rarely (if ever) occur. If relative comparisons were attempted based on the psychological (mental) response, the degree of variance is without limit.

Handgun Bullet Stopping Power

For example, the response could be: "Do less. Do same. Do more. Do less than less. Do less than same. Do less than more. Do more than less but less than more. Do more than less but less than same. Do more than same but less than more. Do more than more – ad infinitum. A graph chart would display randomly occurring peaks (more), plateaus (same) and valleys (less) and random heights of the peaks, plateaus and depths of the valleys.

It is readily apparent, with the exception of immediate (instantaneous) death OR the complete paralysis of both arms/forearms/hands, the possible type and extent of physiological and psychological response variables preclude an accurate prolepsis being made regarding the sequence of events during AND/OR the outcome of any gunfight that <u>has yet to occur</u>.

CHAPTER THREE ENDNOTES

[1] Erich Fromm, *The Anatomy of Human Destructiveness* (New York, New York: Holt, Rinehart and Winston, 1973) p. 8.

[2] Ibid. p. 187.

[3] Video, *Armed Defense*, Cooper's Way. Colonel Jeff Cooper's Personal Defense Course on Video, Tape 4. (Reno, Nevada: Quad Productions, 1995).

[4] J. S. Hatcher, *Textbook of Pistols and Revolvers* (Plantersville, South Carolina: Small Arms Technical Publishing Company, 1935 – reprinted Prescott, Arizona: Wolfe Publishing Company, 1985), pp. 428-429.

[5] Roderick C. Carman, "Guns of the Real Indiana Jones" *Gun Digest 2005* (Iola, Wisconsin: Krause Publications, 2004), pp. 29, 32.

[6] D. McLoughlin, *Wild and Wooly – An Encyclopedia of the Old West* (New York: Barnes and Noble Books, 1995), p. 150.

[7] Donald Chaput, *Virgil Earp, Western Peace Officer* (Norman, Oklahoma: University of Oklahoma Press Printing, 1996), p. 149.

[8] Video, *Deadly Effects – Wound Ballistics* (Pinole, California: ANITE Productions, 1987).

[9] Richard Patterson, *Historical Atlas of the Outlaw West* (Boulder, Colorado: Johnson Publishing Company, 1985 – 3rd printing 1989), p. 16.

[10] Ibid. p. 69.

[11] U.S. Department of Justice, Federal Bureau of Investigation, *Uniform Crime Reports – Law Enforcement Officers Killed and Assaulted, 1993*, pp. 49, 50.

[12] Mark Bowdon, *Black Hawk Down* (NYC, New York: Signet, New American Library, A Division of Penguin Putnam Inc., 2000 – 1st Signet printing, 2001), p. 51.

[13] L. A. Rutledge, "Trial by Fire: 38 vs. Moros." *1985 Handgun Annual* (Los Angeles, California: Petersen Publishing Company, 1985), Volume 2, p. 136.

[14] Louis A. LaGarde, *Gunshot Injuries* (New York: Wm. Wood & Company, 1916 – 2nd edition published Mt. Ida, Arkansas: Lancer Militaria, 1991), p. 70.

[15] U.S. Department of Justice, Federal Bureau of Investigation, *Uniform Crime Reports – Law Enforcement Officers Killed and Assaulted, 1995*, p. 51.

[16] Wayne C. Lee, *Bad Men & Bad Towns* (Caldwell, Idaho: Caxton Printers, Ltd., 1993), p. 59.

[17] McLoughlin, op. cit., p. 96.

[18] Lee, op. cit., p. 71.

[19] U.S. Department of Justice, Federal Bureau of Investigation, *Uniform Crime Reports – Law Enforcement Officers Killed and Assaulted, 1995*, p. 55.

[20] F. Robertson and B. Harris, *Soapy Smith – King of the Frontier Con Men* (New York: Hastings House, 1961), pp. 209-210.

[21] B. T. Traywick, *Tombstone Outlaw Album* (Tombstone, Arizona: Red Marie's, 1984), p. 19.

[22] Patterson, op. cit., p. 75.

[23] U.S. Department of Justice, Federal Bureau of Investigation, *Uniform Crime Reports – Law Enforcement Officers Killed and Assaulted, 1992, p. 44.*

[24] E. Marshall and E. Sanow, *Handgun Stopping Power* (Boulder, Colorado: Paladin Press, 1992), p. 59.

[25] Ibid., p. 90.

[26] Ibid., p. 61.

[27] Joseph G. Rosa, *The Gunfighter: Man or Myth* (Norman, Oklahoma: University of Oklahoma Press, 1969), p. 120.

[28] Ibid. pp. 238, 139.

[29] Ibid. p. 128.

[30] Associated Press, "Across the Nation: Georgia: Fort Valley" USA TODAY, December 2, 2004.

CHAPTER FOUR

TIME-FRAME PARAMETER

OVERVIEW

In discussions and in publications pertaining to bullet-stopping power, the subject of the time-frame parameter is often vaguely defined, given cursory consideration and then conveniently ignored. Yet of all the abstract subjects involved in any dialogue about bullet-stopping power, the time-frame and its major sub-topics (duration, increased risk and reduced bullet efficacy) are one of the most important relative to the final outcome of any gunfight.

DEFINITION

For use within this text, the "Time-Frame Parameter" is defined as the period of time that <u>begins</u> the instant deadly force action begins (e.g., first shot is fired) and <u>stops</u> the instant deadly force action ceases (e.g., last shot is fired).

Other sub-topics that could be considered are concealment, cover, movement, visibility and the distance between combatants. However, they are more properly considered to be subjects of strategy or tactics. Whereas, duration, increased risk and reduced bullet efficacy have a direct bearing on the time frame as defined above.

Duration

Occurring within the time-frame parameter, duration is defined as the period of time that begins the instant the first bullet impacts, penetrates and/or perforates one of the combatants and stops when the last bullet to hit a combatant has occurred. Consequently, any and all shots fired <u>before</u> the first combatant is shot and all shots fired <u>after</u> the last bullet to hit a combatant has occurred are excluded from the time defined as the duration. The reason for this exclusion is that all such shots fired before and after the period of time considered to be the duration usually have little direct import.

It would at first appear that with more shots fired, there would be an increased risk for any of the combatants to be hit. For example, if/when the combatants are behind cover (bullets cannot penetrate) they cannot be hit. Such shots are for the most part ineffective and when done by the officer(s) serve no purpose with the exception of preventing or reducing effective return shots by the suspects. This allows possible movement of the officer(s) to gain a tactical advantage.

However, when the shooting is done by the suspects, there is a different public safety issue, i.e., in addition to the risk to the involved officer(s), these shots pose a real danger to innocent bystanders who may be quite some distance away from the gunfight.

Duration within the time-frame parameter involves someone who has been wounded and the extent of this duration is of **vital** importance, e.g., a Special Forces sergeant was reported to have said:

> The large calibre, slow moving 45 bullet puts the bad guys on the ground. Lighter stuff like the Beretta's 9mm will, too, - eventually - but on the battlefield, you almost always have to double tap, and, in close combat, a gunfighter hasn't the time or ammo to lose firing two rounds.[1]

Another example that emphasizes the vital importance of the duration involved an off-duty deputy sheriff, who at the time of the incident was a patron in a tavern. During a robbery, the deputy shot the suspect in the chest, a wound that proved fatal eventually. However, before dying, the robber engaged the deputy in a struggle and managed to beat him (deputy) to death with a sawed-off rifle.[2] In this incident, for whatever reason, the robber either would not or could not use the rifle as a firearm, but instead used it as a club.

There is little consolation for the officer and/or civilian if the shootee receives an eventually lethal gunshot wound, but because the gunshot wound does not immediately **stop** the lethal threat action, the shootee, before dying, is able to inflict a lethal wound in the officer or civilian – gunshot or otherwise. It is this eventually that is responsible for more pyrrhic victories than any other single factor.

Increased Risk

Even if the results of a gunfight are ultimately favorable to the officer, it is important to remember whenever multiple hits are required to stop the lethal threat action, the risk factor is increased due to the increase in the time-frame available for return shots. The importance of this increased risk should not be glossed over because death or grievous injury can be the consequences of returned shots during any extension of the time-frame of the gunfight. Consider the following:

Each of two individuals in a gunfight can shoot and hit at a rate of two shots per second. Both individuals shoot, and the gunfight is over in one second. This means the risk factor to each person was two hits. Increase the time for the gunfight to two seconds, then to three seconds, and the risk factor for each person then becomes four and six hits. Given a choice, would you want your adversary to shoot at you two, four or six times?

The following example of increased risk, due to the need to make multiple hits, was reported by a soldier serving in Afghanistan:

> To make matters worse, the 9mm round is like firing paint balls. I had to pump four rounds into an al-Quaeda who was coming at me before he dropped. We're dealing with fanatical crazies out here who won't quit until they die for Allah.[3]

No mention was made if the al-Quaeda individual was or was not able to return fire, and if he was able, whether or not he did shoot at the soldier during the time between the impact of the first and the fourth bullet? However, the fact remains that four hits were required and is an indication that the time needed to make four hits would have been about two seconds. Although there are other unknown variables (e.g., the body parts penetrated by the first three bullets and the mindset of the individual), available time (opportunity) appears to have existed for the al-Quaeda member to return fire?

Reduced Bullet Efficacy

Although not always concomitant with the increased risk due to the prolonged duration of a gunfight, reduced bullet efficacy is often an important factor that contributes to prolonged duration. Reduced bullet efficacy can be the result of the shootee's physical and/or mental condition, i.e., the shootee's response to the shot (bullet) placement and/or to specific bullet performance characteristics.

1. Physical Condition. This includes agility, body size, strength and stamina. Some may question the inclusion of agility. However, a person's agility sometimes enables physical movement to be made that results in a bullet missing a body part that would have otherwise been hit. The greater the person's agility ability, the more effective the movement can be, which means a person may sometimes avoid being hit altogether.

A person's body size (bulk/weight) can and often does affect bullet performance. Consider three body sizes. First, a one hundred (100) pound individual; second, a two hundred (200) pound individual; third, a three hundred (300) pound individual. The amount of body mass the bullet must penetrate/perforate in order to reach and disrupt vital body organs can and does vary significantly. Using the same load and with similar bullet placement: In one person (100 pounds) the bullet penetration may be excessive. In another person (200 pounds) the bullet penetration may be adequate. In another person (300 pounds) the bullet penetration may be inadequate. As it relates to bullet performance, a person's body size determines to a large extent what, in fact, a bullet can or cannot do. The subject of bullet efficacy is addressed in the next chapter.

A person's physical strength need not be Herculean. There are numerous incidents of people, who, possessed of presumed average or even less than average strength, after being shot reacted in ways that cannot be adequately explained based on body strength alone. The fact that physical strength varies between individuals is of less importance than what the individual can do with what strength is available after being shot.

Physical stamina is a complex consideration and is addressed as a dual aspect of the person's physical and mental state.

2. Mental Condition. When modified by the use of chemicals a person's mental condition can cause unusual and/or unexpected reactions to being shot. One result can be an extension of the available time to commit a lethal threat action before the physical affect of the bullet results in the cessation of the lethal threat action. For example, in Mogadishu, Somali, many Somali men, particularly the young men who cruised around Mog on "technicals," vehicles with .50 calibre machine guns bolted in back, were addicted to **khat**, a mild amphetamine that looked like water cress.[4] The use of chemicals to modify behavior patterns appears to be, if not common, at least not a rare practice among certain groups. The following is one example that occurred in Afghanistan, during operation Anaconda:

> In another fight, one Ranger fired several torso shots with a 45 pistol before his foe fell. When we looked at the corpses, we found their mouths full of khat.[5]

Mental condition modified by fanaticism can also cause unusual and/or unexpected reactions after being shot. Fanaticism can be based on the political, religious and/or social ideology of a group or of an individual. While it is true that acts of fanaticism can be more easily directed or intensified by the use of chemicals, the use of chemicals is NOT essential in order for fanatical behavior to occur. Fanaticism should not be confused with dementia – a person need not be psychotic to be a fanatic. However, as it refers to the reaction to an eventually lethal gunshot wound, both the fanatic and the psychotic are often able to continue the lethal threat action as though nothing of enervating physical OR mental consequence had occurred.

Whereas, an otherwise normal person, who has the same abilities (strength and stamina) is less likely to display the same degree of mental indifference to a gunshot wound. A person can possess great physical stamina, but because of a neutral or even an angry mindset, the actual demonstrated stamina is often considerably less, and if it was not so serious, sometimes almost to the extent of being ridiculous, for example:

Handgun Bullet Stopping Power

> One Illinois officer fell down and died after being shot in the arm with one .22 calibre bullet. What doctors call "psychosomatic death" – that is, sudden death in which emotional states like hopelessness and feeling of abandonment are primary contributing factors. . . .[6]

The last subject to be addressed within this chapter concerns what many people refer to as action versus reaction. This is a somewhat controversial subject, and it is often incorrectly or at least incompletely described. Many persons profess to know the difference between action and reaction, but are unable to articulate how, where and when the supposed differences occur.

Before an explanation of the differences can be given, it is first necessary to identify and define the elements that are involved.

First, and perhaps surprising to many, there is NOT any actual difference in the physiology (physical mechanism) between decisions of action or reaction. How can this be? Reaction is defined:

> The chain of body responses can be understood through the S-O-R (Stimulus-Organism-Response) concept; also, in this concept the introduction of a stimulus is perceived by the organism, the organism then processes the essential data and picks an appropriate reaction, which is translated into motor responses.[7]

This description of reaction also applies to action – in that both require and use electrochemical pulses. Whether action or reaction, the electrochemical pulses travel at nearly the same speed through the nervous system, between 0.15 and 0.20 second. . . .[8] The sole distinction between action and reaction is that with action the "S" (stimulus) occurs prior to the time-frame and with reaction, the entire S-O-R occurs within the time frame.

Misunderstanding can exist because it is mistakenly thought by some that NO TIME is needed to initiate action; i.e., action occurs without any need for a physiological lag time. While both combatants utilize these electrochemical pulses, only the person <u>reacting</u> has the time (0.15 to 0.20 second) included in the actual time required to physically press/pull the trigger (fire a shot). Consequently, the quickest time to react and shoot to other than a practiced stimulus is about 0.20 second. Remember, the internal S-O-R time (about 0.15 to 0.20 second) involved in initiating the movement of the trigger cannot be discerned by the <u>reacting</u> combatant.

With gun in hand and finger on the trigger, forty-six (46) police officers were tested for the response time (beep signal of a timer) needed to react and fire a shot. The result was a mean (three attempts average per officer) reaction/shoot time of about **0.37** second, with 0.17 second the fastest and 0.89 second the slowest.[9]

However, there are techniques that can be used to reduce the total S-O-R reaction time to the degree the reaction can almost be considered a conditioned reflex action. That is, a reaction triggered by anticipation. Where range commands are known and given in a consistent manner, i.e., voice command, whistle, horn, light or some combination of same; the technique of anticipating the start signal is used by some individuals. Should a person "jump the gun" in organized shooting competition, the penalty can be forfeiture of the shot value or even the forfeiture of the total score for a stage of fire. If a person's behavior is flagrant and/or repeated, he can be removed from the competition and he may be prohibited from participating in one or more future scheduled events.

However, when done in the field, the results can be disastrous. For example, while being interviewed/interrogated, the subject/suspect makes a furtive move and the officer's instant reaction is to shoot him, only to determine the subject/suspect is unarmed and was only reaching for his wallet (ID). *Possible consequences* of behavior based on anticipation: Criminally liable = suspension, arrest, trial, conviction and incarceration.

CHAPTER FOUR ENDNOTES

[1] David H. Hackworth, (Col. USA Ret.), "Sound Off," *Soldier of Fortune*, Volume 27, No. 11 (November 2002), p. 82.

[2] Ronald J. Adams, Thomas M. McTernan and Charles Remsberg, *Street Survival* (Northbrook, Illinois: Calibre Press, 1980 – 13th printing 1989), p. 216.

[3] Hackworth, loc. cit.

[4] Mark Bowdon, *Black Hawk Down* (New York: SIGNET, New American Library, a Division of Penguin Putnam, Inc., 2000 – 1st Signet printing 2001), p. 23.

[5] Hackworth, loc. cit.

[6] Adams, McTernan and Remsberg, loc. cit., p. 218.

[7] James D. Mason, *Combat Handgun Shooting* (Springfield, Illinois: Charles Thomas Publisher, 1976), p. 45.

[8] Ibid. p. 47.

[9] Ernest J. Tobin and Martin L. Fackler, M.D., "Officer Reaction-Response Times in Firing a Handgun," *Wound Ballistics Review* (1997), 3(1):7-8.

CHAPTER FIVE

BULLET EFFICACY

OVERVIEW

There are four core factors that contribute to the reality of any "stopping" phenomenon within the term Effective Stopping Power (ESP). The first three (the Physiological Response, the Psychological Response and the Time-Frame Parameter) have been previously addressed. As important as these three are, in the final analysis it is Bullet Efficacy that contributes the most to the type and extent of the <u>shootee's</u> response. In this chapter, if or when relative comparisons of bullet efficacy are made, it presupposes that each bullet has the same point of impact AND makes the same type of penetration trajectory (wound track). The only variables are the quantity of tissue displaced/disrupted due to the differences in bullet diameter and/or meplat diameter AND the distance (depth) of bullet penetration.

Bullet Efficacy is the basis upon which concepts and formulae have been and continue to be developed in order to articulate arguable indicators of the comparative and relative probability of bullets (various loads) achieving ESP. As with the definition of ESP given in chapter one, there can be more than one acceptable definition of Bullet Efficacy. The following is the definition used by the author and it is the definition referred to whenever Bullet Efficacy is discussed:

> A numerical value indicating the relative position of a bullet's effectiveness when compared with other bullets as it pertains to the probability of achieving ESP.

DETERMINANTS

What are the determinants that enable bullet efficacy values to be derived? The primary determinants are considered to be Calibre (Diameter), Cross Sectional Area, Design, Meplat, Penetration, Shape, Velocity and Weight. Each determinant affects the performance characteristics of one or more of the other determinants. While describable, this affect cannot be categorically ascribed with an absolute value of relative importance. This is due to the affect of random variables on combinations of these determinants. This can be and usually is further complicated by the affect of other random variables disassociated from the bullet itself, e.g., distance, variations in anatomical resistance to bullet penetration and/or intervening media.

Each determinant is described as if it exists by itself and after all determinants

Calibre (Diameter)

The diameter of a bullet and/or a bullet within a cartridge is usually indicated in either millimeters or inches. Cartridges identified using millimeters may or may not have an accompanying name, e.g., 7mm Mauser or 7x57mm. Cartridges identified using inches almost invariably are identified (at least initially) using a number/letters combination, e.g., 375 H&H Magnum or 444 Marlin. The number can be the actual, the approximate or the nominal bore or groove diameter[1] - e.g., the actual (.375 = .375"), the approximate (10mm = .400") or the nominal (.44 = .429"). When identifying a cartridge, the number can refer to the actual (257 Roberts = .257"), the approximate (45 Colt = .451") or the nominal (405 Winchester = .411") bullet diameter. Whether a bullet is a non-expanding or expanding type, there are several reasons to know or ascertain the actual diameter of the bullet in question.

1. Non-Expanding Bullet.

First, unless fired from a smooth bore barrel, the actual diameter of a fired bullet will usually be measurably less than its advertised calibre (diameter). A recovered non-expanding bullet will be smaller in mean diameter than it was before being fired. This is due to the displacement of bullet material by the lands in the barrel – they cause the grooves in the bullet. Second, even when chambered for the same cartridge, there can be and often are discernible differences in bore and groove diameters between firearms made by different manufacturers. A more precise diameter measurement would included the weighted average of the bore and groove diameter.[2] Third, when calculations are made where the diameter of the bullet is required, e.g., sectional density, a more precise answer will result when the measured (actual instead of advertised) diameter is used.

2. Expanding Bullet.

First, if the bullet did not expand, it is obviously measured as if it is a non-expanding bullet. Second, if bullet expansion is asymmetrical two measurements are needed, i.e., the largest and the smallest diameters of the expanded part of the bullet are added and the sum is divided by two, this gives the mean expanded diameter. Third, if the bullet expansion was symmetrical and is larger than the original unfired diameter, a single measurement of the diameter will suffice. However, of the literally hundreds of recovered test bullets and numerous bullets recovered from big game animals, NONE resulted in symmetrical expansion. In reality, symmetrical expansion is virtually impossible to achieve. Measure the so-called symmetrical expansion as if it is asymmetrical, because it almost invariably is. <u>Fourth</u>, without the necessary technical support equipment, it is extremely difficult to determine where maximum bullet expansion (if any) occurred and if applicable at what depth of penetration bullet fragmentation began.

Another consideration that applies to both non-expanding and expanding bullets is yaw. Somewhere between the muzzle and the target, most (if not all) bullets exhibit some degree of yawing. The degree of yaw is generally very small (usually 3 degrees or less), but when the conditions are least favorable, a bullet can yaw as much as 180 degrees – the base of the bullet rotating to the forward position in the trajectory path.

It is rare for a bullet to yaw 180 degrees while penetrating the atmosphere. For this to happen, the rate of twist and/or the bullet velocity is too slow for the length and shape of the bullet. Some bullets that have a stable flight in the atmosphere exhibit a tendency to yaw after penetrating into tissue. This is mentioned because, depending upon the extent of the bullet yaw, the profile of the longitudinal axis of the yawing bullet may present a larger cross sectional surface area than does the frontal area of a nonexpanding or even an expanding bullet that penetrates in a so-called straight line. Where and when yawing occurs can be determined/observed by using calibrated 250A ordnance gelatin, specialized photography equipment and/or by witness panels.

Cross Sectional Area (CSA)

The cross sectional area (CSA) indicates the largest frontal surface area within the perimeter of the circumference of the calibre (bullet).[3] This frontal surface area can be of various configurations, e.g., it may resemble a pointed steeple, a round hill, a round hill with a pronounced ledge, a flat hill with a pronounced ledge or it can be flat as the proverbial pancake. This CSA may or may not correspond to the CSA of the bullet's meplat. To calculate CSA, multiply the radius squared times pi (3.14159) OR multiply 0.7854 times the diameter squared. For example, given a diameter of 0.451" (radius = 0.2255"), thus radius squared = 0.05085 x 3.14159 = 0.15975 = **0.160** OR 0.7854 times the diameter squared = 0.7854 x 0.203401 = 0.15975 = **0.160** – in both instances rounded to the nearest thousandth.

An important consideration regarding CSA is with a proportional increase in the diameter there is a disproportional increase in CSA. The following illustrates the significance of an increase in CSA:

Diameter	Diameter % Increase	CSA (inches)	CSA % Increase
From .357"	-	0.100	-
To .714"	**100**	0.400	**400**

Since cross-sectional area increases as the square of diameter, this is a subtle way of saying that the most important element of stopping power is bullet diameter. In other words, the easiest way to realize a significant increase in stopping power is to go to a larger calibre handgun. Bullet weight and velocity, hence recoil can remain the same, but if bullet diameter is increased, stopping power will increase appreciably.[4]

As an interesting aside, provided adequate penetration is not adversely affected, this author is unaware of any known wound ballistics authority who opines an increase in bullet cross sectional area will result in a <u>decrease</u> in stopping power.

Another important, yet seldom discussed or mentioned consideration is the fact that for about the last one-fourth (¼) to one-third (⅓) of the bullet's penetration in tissue, the size of the wound channel is considerably <u>smaller</u> than the actual cross frontal surface area of the bullet. While not confirmed by autopsy examinations of humans shot with bullets that did not perforate the body, the author has examined and measured the wound tracks of multiple dozens of big game animals taken by him and other hunters; this characteristic of there being a wound track that is smaller than the recovered bullet has been observed. This characteristic has also been observed during tests conducted by the author shooting into calibrated 10% 250A ordnance gelatin – a tissue simulant (formula developed by Dr. Martin Fackler) that offers similar resistance to bullet penetration as does animal tissue. The results of these tests consistently disclosed, from about the last one-fourth (¼) to one-third (⅓) of the bullet penetration track, the permanent cavity to be considerably smaller (from about one-third [⅓] to one-half [½] the size) than the actual cross frontal diameter of the recovered bullet. This occurs regardless of the final bullet shape.

This is the result of the bullet decelerating to a velocity of about 300 (± 10%) feet per second (fps). The velocity of about 300 fps was determined by firing a bullet into a single block of calibrated 250A ordnance gelatin of sufficient length to stop the bullet, then measuring the distance where the visible point of the smaller channel began. Additional blocks of calibrated 250A ordnance gelatin were then separated at this (average of several shots) penetration depth and a chronograph was placed between the two blocks and a shot was taken. After perforating the first block the bullet crosses over the chronograph screens before penetrating into the second block and the velocity value is indicated/recorded.

As a result of several such tests and pending the results of additional and more comprehensive tests, the velocity of about 300 (± 10%) fps is tentatively considered to be correct. At this velocity and until it comes to a stop, the bullet is penetrating the medium with enough force to displace/disrupt only a small percentage of the 250A ordnance gelatin contacted by the frontal area of the bullet. The resilience of the medium causes the hole to partially close after the bullet has penetrated forward.

It should also be mentioned that this phenomenon can and does occur in some penetration trajectory paths or tracks for a considerably greater depth of penetration; i.e., occasionally as much as approximately ninety (90%) percent of the total distance penetrated. Examples would include certain loads (bullets) from the 25 ACP, the 9mm Luger and the 45 ACP. However, it is important to recognize that a reduced size of the wound track occurs with any type of conventional bullet.

Design

Since the days when the patched lead ball was the state-of-the-art "bullet" efforts have been made and are continuing to be made to design and produce bullets that will result in performance improvements within the three main divisions of ballistics (interior, exterior and terminal). For example, <u>interior ballistics</u>: less peak pressure or a change in the pressure curve; <u>exterior ballistics</u>: shorter time of flight or less deflection and/or drift; <u>terminal (wound) ballistics</u>: more retained bullet mass integrity or more controlled expansion and penetration.

While bullet design affects interior and exterior ballistics, this work is concerned with the affect of bullet design as it pertains to terminal (wound) ballistics. Consequently, consideration is given to past and contemporary bullet designs that have been and are intended to be used as a means by which a lethal threat action can be effectively stopped.

What is meant by design? Design refers to the bullet's composition, structure and shape (configuration).

1. Composition.

Bullets have been made and continue to be made from a variety of substances. Until the early 1990s lead was the principal material used to manufacture bullets. About that time (early/mid 1990s) the ammunition companies became serious in their efforts to find ways to reduce/replace the lead and other heavy metals used in the manufacture of ammunition. The trend is to find and use materials that are less harmful to people and the environment. This type of ammunition is referred to as Non-Toxic, Less Toxic or Reduced Hazard and there has been significant progress.[5~6]

Nonetheless, the main constituent of many bullets continues to be lead (pure lead for muzzle and front loading firearms) and/or lead alloys (varying percentages of tin and antimony) for numerous fixed cartridges. Other types of bullets are referred to as "leadless" – which is a misnomer because these bullets are merely a modified version of either a soft point or a full metal jacket bullet that has the lead core completely enclosed by some form of jacket material. Other bullets are manufactured that incorporate a pure copper jacket, a gilding metal (copper/zinc alloy, typically a 95:5 ratio) jacket or a plated steel jacket – all of which still utilize a lead core.

However, jacketed bullets have been or are being made that do not use lead for the core. In place of a lead core can be one of pure bismuth that has been cast, swaged or plated with a jacket of gilding metal or pure copper – molded metal powder with a nylon (synthetic) binder – compressed tungsten powder – stranded zinc or combinations of other less toxic substances. There are also bullets that are made using a single less toxic material, e.g., heat-treated copper.

2. Structure.

One purpose of bullet structure is to help maintain mass integrity while the bullet is penetrating the target. Depending upon the end use or purpose, the structure can be cast or swaged lead, water quenched or heat treated cast lead alloy, a front and rear lead core swaged into an "H" partition jacket of gilding metal, a lead core chemically bonded and swaged into an "H" partition jacket or solid heat-treated copper. The last mentioned structure also happens to be the bullet's composition. Regardless of what the composition and structure are, these designs can also include nose/ogive features such as a hollow point, a soft point, a protected soft point that are not restricted to a particular bullet shape.

3. Shape (Configuration).

This topic is defined and described under its own heading.

Meplat

"A meplat is the maximum frontal surface area of the bullet, presented as a single flat surface, impacting/penetrating the target."[7] The meplat's diameter relative to the original bullet shape and in conjunction with a threshold impact and penetration velocity determines whether the displacement/disruption of tissue is caused by the meplat's CSA or by a combination of the meplat's CSA and the diameter/shape of the bullet behind the meplat.

Point (meplat) Cavitation Criterion:

> "We now come to a very important question about the flow over composite nose forms. Does the flow cavitate at the point or does it cavitate at the bullet shoulder? If the flat point is small, the flow will

remain attached over the shoulder portion of the nose. But if the flat point is large . . . cavitation will begin at the point, in this case the shoulder portion of the bullet contributes nothing to the drag and . . . if the flow remains attached over the entire bullet nose then the shoulder portion contributes much of the bullet drag.[8]

The initial meplat's CSA can be comparatively small, e.g., the various Sierra, Hollow Point Boat Tail (MatchKing) bullets or the initial meplat's CSA can be comparatively large, e.g., the various Veral Smith, Ogival Wadcutter bullets. In addition, while the bullet is penetrating, the CSA of the meplat may not increase. It may increase but the extent of the increase does not exceed the CSA of the bullet's original diameter. It may increase significantly, i.e., more than ten percent larger than the original meplat or the bullet's original diameter. Finally, the meplat's CSA may increase until bullet fragmentation occurs.

The meplat diameter should NOT be considered to be synonymous with either the original diameter of the bullet that does not expand or the final diameter of a bullet that does expand. It can be, but it occurs only on rare occasions. When there is NO bullet expansion and for the meplat diameter and the original bullet diameter to be the same, the design has to be such that the meplat's diameter is the same as the actual bore and groove diameter of the barrel. It would have the profile of a fifty-five gallon drum with 90-degree sharp shoulder (edges) at the periphery of the front end. When there is bullet expansion and the bullet profile resembles the proverbial mushroom, the diameter of the meplat is usually less than ninety (< 90%) percent of the maximum diameter of the expanded bullet.

Penetration

This is perhaps the easiest of all determinants to define and describe. Bullet penetration simply means the bullet makes a hole in whatever it strikes. Not a part of the general definition is a specific required distance (depth) of penetration. However, as it pertains to bullet efficacy, the factors to consider are the type of penetration trajectory the bullet (specific load) makes and whether or not the longitudinal axis of the bullet, either temporarily or permanently deviates (yaws) from the longitudinal axis of the penetration track. Also important is an answer to the question: Will the bullet (specific load) penetrate the necessary depth to cut/sever major blood vessels, disrupt vital organs or reach and make dysfunctional the CNS (brain/cervical/upper thoracic spinal cord) from any angle OR will the bullet penetrate the necessary depth only from an ideal frontal chest or lateral head shot? It becomes obvious that equally as important as shot (bullet) placement is adequate penetration. What is accomplished if the bullet hits the intended external spot, but the bullet penetration is insufficient to reach and disrupt vital body parts? This is not mere conjecture, e.g., the following shooting incident occurred (April 1862) and was reported by Captain Harrison Trow:

> I shot him in the forehead just above his eyes. I even put my finger in the bullet hole to be sure I had him. The ball never entered his skull, but went round it. To make sure of him, I shot him in the foot and he never flinched, so I left him for dead.[9]

In the final year of the American War Between the States, another similar incident involving inadequate bullet penetration occurred (December 1865):

> According to the doctor who examined him, the first bullet had hit him near the top of his forehead, cutting through to the skull bone, cutting out a round crease and glancing off. . . . The ball (second shot) entered about three-fourths of an inch directly under his right eye, penetrating some two and one-half inches on a level with the base of the brain, inclining downwards and inwards, where it yet remains. Though the ball struck Dennison Crandall slightly below the eye, he did not fall, but advanced toward the outlaws after being shot.[10]

Another example of inadequate bullet penetration occurred (September 1882) in El Paso, Texas during the gunfight between "Doc" Manning and Dallas Stoudenmire. Doc got his gun, a double action .44, into action and shot Dallas. The ball lodged in a large pocketbook and a packet of letters in Stoudenmire's right breast pocket.[11] Shot placement, although not ideal, was still acceptable, while penetration was not. Another perhaps more apropos example, occurred in Cleveland, Ohio (no date given):

> They (police officers) found the subject on the second floor during a room by room search. . . . the subject jumped out from a cubbyhole and started down the stairs firing his .38 revolver. Two slugs buried themselves in Melton's armor as Melton and two other officers returned fire. . . . Melton's armor stopped the first slug directly over his heart and the second shot dead center on his sternum.[12]

Some readers might consider the first three examples to be interesting but, because of the "black powder" handgun ballistics then available, to have little relevance to the ballistics of today's handgun ammunition? To help rectify that misconception, compare (location and date not indicated) with:

> The smuggler was hit once in the forehead with a 45 Automatic bullet which glanced on his sloping forehead and passed around under the

scalp. The other bullet entered his mouth and lodged in the solid mass of bone at the base of the skull, and he made a prompt recovery in about three weeks.[13]

Other readers might also disallow the fourth example as not being fair (?) because body armor was involved. However, take note of the second and fifth example where in each case one bullet ricocheted off the skull bone and the other bullet was stopped by the bone at the base of the skull. The point may then be made that the 45 ACP bullet (full metal jacket) is noted for giving adequate but usually not excessive penetration. However, the following incident involved a 9mm Luger (with a full metal jacket bullet it is noted for usually giving excessive tissue penetration) and should give one cause to reconsider:

> Although the Browning (9mm Luger) is high powered, Sieff's strong front teeth absorbed the impact of the bullet, which came to rest a fraction of an inch away from his jugular vein.[14]

Another incident, although not involving a human, illustrates the problematic penetration ability of the 9mm when head (skull) shots are involved:

> State biologist, Larry Lewis investigated the incident. Upon examining the bear's skull, he found one slug under the hide, and marks where two bullets (9mm) had bounced off. None penetrated the skull, even though they were the full-metal-jacket type.[15]

While the actual depth of bullet penetration is determined by the resistance factor of the substance being penetrated, the design of the bullet, the impact velocity, the rate of expansion, the rate of deceleration and other variables; comparative *potential* bullet penetration values can be established. **See Appendix A.** These potential penetration values presuppose all bullets have the same point of impact, make the same type of penetration track and that bullet configuration either does not change during the penetration OR the extent of any change is proportional. Remember, this is the potential penetration and not the actual depth of penetration. The penetration value does not indicate how much of material "x" the bullet will penetrate; instead it indicates the relative depth of potential penetration when compared with other loads (bullets).

Shape (Configuration)

Bullet nose/ogive shape can vary significantly – from an almost needle-like spire or spitzer point to a wadcutter. To further complicate this subject is the fact that almost any nose/ogive shape can include features such as a full metal jacket (aka a full patch or metal case), a soft point, a protected soft point or a hollow point. These bullet shapes have been designed to be either permanent or transient. If permanent, the bullet could (if recovered) be used again in the assembly of a cartridge. If transient, the bullet may expand as designed; however, these types of bullets may also bend, buckle, rivet, split or otherwise deform or even fragment in a manner unintended by the manufacturer. As a result, there are two disparate schools of thought regarding the significance of the initial or original bullet nose configuration.

Those of the first school consider the initial bullet nose configuration to be very important and a major contributing factor to whatever degree of effective stopping power is achieved. The semiwadcutter (a sub calibre wadcutter) or a wadcutter bullet nose configuration is usually the bullet shape of choice. These bullet shapes (SWC – WC) cause more tissue disruption per unit of penetration than do other non-expanding bullet nose shapes and the disruption is also more severe in that the bullet tends to cut or chop as it penetrates tissue – analogous to a biscuit or cookie cutter. Other bullet nose shapes tend to penetrate by *pushing* through tissue and the resilience (elasticity) factor of most tissue results in there being a smaller permanent wound track. Those in this group attach much less significance to whether or not a bullet expands – if the bullet expands it may or may not be a plus but expansion is not considered essential. As indicated in a FBI publication, "Handgun bullets expand in the human target only 60-70% of the time at best."[16] While this percentage may have changed (more or less?) since the date of the publication (1989); bullet "expansion must never be the basis for bullet selection, but considered a bonus when, and if, it occurs."[17]

Those belonging to the second school give scant attention to the initial bullet nose configuration just so the bullet design results in the bullet expanding from 1.5 to 1.75 times its original diameter in the first one-half (½) to one and one-half (1½) inches of penetration. Those in this group consider bullet expansion to be the one essential element if consistent ESP is to be achieved. There are a couple of factors which raise serious questions regarding the consistency and reliability of handgun bullet expansion when combined with adequate penetration.

If the bullet expands as intended so as to resemble a "mushroom" the efficacy of the expanded bullet diameter is less than would at first be indicated. If, for example, a .355" calibre, 115 grain bullet expands 1.75 times to .621" but has a meplat of .559" (about 90% of the expanded diameter) that is the actual working area of the bullet. This .559" represents an effective CSA increase of almost 2.5 times that of the original .355" calibre. In ten inches of penetration the .355" WADCUTTER bullet will disrupt about 0.989 inches of tissue, while the .559" working meplat will disrupt about 2.454 inches of tissue. This would appear to indicate the expanded bullet is much more effective?

Things are not always as what they first appear. First, the ROUNDED periphery of the expanded bullet tends to push through tissue and unless the bullet strike is very close to being perpendicular, major blood vessels are more apt to be pushed aside rather than to be severed or cut as would be the case with the SHARP edge of a semiwadcutter or wadcutter bullet. Second, if other factors are the same or nearly the same, bullet sectional density is an indicator of relative penetration. The sectional density of the 115 gr .355" bullet (no expansion) is about **0.130** and about **0.043** for the same bullet expanded to 0.621" (1.75 times original diameter). If a 115 gr .355" diameter non-expanding bullet gives adequate penetration; when expanded to .621" the bullet (now has about $1/3^{rd}$ the sectional density) penetration potential has been reduced significantly – to the extent that inadequate penetration can occur. A classic example of inadequate bullet penetration due to excessive bullet expansion occurred (11 April 1986) in Miami, Florida during the FBI firefight with two criminals. If the 9mm Luger 115 gr JHP bullet (that hit Platt) expanded to the extent mentioned above, then considering the angle of entry and the subsequent amount of body mass to penetrate, the fact that insufficient penetration occurred should not have surprised anyone. Third, while handgun bullets almost invariable penetrate tissue with some degree of curvature, the penetration track or trajectory of an expanded bullet that has a rounded "mushroom" shape will usually result in a more pronounced curvature than that produced by the semiwadcutter or wadcutter bullet.

Velocity

"Bullet velocity is a vector quantity whose magnitude is the bullet's speed and whose direction (movement) is the bullet's direction of motion."[18] Whenever velocity values are needed, individuals lacking access to a chronograph will of necessity use the velocity values as listed in the catalogs of the various ammunition companies. These velocity values are listed for the muzzle and for specific down range distances, and are usually given in feet per second (fps). From a bullet efficacy perspective, handgun bullet velocity is important to the degree that it affects (positive/negative) bullet stability, the extent and type of bullet expansion, the depth and type of bullet penetration.

Weight

Bullet weights are usually listed in grains and there are 7000 grains to one pound. Stated differently, a 147 grain bullet weighs about 0.021 of one pound and a 230 grain bullet weighs about 0.033 of one pound. Handgun bullets, and for that matter most bullets for rifle cartridges are rather lightweight objects. However, within each calibre (diameter) there is a range of bullet weights wherein the disparity is very large, and weight (actually retained weight) is an important factor that affects what the achieved results will be regarding expansion and penetration.

Handgun Bullet Stopping Power

    As is the case with bullet shape, there are two schools of thought regarding what range of bullet weights contributes to the most consistent ESP. Members of one school advocate the use of a bullet that is light in weight and loaded to at least +P levels in velocity, e.g., not more than about 115 grains for the 9mm Luger, not more than about 155 grains for the 40 S&W and not more than about 185 grains for the 45 ACP – within the pressure and design limitations imposed by both the cartridge and handguns chambered for the cartridge. However, in the futile but never ending search for that "magic bullet" there appears to be little regard for the longevity of the firearm or for the increase in recoil when a load is changed from a standard to a +P to a +P+ to perhaps even a sub-borderline proof load.[19]

    Advocates from the other school are equally adamant that the bullet weight should be in the middle to heavy range for the cartridge; e.g., 124 to 147 grains for the 9mm Luger, 165 to 180 grains for the 40 S&W and 200 to 230 grains for the 45 ACP. Furthermore, the ammunition to be used is loaded to industry standard pressures (CUP and/or PSI). If so-called improved ballistics (heavier bullet and/or faster velocity) are sought, this should be accomplished by the use of either another existing handgun cartridge or the introduction of a new handgun cartridge that produces the "improved" ballistics at standard pressures. For example, without increasing the bullet diameter, improve upon the ballistics of the 9mm Luger by using an already existing cartridge like the 38 Super or a more recent development like the 357 SIG.

    If other factors are the same or nearly the same, a heavier bullet (same calibre/cartridge) will almost invariably penetrate deeper into tissue and if properly designed the heavier bullet will also disrupt more tissue per total units of penetration. However, one forensic scientist believes the weight of the bullet to be more important than calibre, and the higher sectional density bullets will be shown to be the most effective.[20]

    Because some students of wound ballistics base their conclusions about stopping power on concepts and/or formulae that are contrary to the conclusions of other students of wound ballistics, there can be and often are conflicting assessments regarding the comparative significance of the contributory values of the various determinants.

    Therefore, it should be obvious at this juncture that it is virtually impossible to assign relative values to the various bullet determinants that are both definitive and permanent. However, before the concepts and formulae pertaining to ESP are considered, the subject of bullet performance characteristics needs to be addressed. This is done in order to correct some of the blatant misinformation that is considered to be factual by many of the general public and also to provide factual information which the reader can use to conduct a meaningful dialogue with others who express an interest in this subject (ESP).

CHAPTER FIVE ENDNOTES

[1] Federal Law Enforcement Training Center/Firearms Division, *Ammunition Glossary* (Glynco, Georgia: Federal Law Enforcement Training Center, undated), p. 4.

[2] Duncan MacPherson, *Bullet Penetration: Modeling the Dynamics and the Incapacitation Resulting from Wound Trauma* (El Segundo, California: Ballistic Publications, 1994), p. 204.

[3] George Bredsten and John Hillegass, *Ballistics Workbook and Calculator* (Glynco, Georgia: Federal Law Enforcement Training Center/Firearms Division, 1998) Part III.

[4] Michel H. Josserand and Jan A. Stevenson, *Pistols, Revolvers, and Ammunition* (New York, New York: Crown Publishers, Inc., 1972), p. 153.

[5] The author participated in the decision making process pertaining to the establishment of standards for the manufacture of less toxic ammunition that would be used by the Federal Law Enforcement Training Center/Firearms Division (FLETC/FAD). As a ballistics consultant, he was involved in the research, design and implementation of Reduced Hazard ammunition to determine if it complied with the various less-toxic ammunition performance requirements. This included tests of ammunition submitted by both major and minor ammunition companies.

[6] George Bredsten, et al., Handgun Ammunition (Non-Toxic, Lead Free and/or Frangible) Test Number: NT/DEP/2000 (Federal Law Enforcement Training Center/Firearms Division, 2000).

[7] Bredsten and Hillegass, op. cit.

[8] Carroll E. Peters, *Defensive Handgun Effectiveness* (Manchester, Tennessee: Carroll Peters, 1977), pp. 74, 75.

[9] John P. Burch, *Charles W. Quantrell A True History of His Guerrilla Warfare on the Missouri and Kansas Border During the Civil War of 1861 to 1865, as Told by Captain Harrison Trow* (Vega, Texas: J. P. Burch, 1923), p. 58.

[10] E. Fuller Torrey, M.D., *Frontier Justice: The Rise and Fall of the Loomis Gang* (Utica, New York: North Country Books, Inc., 1992), pp. 169-171.

[11] Joseph G. Rosa, *The Gunfighter: Man or Myth* (Norman, Oklahoma: University of Oklahoma Press, 1969), p. 153.

[12] Richard C. Davis, *Now Over 550 Second Chance "Saves"* (Central Lake, Michigan: Second Chance Armor Company, no date indicated), Save No. 56, no date, p. 32.

[13] Allen P. Bristow, *The Search for an Effective Police Handgun* (Springfield, Illinois: Charles C. Thomas, 1973), p. 21.

[14] Christopher Dobson and Ronald Payne, *The Terrorists: Their Weapons, Leaders and Tactics* (New York: Facts on File, Inc., 1982), pp. 112, 113.

[15] "Anglers Kill Bear, Then Swear off Night Fishing," *Alaska Magazine* (December/January 2003), p. 56.

[16] Urey W. Patrick, *Handgun Wounding Factors and Effectiveness* (Quantico, Virginia: FBI Academy, Firearms Training Unit, 1989), p. 11.

[17] Ibid.

[18] Bredsten and Hillegass, op. cit.

[19] Conversations (5 & 8 September 2003) with Tim Fischer, FLETC/FAD gunsmith and later corroborated by Bob Rogers, INS/USBP gunsmith, disclosed the ill-advised effort to "magnumize" the 40 S&W, 155 gr JHP service load resulted in an increase in both accelerated wear and breakage (from about 8 to 12 percent of the pistols per class of 48 students) of the Beretta, 96D, Brigadier service handguns.

[20] Eugene J. Wolberg, *Wound Ballistics Workshop Presentations* (Quantico, Virginia: FBI Academy, January 19-22, 1993), p. 45.

CHAPTER SIX

BULLET PERFORMANCE CHARACTERISTICS

OVERVIEW

It is irrefutable that the previously described determinants exist, but what is often disputed is the importance or significance of each determinant relative to the particular method or system used to quantify, evaluate and rank or grade the probable comparative stopping power of various cartridges (loads).

The application of determinants can be described by quantifying the results of specific bullet performance characteristics (BPC). These BPC include, but are not limited to ENERGY, MOMENTUM, ANATOMICAL DISPLACEMENT / DISRUPTION, HEMORRHAGE and NEURAL DYSFUNCTION. Each of these BPC is described as if it exists by itself. After these BPC have been individually described, the interrelationship of these interacting BPC – as to their affect within each of the described concepts and/or formulae – is addressed in subsequent chapters.

BULLET PERFORMANCE CHARACTERISTICS

Energy

Energy is defined as the ability to do work and Kinetic Energy is the energy of an object by virtue of its motion.[1] Some individuals appear to be enamored by the idea that energy is the definitive and realistic way to evaluate a bullet's performance capabilities relative to stopping power, i.e., the more energy the more effective the stopping power.

Whether or not the use of energy can be a reliable indicator of bullet efficacy is now considered from the perspectives of foot pounds, the time frame for bullet movement within the shootee and the comparative efficiency of a bullet compared with an arrow/spear.

1. Foot pounds.

A formula used to calculate kinetic energy in foot pounds is bullet weight in grains times the velocity squared divided by the grains to pounds conversion factor times a value for the acceleration of gravity. "... kinetic ... energy takes two factors into account: mass and velocity. The emphasis in this formula is placed on velocity ... the ... energy increasing by the square of the increase in velocity."[2] Since a bullet is in motion when it hits the shootee, the kinetic energy involved is easily calculated, e.g., a 230 grain bullet impacting at 975 feet per second (fps) would develop about 485 foot pounds (ft lbs). This is often understood (erroneously) to mean the bullet would move a one pound object a distance of 485 feet or move an object weighing 485 pounds a distance of one foot. Anyone who has done more than a modicum of shooting knows neither will happen.

A person needs only to shoot the bullet into a one pound object, for example a block of wood, that will capture the bullet or shoot into a 485 pound object that will also capture the bullet and then observe the results. If the one pound block of wood is moved 485 feet or the 485 pound object is moved one foot, the author will happily buy you (the reader) the steak supper of your choice. However, if it does not, then you (the reader) will pay for mine! Over the years, I have made this offer to hundreds of persons (firearms instructors, law enforcement officers, hunters, competitive target shooters and plinkers) but, after deliberation, NONE accepted. The one pound object will be moved at most a few feet and any movement of the 485 pound object will be all but indiscernible.

2. Time Frame.

This refers to the measurement of time beginning with bullet impact and ending when the bullet movement stops. Julian S. Hatcher gave an explanation why a person is never "literally bowled over" by a pistol bullet as follows:

> Consider what would happen if you threw a baseball against a heavy safe door that happened to be standing open. It would not move. Even if you threw your whole weight against the heavy safe door, it would hardly move. To shut it, you have to apply a push for a considerable interval of time. In striking a heavy body like a man, the bullet does not have time to put it into motion.[3]

For example, if a bullet impacts the shootee at 975 fps and penetrates six (6) inches and stops, the time for the bullet to stop will be about one-thousandth (0.001+) of a second. If the bullet penetrates twelve (12) inches instead of six inches, the time for the bullet to stop will be about two-thousandths (0.002+) of a second.

3. Arrow/Spear versus Bullet.

This particular type of comparison almost invariably causes many shooters to complain that the comparison is not fair. Why is it not fair? After all, with the centerfire handgun cartridge exception of the 25 ACP and perhaps the 32 S&W, the energy comparison between an <u>arrow</u> and a bullet favors the bullet. In the above example, the 230 grain bullet develops about 485 foot pounds, while a broadhead arrow, weighing 300 grains, with a velocity of 300 fps develops only about 60 foot pounds. The bullet has more than eight times the kinetic energy of the arrow, yet experienced and skilled archers regularly hunt large and even potentially dangerous big game without trepidation. Whereas, one would have to search far and wide to find the hunter who would seriously consider and intentionally hunt – without backup – large big game (e.g., elk, moose or sable antelope, let alone potentially dangerous big game such as Cape buffalo or grizzly bear) using a cartridge, the bullet from which develops only 485 ft lbs.

Consider the results of a <u>spear</u> wound. During the battle in the Teutoburg forest (AD 9), three Roman Legions and auxiliary units (about 20,000 soldiers) were annihilated by Germanic tribes. The spears used by the Germans weighed one and one-half pounds and were hurled at a velocity of about 55 fps. The energy developed by the spear was about 70 ft lbs, yet this weapon easily penetrated the Roman shield and then penetrated into a Roman soldier to either kill or cause a wound of random severity (depending upon the part of the body penetrated).[4]

Without belaboring the point, either a broadhead arrow or a spear will usually penetrate deeper (possible exceptions are very large bones like a ball and socket joint), create a larger and more severe wound track and generally result in as quick or quicker kill than will an *expanding bullet* from most handgun and many rifle cartridges. By expanding bullet, it is understood to mean a bullet that expands to at least one and one-half (1½) times its original diameter, For example, a .308 inch diameter bullet would need to expand to at least .462 of an inch and a 9mm (.354") would have to expand to at least .531 of an inch. Hmmm. Perhaps the type and extent of the physical wound just might be significantly more important than the theoretical number of foot pounds produced by the projectile – be it an arrow, a bullet, or a spear.

Julian S. Hatcher made another very discerning remark regarding energy: "Thus the amount of energy actually expended by the bullet in the body does not measure either the killing effect or the stopping power."[5] An example that supports Hatcher's remark was given by Ross Seyfried:

> First, bullet energy and its transfer to game animals really has very little effect on killing potential. I've watched both impala and pronghorns soak up and stop 300 Magnums at short range, in both cases, bullet performance was perfect; the shots hit the front shoulders and stopped in the opposite hip under the skin. Both little critters, just over 100 pounds, took almost 4000 foot pounds of energy. Neither of the animals showed any visual signs of being hit.[6]

To equate energy per se with either killing or stopping power is a non sequitur.

Momentum

"Momentum is defined as the product of the mass of an object with its velocity."[7] Momentum takes into account the same two factors that are used to determine energy, i.e., mass and velocity. However, momentum is directly proportional to the mass and the velocity; e.g., if the mass or the velocity is increased by two or reduced by half, the momentum is increased or decreased proportionately. Momentum will be described from the perspective of the bullet's momentum, the momentum given to the displaced/disrupted body part(s) and to the momentum given to the shootee.

1. Bullet Momentum.

To calculate momentum, first obtain the mass of the object and convert it to pounds. Then divide that quotient by the gravitational value (32.16) and then multiply the new quotient by the velocity in fps. For example, a 230 grain bullet with a velocity of 975 fps (230 ÷ 7000 equals 0.0328 pounds, then 0.0328 ÷ 32.16 equals 0.00102, then 0.00102 × 975) equals a momentum value of 0.9945 pounds feet. Contrast this with a man weighing 200 pounds (1,400,000 grains) moving at five (5) fps (200 ÷ 32.16 equals 6.2189 × 5) equals a momentum value of 31.0945 pounds feet.

If a similar degree of importance is attached to momentum that some people attach to energy, a 200 pound man moving at five (5) fps should produce more ESP than a bullet? The man moving at five fps (approximately 3.4 miles per hour) produces more than 31 times the momentum than does the 230 grain bullet moving at 975 fps. Does this mean when the walking man impacts another person, the ESP will be superior to that of a well placed 230 grain bullet impacting and penetrating at 975 fps? 'Tis most improbable.

2. Body Part(s) Momentum.

Essentially this is a transfer of some of the bullet's energy as the momentum of the displaced/disrupted body part(s). The movement of the affected body part is a manifestation of the transferred amount of bullet momentum. This displacement / disruption of body part(s) may be either permanent or temporary, but this momentum is distinct and separate from the momentum imparted to the body as a whole. Unable to locate empirical data regarding the measured velocity at which various body parts move as a result of transferred momentum, some apriori assumptions are made. A hypothetical body part weighs one-tenth of one pound and acquires an initial velocity of fifteen (15) fps. The momentum of the body part equals 0.1 (700 grains) divided by 32.16 equals 0.0031 times 15 equals 0.0466 pounds feet.

3. Shootee Momentum (Movement).

Contrary to the unlimited and unfortunately unrealistic imagination of some, many or perhaps most of the movie/TV scene and script writers, no bullet from any conventional handgun, rifle or shotgun can knock a person down – period. What velocity does a person acquire from the effect of a bullet that stays within his torso? Given: a 200 pound man impacted by a 230 grain bullet at 975 fps. Thus 230 ÷ 7000 equals 0.0329, then 975 × 0.0329 equals 32.08, then 32.08 ÷ 200 equals **0.1604 fps** OR somewhat less than two inches (0.1666') per second. It should now be obvious that neither energy nor momentum values, in and of themselves, are either representative or reliable indicators of reality insofar as ESP is concerned.

Anatomical Displacement/Disruption

This is the first of the bullet performance characteristics to be described that can be physically verified, i.e., the type and extent of the body part(s) displacement / disruption can be observed, measured and recorded. From the standpoint of bullet efficacy the anatomical disruption can be considered to be either insufficient or sufficient.

1. Insufficient.

This refers to the quantity of anatomical disruption that does not result in ESP. If the disruption (tissue, organs or skeletal parts) *DOES NOT* involve a critical time frame, the quantity of disruption can be small and of minor severity OR large and of major severity, e.g., small and minor severity: a subcutaneous flesh wound in the sartorius (thigh muscle); large and major severity: the comminution of the patella (kneecap). However, even though amputation could become necessary at a later time to safeguard the life of the individual; at the time of the incident neither the affect nor the seriousness of such a wound prevents the shootee from initiating, continuing or resuming a lethal threat action.

When the disruption (tissue, organs or skeletal parts) *DOES* include a critical time frame, the quantity disrupted does not produce ESP although it may eventually cause death. While the following example was previously described (page 24, paragraph three) to illustrate that the *ability* to commit deadly force can exist after receiving a fatal gunshot wound, it is again mentioned here to illustrate that if a wound, even though properly placed so as to penetrate vital organs, does not disrupt sufficient quantities of the vital organs, it is unlikely to produce ESP:

> In Deming, New Mexico (July 2002) after being shot through the left lung and heart from a 25 Auto, the shootee was able to shoot his opponent in the head with a 357 Magnum – both persons died and were found about five feet from each other.[8]

Even though a shootee eventually dies from the bullet wound, as in the above example, it can be considered to be at best a pyrrhic victory for the shooter. This does not necessarily mean all fatal gunshot wounds involving insufficient anatomical disruption will fail to cause ESP. Some fatal gunshot wounds will not, but others will – and under these conditions, when ESP does occur, it most likely can be attributed to the psychologically induced physiological response of the shootee.

2. Sufficient.

This refers to the quantity of anatomical disruption that results in ESP and it is axiomatic that when ESP occurs, a critical time frame is a non-issue. Since the disruption (tissue, organs or skeletal parts) DOES NOT include a critical time frame, the quantity of disruption can be minor, major or both. For example, relatively <u>minor</u> disruption occurred when a bullet was fired into the cranium that resulted in a small wound track in the brain and no visible external damage except for the bullet wound entry hole caused by a "44 calibre round ball fired from a Henry Deringer single shot pistol"[9]~[10] as was the case with the assassination of President Abraham Lincoln.

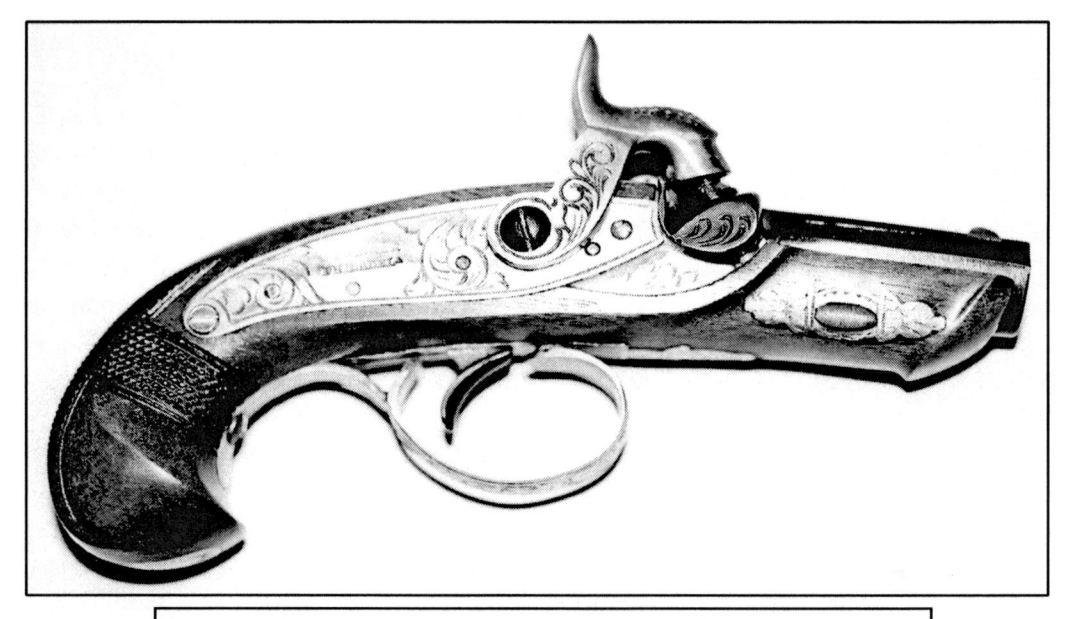

Replica of the Henry Deringer single shot pistol

Contrast this with the <u>major</u> disruption that occurred when a bullet was fired into the cranium that resulted in skull (bone) fragments and parts of the brain being expelled out of and away from the head, allegedly caused by a "Model 31/98, 6.5 mm Mannlicher-Carcano . . . "[11] as was the case with the assassination of President John F. Kennedy.

Both <u>minor and major</u> disruption can occur simultaneously when the bullet's penetration trajectory (wound track) includes the penetration and perforation of more than one anatomical part, none of which includes a critical time frame. An example might be where the bullet's penetration trajectory includes perforation of the thoracic spinal cord and the comminution of the ball and socket joint of each arm. When these anatomical parts are made dysfunctional ESP is the result. Either the dysfunction of the ball and socket joint of each arm OR the thoracic spinal cord result in ESP and the achieved results are not interdependent. However, the damage to the two ball and socket joints would be extensive when compared to the relatively minor damage to the thoracic spinal cord.

Hemorrhage

Not being versed in hemodynamics or fluid mechanics and not having had either medical training (except for basic first aid and CPR) or a hydraulic engineering background, what follows are the author's opinions regarding hemorrhaging and why hemorrhaging bullet wounds are not very reliable in that they cannot (in and of themselves) be depended upon to cause ESP. While other kinds of anatomical disruption may or may not include a critical time frame, hemorrhaging will always include a critical time frame. ESP cannot be expected to occur whenever hemorrhaging is the only bullet performance characteristic contributing to the type and kind of stopping power that is achieved. Even if it was possible to instantly cause the blood pressure to drop to zero, the oxygenated blood that has already reached the brain allows for volitional physical behavior to occur for about five to perhaps fifteen seconds regardless of the severity of the bleeding.

There are three basic types of bleeding: capillary, venous and arterial and the general affect and effect of each type varies:

1. Capillary.
"This is where the important functions of the circulation take place: exchange of material between circulation and cells."[12] From the perspective of ESP, capillary bleeding is irrelevant. A bullet wound of this type would involve penetration and/or perforation of muscle tissue without concomitant damage to either major veins or arteries. While undoubtedly more painful and obviously more serious, this type of bleeding can be likened to that from a cut that occasionally occurs while shaving.

2. Venous.
"Beginning at their smallest branchings, called venules, they transport blood laden with waste products collected throughout the body and partly depleted of oxygen, back to the heart."[13] From the perspective of ESP, venous bleeding is much more effective than capillary bleeding. However, because blood flow in the veins is done under relatively low pressure, a cut or severed vein bleeds in a steady, even

Handgun Bullet Stopping Power

flow. Even if a pulmonary vein has been severed, at its fastest rate of hemorrhaging it should not be surprising that the shootee can have the physical ability to commit a lethal threat action for an indeterminate time.

3. Arterial.

This is rhythmic, pulsating and visually can be the most spectacular type of bleeding. Contrary to some popular opinion arterial bleeding, if not stopped can continue for considerably more time than a minute or two. To a large extent, the exact length of time depends upon which artery was cut/severed and where within the body it occurred. Before "gray-out" begins, the shootee has the potential to begin, continue or resume a lethal threat action for a time ranging from at least five to fifteen seconds. Thus, regardless of the type of hemorrhaging, it is virtually impossible for an instantaneous stop to occur due <u>only</u> to blood loss.

Yet, excluding psychological decision(s) to stop, a reason many, if not most lethal threat actions of the shootee stop is due to the hemorrhaging caused by a bullet wound. This is an important consideration regarding bullet efficacy and by its very nature is one that should dampen any fervent advocacy of a particular calibre, cartridge or load. This is not to suggest that there aren't differences in the rate of hemorrhaging between bullets having different diameter meplats. There are differences, but nonetheless, in no instance can a bullet wound that depends solely upon hemorrhaging to cause ESP negate the five to fifteen seconds of potential volitional behavior available to the shootee.

Presupposing the same point of impact, the same type of wound track and the same bullet penetration trajectory, the rate of blood flow will vary disproportionately with the cross sectional area of the bullet's diameter or the bullet's meplat. For example, <u>given</u> that incapacitation due to hemorrhaging occurs in ten seconds for a bullet with a meplat of .357" – doubling the meplat diameter to .714" results in an incapacitation time of 2.5 seconds.

To illustrate the significance of an increase in meplat diameter (entry hole and wound track), the author has prepared attachments where the only variable is the difference in the bullet's meplat diameter. While any diameter could have been used, the author selected .357" and .62" as base lines. To the base line diameter was assigned a <u>given</u> rate of time for incapacitation to occur. All other meplat diameters are then relative to the base line. The <u>given</u> times for .357" are 10 seconds, 20 seconds, 30 seconds, and the <u>given</u> times for .62" are 240 seconds and 300 seconds. **See Appendices B through F.**

The 240 and 300 seconds were selected because according to some accounts regarding the infamous Miami, Florida FBI firefight of 11 April 1986, Platt (after sustaining an allegedly non-survivable gunshot wound) was able to commit successful lethal threat actions for a time period estimated to be <u>more</u> than four minutes.[14] If the bullet (9mm JHP) that cut/severed Platt's brachial artery had expanded to have a meplat diameter of about 0.621" within about the first inch of penetration into the arm and the time needed to incapacitate as a result of hemorrhaging was about four minutes – how could the <u>time</u> for ESP have been reduced?

In this respect the use of a larger calibre handgun bullet, with a smaller working meplat diameter and with the same depth of penetration, would NOT have reduced the time needed to incapacitate. In fact the time needed to incapacitate as a result of hemorrhaging alone would have been significantly increased. For example, any expanding bullet from a 40 S&W, a 44 S&W Special, a 45 ACP or a 45 Colt with a working meplat diameter of .52" would have required about five and seven-tenths (5.7) minutes to incapacitate. This would have allowed about an extra one hundred (100+) seconds for Platt to continue his lethal threat actions. In this particular shooting affray, the problem was not inadequate bullet expansion – it was *inadequate bullet penetration*.

Had the bullet penetrated from about three to five more inches, it could have penetrated the aorta, the heart and possibly into the left lung. As a result, the time needed to incapacitate would have been reduced. How much time reduction is problematical, but nonetheless with all other factors the same, there would have been a reduction. Again, the problem was not inadequate bullet expansion – it was *inadequate bullet penetration*.

Worth repeating for emphasis: Keep in mind that between the time of critical blood loss (insufficient or zero blood pressure) and the time of actual incapacitation there must be considered, a <u>possible</u> five to fifteen seconds of volitional behavior that might be used by the shootee.

Neural Dysfunction

This can be a very controversial subject. However, whenever a controversy develops it almost invariably centers on the phrase "remote neural dysfunction" and regarding this there are two schools of thought.

Members of one school insist remote neural dysfunction can and does occur. To some it is thought to be analogous to being struck or punched in the solar plexus or struck on the jaw with sufficient force to result in either a temporary or permanent disconnect between the brain and the muscle or muscle groups needed to continue further physical activity. In other words, there is a failure to communicate a command from the brain and/or a failure to execute the command due to a short circuit somewhere in the nervous system.

Members of the other school contend remote neural dysfunction that would achieve effective stopping power is illusory and the product of wishful and wildly imaginative thinking. The idea that <u>handgun bullets at typical handgun bullet impact velocities</u> can cause remote neural dysfunction, foisted by some as scientific fact, is considered to be nothing more than fallacious speculation.

In order to maintain objectivity and from a medical perspective a number of physicians, registered nurses, emergency medical technicians and/or paramedics were contacted and asked to answer a few basic questions about neural dysfunction and "remote" neural dysfunction. Some of those contacted chose not to go on record regarding their opinions – period. Others chose not to participate because they claimed the extent of their medical training did not qualify them as specialists in the field of neurology. Why these individuals could not or would not at least define neural dysfunction remains a mystery. However, among those individuals that participated there was general agreement that "remote" neural dysfunction was a nebulous concept and before the questions could be accurately and adequately answered, it would first require many agreed upon stipulations (e.g., <u>the specific nerve[s] affected, the duration of any neural damage, the wound proximity to specific nerve[s] that could result in physical incapacitation, the quantity and severity of adjacent tissue displaced and/or disrupted</u>).

However, if the reader should disagree with the need for agreed upon stipulations, it is suggested that he conduct his own inquires (requesting answers to the same questions) among medical personnel and IF THEIR ANSWERS CONTRADICT THE ABOVE, contact/notify the author (through the publisher) and perhaps mutual efforts can be undertaken that would resolve any alleged differences. The five questions are:

1. What is (Define/describe) neural dysfunction?
2. What is meant by "remote" neural dysfunction?
3. If remote neural dysfunction can occur, can it result in the physical incapacitation of an individual, i.e., cause the cessation of a lethal threat action?
4. If remote neural dysfunction can occur, what is the time-frame parameter; i.e., instantaneous, a couple of seconds, several seconds OR?
5. If remote neural dysfunction can occur, can it be caused by a handgun bullet wound and if so, what is the maximum distance, between the bullet wound and the affected nerve(s), that this can occur?

It is apparent that variations in the numerical values assigned to one or more BPC used to quantify, evaluate and rank or grade the probable comparative stopping power <u>will</u> produce disparate results, sometimes even to the degree of being diametric. In subsequent sections the various stopping power concepts and/or formulae are described, examples given and then evaluated. When perused, it will become obvious to the reader that some formulae use as facts that which are either aposteriori or apriori musings, while other formulae incorporate the tangible evidence of biology, physics and physiology.

CHAPTER SIX ENDNOTES

[1] Karl F. Kuhn, *Basic Physics* (New York, John Wiley and Sons, Inc., 1979), pp. 24, 26.

[2] Bill Steigers, "The Muzzle Energy Myth," *Bitterroot Bullet-In* (1980): first page (unnumbered).

[3] Julian S. Hatcher, *Textbook of Pistols and Revolvers* (Originally published Small Arms Technical Publishing Company, 1935 – Reprinted Prescott, Arizona: Wolfe Publishing Co., Inc., 1985), p. 407.

[4] Peter S. Wells, *The Battle that Stopped Rome* (New York, New York: W. W. Norton & Company, 2003), pp. 170, 179.

[5] Hatcher, op. cit., p. 408.

[6] Ross Seyfried, "Bone-Bashing Big Game Bullets," *Guns & Ammo* (January 1990): p. 41.

[7] Kuhn, op. cit., p. 33.

[8] Associated Press, "Deming Man, teen-ager kill each other," Silver City Daily Press [Silver City, New Mexico], (17 July 2002): pp. 1, 9.

[9] Charles E. Chapel, *Guns of the Old West* (New York: Coward-McCann, Inc., 1961 – Special Edition privately printed by Odysseus Editions, Inc. for the National Rifle Association, 1995), p. 117.

[10] Michael W. Kauffman, *American Brutus* (New York: Random House, 2004), the seventh page of sixteen unnumbered pages of photographs located between pages 240 and 241.

[11] Bonar Menninger, *Mortal Error: The Shot That Killed JFK* (New York: St. Martin's Press, 1992), p. 6.

[12] The Reader's Digest Association, *ABC's of the Human Body* (Pleasantville, New York: Reader's Digest Association, Inc., 1987), p. 93.

[13] Ibid. p. 92.

[14] W. F. Anderson, M.D., *Forensic Analysis of the April 11, 1986, FBI Firefight* (Los Angeles, California: University of Southern California School of Medicine, 1996 – Second printing February 1997), p. 3.

CHAPTER SEVEN

STOPPING POWER CONCEPTS/FORMULAE

OVERVIEW

It is in this area of discussion that acrimony often occurs, due primarily to perceived affronts (imagined or real) to personal character, education, integrity and knowledge. What one individual considers to be a valid concept another individual may consider that concept to be fraught with illogical and invalid conjecture. A similar situation exists regarding the formulae used to postulate comparative as well as probable stopping power values. All stopping power concepts and formulae are speculative since *none* are based on the results of *scientific tests* that would have involved living human beings.

However, these concepts and formulae can be individually studied, analyzed and comparisons can then be made that permit an assessment of relative worth that is based on both logic and science. Rather than becoming embroiled in argumentative issues, e.g., smaller calibre, lighter bullet weight and faster velocity versus a larger calibre, heavier bullet weight and somewhat slower velocity; three handgun cartridges (calibre, bullet weight and velocity), will be used as examples to describe, explain and otherwise set forth bullet efficacy relative to achieving ESP as determined by each of the various concepts and/or formulae.

These three handgun calibres (9mm Luger, 40 S&W and 45 ACP) are representative of what are currently popular semi-automatic handgun cartridges among law enforcement officers and civilians for the purpose of self defense in a life threatening situation. It is important to avoid succumbing to the advertisement messages (hyperbole) that imply almost mystical bullet performance characteristics to any cartridge – especially those that are the "newest" and/or are riding the crest of current popularity. It is more important to recognize the fact that the name of the cartridges used as examples could just as well have had other nominal and/or numerical designators, and that It is the specifics of the bullet design, diameter, velocity and weight (not the name of the cartridge) that determine the values used to calculate the relative ESP of the particular concept or formula under consideration.

In order to provide a more detailed coverage, each cartridge (bullet) will be considered in three ways; i.e., first, no bullet expansion; second, bullet expansion to 1.5 times the original diameter and third, bullet expansion to 1.75 times the original diameter.

If the reader is interested in the specifics about more or less bullet expansion or data pertaining to other cartridges, e.g., 357 Magnum, it remains for the reader to undertake the mathematics involved. For the author to have included data for all currently available commercial centerfire handgun cartridges (loads) would have required a voluminous series of tables.

It is also believed such an endeavor would have proven to be counterproductive, because it would have been far too easy for the reader to become enmeshed by the numbers and avoid or ignore the explanation and reasoning for the data or information provided with each concept and/or formula.

The three loads selected are used as examples to explain and illustrate how each concept and/or formula establishes values relative to ESP. Numbers 1, 4 and 7 are the original calibres of the bullets (shown in **bold**) that do <u>NOT</u> expand, while numbers 2, 3, 5, 6, 8 and 9 are the calibres (diameters) of the bullets that expand to the extent indicated.

9mm Luger (Parabellum)

	Bullet Weight	Bullet Velocity	Calibre Bullet Diameter	Bullet Cross Sectional Area
1.	124 gr	1200 fps	**0.355"** (original diameter)	0.099"
2.	124 gr	1200 fps	0.533" (1.5 times O.D.)	0.223"
3.	124 gr	1200 fps	0.621" (1.75 times O.D.)	0.303"

40 Smith & Wesson

	Bullet Weight	Bullet Velocity	Calibre Bullet Diameter	Bullet Cross Sectional Area
4.	155 gr	1150 fps	**0.400"** (original diameter)	0.126"
5.	155 gr	1150 fps	0.600" (1.5 times O.D.)	0.283"
6.	155 gr	1150 fps	0.700" (1.75 times O.D.)	0.385"

45 ACP (45 Auto)

	Bullet Weight	Bullet Velocity	Calibre Bullet Diameter	Bullet Cross Sectional Area
7.	230 gr	0850 fps	**0.451"** (original diameter)	0.160"
8.	230 gr	0850 fps	0.677" (1.5 times O.D.)	0.359"
9.	230 gr	0850 fps	0.789" (1.75 times O.D.)	0.489"

George B. Bredsten

Examples of various 9mm ammunition

Examples of various 40 S&W ammunition

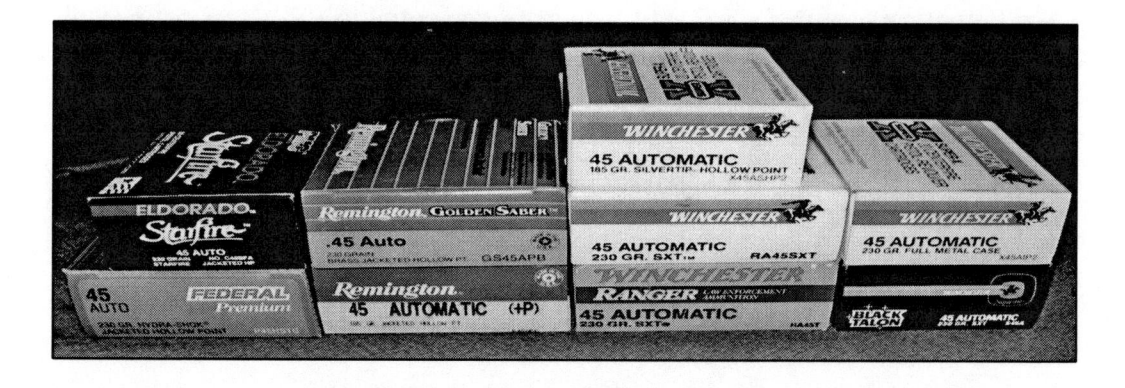

Examples of various 45 ACP (45 Auto) ammunition

After each concept and/or formula has been described, discussed and illustrated using the above three cartridges, comments are made that point out some of the possible positive and negative aspects associated with that concept and/or formula. At this time the reader is probably thinking: What is the decisive consideration or factor that permits one formula to be ***the*** standard by which all others are compared? Ah, there is the crux of the problem. No person, repeat, no person can state with certainty that concept "A" and/or formula "A" is categorically and unequivocally more accurate in assessing relative ESP than ALL of the other concepts and/or formulae.

Which concept and/or formula is favored by the reader may depend upon the propaganda affect of the "gun press" media (favorable or unfavorable articles), the influence of the opinion/views of the reader's associates and friends, the reader's experience/knowledge and finally the predilection of the reader.

After each concept and/or formula has been described, discussed, and where possible examples given and evaluated, it then becomes the reader's responsibility to determine whether or not the particular concept and/or formula then merits either dismissal or additional consideration.

Nota bene: The concepts and/or formulae described and discussed together with the given examples represent the author's understanding and opinions and consequently should not be considered to be either a pro or con presentation. If that is the reader's impression it is incorrect and the reader (if of the third category mentioned in the exordium) should not allow perceived author bias (either imagined or real) influence how this information is assimilated and evaluated.

That there are errors in this work are possible, but whatever the errors they are assuredly not intentional and it is hoped that the quality of this work has not suffered greatly because of any such errors. It is the author's recommendation that the reader peruse the material in order to reach decisions based on a serious contemplative and objective evaluation of the contents (evidence and facts) presented in this chapter.

The following list of concepts/formulae is not all inclusive, but is representative of what the author believes to be a reasonable number that address the subject of ESP from different perspectives – some of which are tangential to ESP. It is believed that some concepts/formulae have a more logical and/or scientific basis than do others, but that is for the reader to decide.

STOPPING POWER CONCEPTS/FORMULAE
(Listed in alphabetical order by last name or agency)

1. ARCHIBALD, Bob   - "One Shot Stop Ratio"   A/OSSR
2. COOPER, Jeff   - "Cooper Short Form"   C/SF
3. DiMIAO, Vincent   - "Energy Loss"   D/EL
4. FULLER, Steve   - "Fuller Index Technique"   F/FIT
5. HATCHER, Julian S.   - "Hatcher's Relative Stopping Power" H/RSP
6. KEITH, Elmer   - "Pounds Feet"   K/PF
7. MATUNAS, Edward   - "Power Index Rating"   M/PIR
8. MATUNAS, Edward   - "Optimum Game Weights"   M/OGW
9. PETERS, Carroll   - "Impulse Ratio"   P/IR
10. SMITH, Veral   - "Terminal Sectional Density"   S/TSD
11. SMITH, Veral   - "Terminal Displacement Velocity"   S/TDV
12. STOLINSKY, David   - "Stopping Power – A Physicians Report" St/SPPR
13. TAYLOR, Chuck   - "Taylor Modified Short Form"   TC/MSF
14. TAYLOR, John   - "Taylor Knock Out"   TJ/KO
15. USDJ   - "Relative Incapacitation Index"   RII
16. WALKER, Louise   - "Defensive Ammo Performance"   WL/DAP
17. WALTERS, Kenneth   - "Contrast/Comparison SP Formulae"   WK/CSPF
18. WOOTTERS, John   - "Wootters' Lethality"   W/L

1. ARCHIBALD, Bob – "ONE SHOT STOP RATIO" (A/OSSR)
REFERENCE: *2004 HANDGUNS* Annual[1]

==========

Formula: Bullet weight (grains) × 0.16
+
Muzzle Velocity (fps) × 0.04
+
Recovered diameter (inches) × 72 - 32

=====

Calculated "One Shot Stop Ratio" (A/OSSR)
9mm Luger
1) 124 × 0.16 + 1200 × 0.04 + **0.355** × 72 - 32 = **61.4**
2) 124 × 0.16 + 1200 × 0.04 + 0.533 × 72 - 32 = 74.2
3) 124 × 0.16 + 1200 × 0.04 + 0.621 × 72 - 32 = 80.6
40 S&W
4) 155 × 0.16 + 1150 × 0.04 + **0.400** × 72 - 32 = **67.6**
5) 155 × 0.16 + 1150 × 0.04 + 0.600 × 72 - 32 = 82.0
6) 155 × 0.16 + 1150 × 0.04 + 0.700 × 72 - 32 = 89.2
45 ACP
7) 230 × 0.16 + 0850 × 0.04 + **0.451** × 72 - 32 = **71.3**
8) 230 × 0.16 + 0850 × 0.04 + 0.677 × 72 - 32 = 87.5
9) 230 × 0.16 + 0850 × 0.04 + 0.789 × 72 - 32 = 95.6

==========

Comments:

There are possible combinations of bullet diameter, bullet weight and bullet velocity that can result in a <u>positive</u> one-shot stop ratio value of more than one hundred (100%) percent, e.g., one commercial 44 Remington Magnum load (180 grain bullet at 1600 fps), if it expands to 0.75" it has a one-shot stop value of **114.8**. Because the value is expressed as a percentage relating to none, some or all, the positive value expressed cannot exceed one hundred (100%) percent. If it does, Archibald recommends the value be changed to 100%.

Currently the least powerful, readily available commercial centerfire handgun cartridge is the 25 Auto (e.g., 50 grain bullet at about 760 fps) and it has a **24.5** one-shot stop ratio. Even the obsolete and extremely rare 2.7mm Kolibri (3 grain bullet at about 675 fps) has about a **3.1** one-shot stop ratio. However, of more importance is the remaining velocity after the bullet has first perforated an intervening medium. If after first penetrating an intervening medium, e.g., an arm, a door or drywall (gypsum board), the above mentioned 25 Auto bullet has an impact velocity of 125 fps, it then has a **minus 0.928** one-shot stop ratio. However, since the value is expressed as a percentage relating to <u>none</u>, <u>some</u> or <u>all</u>, the negative value expressed cannot be less than zero (0%) percent. If it is, Archibald recommends the value be changed to zero.

1. ARCHIBALD, Bob – "ONE SHOT STOP RATIO" (A/OSSR)
==========

There is no conventional bullet from any conventional handgun cartridge in general use by law enforcement officers or civilians that will *ALWAYS* SUCCEED in producing a one-shot STOP with a hit <u>somewhere</u> in the thorax. Conversely, there is no conventional bullet from any conventional handgun cartridge in general use by law enforcement officers or civilians that will *ALWAYS* FAIL to produce a one-shot stop with a hit <u>somewhere</u> in the thorax. The basic premise of this formula appears to be flawed, i.e., the formula can indicate that a given cartridge (load) is always (100%) effective or always (100%) ineffective in producing one-shot stops.

This concept/formula appears to be fraught with the possibility and/or probability of an unrealistic number of "random" anomalies and exceptions regarding shootee response to a bullet wound someplace within the thorax. Nonetheless, *100% means all* and *0% means none* – thus, NONE and/or ALL preclude there being any more than ALL or less than NONE. This hypothesis is therefore considered to be flawed and to have very limited pragmatic or theoretic utility.
==========

2. COOPER, Jeff – **"COOPER SHORT FORM RSP"** (C/SF)
   REFERENCE: FIRST FORMULA – Kenneth L. Walters[2]
===========
   First Formula: C/SF = (W × V ÷ 10000) × (CSA ÷ 0.102)
      W   = Bullet weight in grains
      V   = Bullet velocity in feet per second (fps)
      CSA = Cross sectional area in inches (r^2 × pi = CSA)
= = = = =

<u>Calculated "Cooper Short Form"   (C/SF)</u>
9mm Luger
1) 124 × (1200 ÷ 10000) × (0.099 ÷ 0.102) = 14.4 = **14**
2) 124 × (1200 ÷ 10000) × (0.223 ÷ 0.102) = 32.5 = 33
3) 124 × (1200 ÷ 10000) × (0.303 ÷ 0.102) = 44.2 = 44
40 S&W
4) 155 × (1150 ÷ 10000) × (0.126 ÷ 0.102) = 22.0 = **22**
5) 155 × (1150 ÷ 10000) × (0.283 ÷ 0.102) = 49.5 = 50
6) 155 × (1150 ÷ 10000) × (0.386 ÷ 0.102) = 67.5 = 68
45 ACP
7) 230 × (0850 ÷ 10000) × (0.160 ÷ 0.102) = 30.7 = **31**
8) 230 × (0850 ÷10000) × (0.359 ÷ 0.102) = 68.8 = 69
9) 230 × (0850 ÷ 10000) × (0.489 ÷ 0.102) = 93.7 = 94

===========
Comments:
   As given this formula factors in the affect due to the difference in bullet diameter, but it does <u>not</u> factor in the affect of a difference in the bullet's shape. Whether or not a bullet pushes into or chops/cuts tissue while penetrating has an affect on both the degree of wound severity and the shootee's subsequent reaction to the affect of the bullet wound.

George B. Bredsten

2. COOPER, Jeff – "**COOPER SHORT FORM RSP**" (C/SF)
   REFERENCE: SECOND FORMULA – Chuck Taylor[3]
= = = = = = = = = = =

Second Formula: C/SF = (W × V × BF)
    W   = Bullet weight in grains (nearest ten)
    V   = Bullet velocity in feet per second (nearest hundred)
    BF = Bore factor (CSA) with .357" = .100
= = = = =

<u>Calculated "Cooper Short Form" (C/SF)</u>
9mm Luger
1) 12 × 12 × 0.099 = 14.3 = **014**
2) 12 × 12 × 0.223 = 32.1 = 032
3) 12 × 12 × 0.303 = 43.6 = 044

40 S&W
4) 16 × 12 × 0.126 = 24.2 = **024**
5) 16 × 12 × 0.283 = 54.3 = 054
6) 16 × 12 × 0.386 = 74.1 = 074

45 ACP
7) 23 × 09 × 0.160 = 33.1 = **033**
8) 23 × 09 × 0.359 = 74.3 = 074
9) 23 × 09 × 0.489 = 101.2 = 101

= = = = = = = = = = =

Comments:

   160 (W) × 1000 (V) × **1** (Taylor's fractional designator for .357 diameter bore) = 1600. Then 16 × 10 × **1** = 160 (but Taylor says 16 is the correct answer), thus 16 × 10 × **0.1** = 16 (the number given as correct by Taylor). Then the fractional designator value of **0.1** and NOT 1.0 is correct for the .357" diameter bore. In addition by rounding bullet weight to the nearest ten grains and velocity values to the nearest hundred – the answers will be even more approximate than those calculated using the first method.

   In addition to the above mentioned consequences of using either of these two methods to determine Cooper's RSP, another problem with the Cooper formulae is that because the answers are much more approximate some answers can indicate a greater disparity between cartridges (loads) than probably actually exists. For example, using the first load given for the above 9mm Luger and the 45 ACP where neither bullet expands, the Cooper value(s) are 14:31 and 14:33. The Hatcher RSP values for those same loads are 34:73. This indicates the following:

    Cooper's 1st formula: about a 2.2 to 1 ratio (2.214:1)
    Cooper's 2nd formula: about a 2.3 to 1 ratio. (2.357:1)
    Hatcher's formula: about a 2.1 to 1 ratio (2.147:1)

2. COOPER, Jeff – "**COOPER'S SHORT FORM RSP**" (C/SF)
==========

Thus, *if* Hatcher's assertion is correct – i.e., a RSP value of about 60 is approximately 90% effective as a fight (lethal threat) stopper, and a RSP value of about 30 is approximately 50% effective – then Cooper's formulae values indicate the 9mm Luger load is between about 45% and 48% as effective as the 45 ACP load. This represents a significant difference in relative stopping power, i.e., about 45 to 48 percent instead of about 50 percent, and thus it can be reasonably inferred that the Cooper values are negatively skewed.

As is mentioned in the first paragraph of chapter five of this opuscule, when any relative comparisons of bullet efficacy are made, it presupposes that each bullet has the same point of impact AND makes the same type of penetration trajectory (wound track). The only variables are the quantity of tissue displaced/disrupted due to the differences in bullet and/or meplat diameter AND the distance (depth) of bullet penetration.
==========

3. DiMAIO, Vincent J. – **"ENERGY LOSS"** (D/EL)
    REFERENCE 1: V. J. M. DiMaio, M.D. et al.[4]
    REFERENCE 2: V. J. M. DiMaio, M.D.[5]
==========

    Formula: **D/EL** =   **Ei − Ee**
                  E   =   W × V²/450240
                  Ei   =   Energy (on entry/impact) in foot pounds
                  Ee   =   Energy (after exiting) in foot pounds
=====

Calculated "Energy Loss" (D/EL)
9mm Luger

1) .355" = 124 gr : 1200 fps : 397 ft lbs = 31" ± penetration
   CSA = 0.099
2) .533" = 124 gr : 1200 fps : 397 ft lbs = 13" ± penetration
   CSA = 0.233
3) .621" = 124 gr : 1200 fps : 397 ft lbs = 10" ± penetration
   CSA = 0.303

40 S&W

4) .400" = 155 gr : 1150 fps : 455 ft lbs = 28" ± penetration
   CSA = 0.126
5) .600" = 155 gr : 1150 fps : 455 ft lbs = 12" ± penetration
   CSA = 0.283
6) .700" = 155 gr : 1150 fps : 455 ft lbs = 09" ± penetration
   CSA = 0.385

45 ACP

7) .451" = 230 gr : 0850 fps : <u>369</u> ft lbs = 18" ± penetration
   CSA = 0.160
8) .677" = 230 gr : 0850 fps : <u>369</u> ft lbs = 08" ± penetration
   CSA = 0.359
9) .789" = 230 gr : 0850 fps : <u>369</u> ft lbs = 06" ± penetration
   CSA = 0.489

==========

Comments:

    Each number within each trio of numbers, i.e., (1, 2 and 3), (4, 5 and 6) and (7, 8 and 9) has the same comparative kinetic energy upon impact and each trio of numbers would lose their kinetic energy over the distance penetrated. Obviously more kinetic energy is dissipated quicker when the bullets penetrate less. According to DiMaio, et al. (page 3 of first reference) "… the **_wounding_** effectiveness of different types and calibers of cartridges could be evaluated and compared by determining the amount of

3. DiMAIO, Vincent J. – "**ENERGY LOSS**" (D/EL)
==========

energy lost by each bullet in passing through tissue."

However, no consideration is given to the differences where within the penetration track the "energy" is transferred. If a penetration of 12 ± inches was needed to reach the vitals (e.g., intervening medium, an oblique angle for the shot) bullets 1, 2, 4, 5 and 7 would provide more than adequate penetration, but because of a significant increase in cross sectional area, bullets 3, 6, 8 and 9 would give insufficient penetration. Yet, each bullet would have transferred all of its energy to the target.

The penetration potential value of 1264 (Appendix A) equates to about nine (9 ± 1") inches in muscle/tissue, and is based on the approximate nine (9 ± 1") inches for the 9mm bullet (115 gr STHP: 1225 ± fps) that penetrated through the right arm and into the thorax of Platt (FBI Miami firefight of April 1986) **and** numerous test shots with this cartridge (bullet) fired into calibrated 10% 250A Ordnance Gelatin, that resulted in a mean expansion diameter of 0.621" and a penetration of nine (9 ± 1) inches.

To postulate these loads will produce relative results in relation to the amount of "energy transfer" is an example of reasoned speculation that denies, excludes or ignores the affect of such differences as what anatomical parts are <u>actually</u> impacted/penetrated, what penetration trajectory (type and depth) occurs and what the wound severity is at the critical depth (distance) of penetration..
==========

4. FULLER, Steve – "FULLER INDEX TECHNIQUE" (F/FIT)

REFERENCE 1: E. Marshall & E. Sanow[6]
REFERENCE 2: E. Marshall & E. Sanow[7]
REFERENCE 3: E. Marshall & E. Sanow[8]

==========

The F/FIT addresses several factors that are alleged to be important/essential if predictable stopping power values are to be determined. These are:

1. **Muzzle Energy**
   a. For hollow points: Energy FIT = 96.34 - 78.24 × e *
      - Energy ÷ 215
   b. For solid points: Energy FIT = 89.41 - 59.95 × e *
      - Energy ÷ 412

2. **Gelatin Tests**
   a. "Jello" FIT (Crush [permanent] cavity) = 89.30 - 87.26 × e *
      - crush volume ÷ 1.888
   b. "Jello" FIT (Stretch [temporary] cavity) = 90.68 - 90.80 × e *
      - stretch volume ÷ 10.139
   c. "Jello" FIT (Both cavities) = 91.38 - 34.38 × e *

$$\frac{\text{crush volume}}{0.851} \qquad \frac{\text{stretch volume}}{11.65}$$

      - 68.71 × e *

3. **Muzzle Energy and Gelatin**
   a. Best FIT (Combined muzzle energy and gelatin tests)
      90.52 + 0.896 × depth - 0.0534 × depth^2 - 87.65 × e *
      dia. × energy ÷ 63.93

4. **Strasbourg Tests**
   a. Goat FIT = 100 – 73.52 x e *

$$\frac{9.461}{\text{AIT} - 2.5}$$

   *   e   = base of exponential term = 2.71828
        AIT   = Average Incapacitation Time

4. FULLER, Steve – "**FULLER INDEX TECHNIQUE**" (F/FIT)
==========

Comments:

Not being versed in the more advanced mathematics, I do not challenge the appropriateness of the mathematics used, nor do I dispute the accuracy of the numerical values presented. However, regardless of the mathematics used or the preciseness of the calculated numerical values, two fundamental errors exist that negate the relevance of Fuller's data.

Fuller's *first* error (intentional or unintentional) is his unquestioned (?) acceptance of Marshall and Sanow's shooting incidents data as being <u>factually obtained</u>, <u>factually recorded</u> and then <u>objectively reported</u>.

Consider "<u>factually obtained</u>." Marshall and Sanow set forth (*Handgun Stopping Power: The Definitive Study* – Boulder, Colorado: Paladin Press, 1992, pp. 43 and 44) the data collection methodology as follows:

> In order to be included in this study, I **insisted** [emphasis added] on either having or at least being able to review some of the following: police reports, evidence technician reports, statements of the victim (if he survived), homicide reports, autopsy results and photos. Whenever possible, I also talked to the emergency room doctors and attending physicians. Recovered bullets were either personally examined or photographed by me, or I was provided with photographs of the bullets.

On page 121, Marshall and Sanow state to the effect that five Glaser shootings came from Gene Wolberg, senior criminologist, San Diego Police Crime Lab. Wolberg (*Soldier of Fortune* Magazine, December 1992, page 40) DENIES ALL knowledge of the first two shooting reports that Marshall and Sanow attribute to him. In the same magazine article, "Wolberg never provided Marshall or Sanow any of the reports, test results, photos or evidence which they insist they inspected prior to including a shooting in their database." In addition, IF Marshall and Sanow had actually contacted Wolberg, they should have realized that Wolberg was a senior criminalist and not a senior criminologist.

Next consider <u>factually recorded (stated)</u>. Marshall and Sanow on page 35 of their book assert that "The <u>single</u> instance of under penetration in the FBI/Miami shoot-out (11 April 1986) is not grounds for withdrawal from service." The word "single" is underlined because it is reasonable to understand that it is meant there has been only one instance where this bullet (9mm 115 gr STHP) failed to give adequate penetration. Again, Roberts and Wolberg in their article in the before mentioned magazine responded:

4. FULLER, Steve – "**FULLER INDEX TECHNIQUE**" (F/FIT)
= = = = = = = = = = =

>This statement is incorrect. Numerous failures due to insufficient penetration have been documented with the 9mm Winchester Silvertip 115 gr JHP. One infamous incident occurred on Easter Sunday in 1989, when San Diego Sheriff's Department Tactical Unit officers were forced to shoot a criminal 27 times over several minutes because their 9mm Silvertips **failed to penetrate deeply enough** [emphasis added] to damage any vital organs and cause physiologic incapacitation, despite solid torso hits. A bullet finally severed the relatively superficially placed carotid artery and jugular vein in the neck, resulting in a fatal hemorrhage which ended the encounter.

Regarding the last part of the first error, there is the objectively reported to consider. Again, Marshall and Sanow, page 62, state "Ballistic gelatin results clearly predict the 115 gr JHP to be the top load in 9mm." However, Roberts and Wolberg (page 69) reply that: " … the authors offer no justification to support their assertion. In fact, the actual published data on 9mm JHP ammunition shows their comments to be utterly false and inaccurate."

Fuller's second error is apparently a wanton disregard for the disparate data of Marshall and Sanow that egregiously fails to consider the dissimilarity in the effects of bullet wounds due to the bullets penetrating different anatomical body parts located within the torso, e.g., the heart versus the right clavicle. Should such distinctly different anatomical torso wounds produce the same stopping power effect? Apparently Marshall and Sanow believe bullets shot anywhere into the torso will or should produce the same relative results?

This comparative effectiveness is not established or considered by comparing "apples with apples" – it is instead a vague comparison of "apples with anything." This non-scientific approach is sufficient reason to invalidate the conclusions reached by the authors – and by extension the conclusions reached by Fuller will have been based on the same *ambiguous*, *distorted*, *faulty* and *unverifiable* source data.

There is another aspect of the Marshall/Sanow reported data that raises an additional suspicion regarding the validity of the reports. This is found in the *alleged* "Strasbourg" test data. *Supposedly* a few of the goats that were shot, did not react as expected and because of this unexpected reaction to bullet impact/penetration, the incapacitation time (IT) was excluded, discounted, disregarded or otherwise considered to have NOT taken place. These IT values were excluded simply because the particular goat(s) failed to respond in a manner consistent with the "rules" of the test conditions. **If** this "Strasbourg" test took place and **if** the reported data was not *concocted*, then the unexpected reaction of a few goats to bullet impact/penetration is

4. FULLER, Steve – "**FULLER INDEX TECHNIQUE**" (F/FIT)
==========
not unlike what can happen in the "real world" – i.e., things do not always go as expected or planned.

Nota bene: By selective inclusion and/or exclusion, irrelevant and relevant data can be skewed to project conclusions or results that seem to be supported by facts but are actually only the product of dubious but skillfully manipulated speculation.
==========

5. HATCHER, Julian S. – "RELATIVE STOPPING POWR" (H/RSP)
REFERENCE: Julian S. Hatcher[9]
==========

Formula: H/RSP = M × CSA × BSF
M = Momentum (energy divided by velocity)
CSA = Cross sectional area (r^2 × pi [3.14159])
BSF = Bullet shape factor, i.e.:

1. Jacketed Bullets with Rounded Nose   0900
2. Jacketed Bullets with (small) Flat Point   1000
3. Lead Bullets with Rounded Nose   1000
4. Lead Bullets with Blunt Round Point or with
        Small Flat on Point   1050
5. Lead Bullet with Large Flat on Point   1100
6. Lead Bullets with Square Point or Equivalent 1250

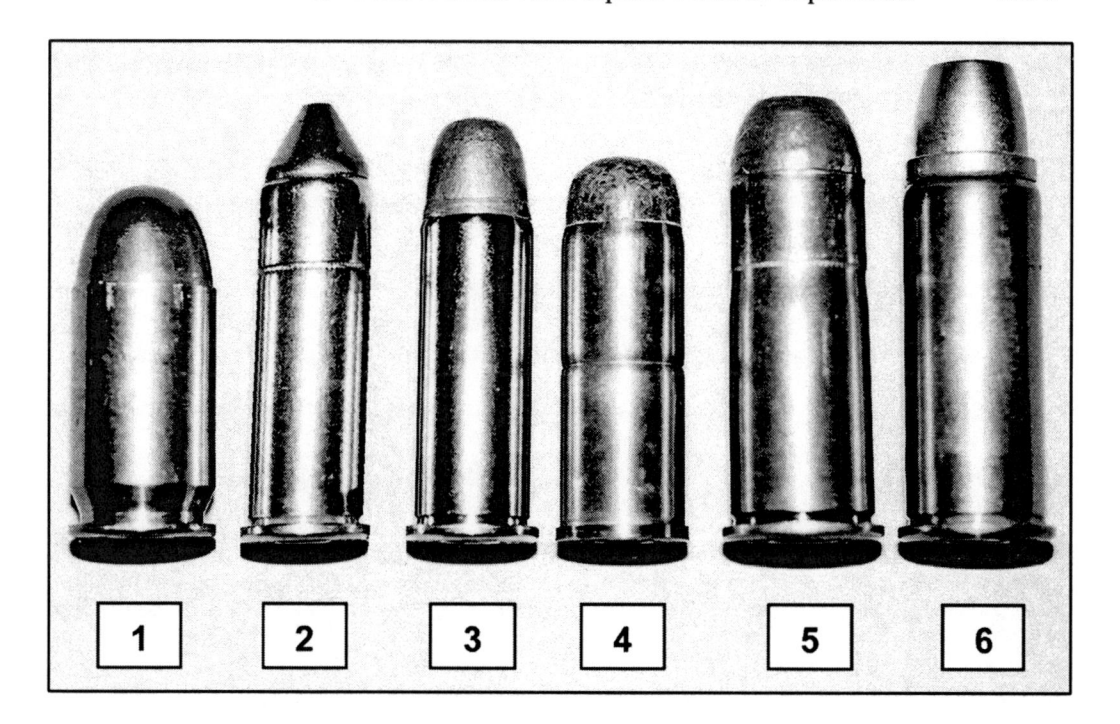

Examples of Bullet Shape factors:
1. **Jacketed Round Nose (JRN)**
2. **Jacketed Small Flat Nose (JSF)**
3. **Lead Round Nose (LRN)**
4. **Lead Blunt Round Nose (LBRN)**
5. **Lead Large Flat Nose (LLFN)**
6. **Lead Wadcutter/Semi Wadcutter (LWC/LSWC)**

5. HATCHER, Julian S. – **"RELATIVE STOPPING POWER"** (H/RSP)
==========

Calculated "Relative Stopping Power"

9mm Luger (Parabellum)

1) 124 gr – 1200 fps – 0.355" (original diameter)

    M   = 0.331
    CSA = 0.099
    BSF = 1050

    RSP = 34.41 = **034**

2) 124 gr – 1200 fps – 0.533" (expanded diameter)

    M   = 0.331
    CSA = 0.223
    BSF = 1050

    RSP = 77.5 = **077**

3) 124 gr – 1200 fps – 0.62125" (expanded diameter)

    M   = 0.331
    CSA = 0.303
    BSF = 1050

    RSP = 105.31 = **105**

40 Smith & Wesson

4) 155 gr – 1150 fps – 0.400" (original diameter)

    M   = 0.396
    CSA = 0.126
    BSF = 1050

    RSP = 52.39 = **052**

5. HATCHER, Julian S. – **"RELATIVE STOPPING POWER"** (H/RSP)
===========

40 S&W – continued

5) 155 gr – 1150 fps – 0.600" (expanded diameter)

   M = 0.396
   CSA = 0.283
   BSF = 1050

   RSP = 117.7 = **118**

6) 155 gr – 1150 fps – 0.700" (expanded diameter)

   M = 0.396
   CSA = 0.385
   BSF = 1050

   RSP = 160.1 = **160**

45 ACP (45 AUTO)

7) 230 gr – 0850 – 0.451" (original diameter)

   M = 0.434
   CSA = 0.160
   BSF = 1050

   RSP = 72.91 = **073**

8) 230 gr – 0850 – 0.6765" (expanded diameter)

   M = 0.434
   CSA = 0.359
   BSF = 1050

   RSP = 163.6 = **164**

5. HATCHER, Julian S. – **"RELATIVE STOPPING POWER"** (H/RSP)
==========

45 ACP (45 AUTO) - continued
9) 230 gr – 0850 – 0.78925" (expanded diameter)

$$M = 0.434$$
$$CSA = 0.489$$
$$BSF = 1050$$

$$RSP = 222.8 = \mathbf{223}$$

Comments:

Hatcher obtained the momentum value by dividing the energy by the velocity. The value thus obtained is incorrect by one-half, but when all calculations for Hatcher's momentum are made in this manner, the answers remain relative.

While Hatcher did not give a specific value for a jacketed bullet with a large flat, he did differentiate between a lead bullet with a small flat point (LBSF = 1050) and a jacketed bullet with a small flat point (JSF = 1000). He also assigned a lead bullet with a large flat point the BSF of 1100. Consequently, it is logical that a jacketed bullet with a large flat point be assigned the BSF of 1050. Thus, all the bullets in these examples have been given a BSF value of 1050.

If/when bullet expansion occurs, many perhaps even most bullets will have a profile similar to that of a mushroom. The flat (meplat) may be large but its perimeter will usually be one that has a rounded edge. Few expanding bullets will have permanent shapes that have sharp edges and that is what separates the bullet shape that has a large flat from the bullet shape that has a large flat with a sharp perimeter edge. A true wadcutter or Keith type semiwadcutter (in reality a subcalibre wadcutter) has the ability to cut, sever or separate tissue and blood vessels that a similarly placed "mushroom" shaped bullet might just temporarily push aside.
==========

6. KEITH, Elmer – "POUNDS FEET" (K/PF)
REFERENCE: Elmer Keith[10]

==========

Formula: K/PF = (BWgr ÷ grlbc) × BV
BWgr = Bullet weight in grains
Grlbc = 7000 (grains to pounds conversion)
BV = Bullet velocity in fps

=====

Calculated Keith's Pound Feet (K/PF)

9mm Luger
1) (124 ÷ 7000) × 1200 = 21.257 = **21**

40 S&W
2) (155 ÷ 7000) × 1150 = 25.464 = **26**

45 ACP (45 Auto)
3) (230 ÷ 7000) × 0850 = 27.928 = **28**

==========

Comments:

This formula is similar to, but not the same as the formula used to determine momentum. Momentum is determined by multiplying the mass (not weight) of the object by its velocity. Thus, e.g., the 9mm 124 gr bullet would have a mass (124 ÷ 7000 ÷ 32.16) = 0.00055. The momentum would then be (0.00055 × 1200) **0.66** and not the **21** as arrived using Keith's method.

Keith mentioned on page 4 of the reference: "The only place it is seriously in error is in the tabulation and classification of **very high velocity rifles** [emphasis added] on thin shelled game of light weight, like the deer class." This qualifying statement makes allowances for the relatively light weight, minimum high _impact_ velocity (1800 to 2200 fps) bullet that also has sufficient penetration to reach the vitals where a temporary wound cavity is formed that can result in intensified/increased wound disruption due to tissue elasticity limits being exceeded and/or fragmentation occurring while the temporary cavity exists. It is evident that there are very few "handgun" cartridges that can provide this kind of ballistics (impact velocity 1800 – 2200 fps), and none of these are "handgun" cartridges in typical use by law enforcement officers.

By comparison, a 223 Remington bullet (55 gr at 3200 fps) that DOES NOT expand, yaw or fragment is indicated to be somewhat less effective than a 40 S&W bullet (155 gr at 1150 fps) that also DOES NOT expand, yaw or fragment:

223 Remington (055 ÷ 7000) × 3200 = 25.142 = **25**

Also by comparison, both the 308 Winchester and the 12 Gauge slug are calculated to be from about 2.6 to 3.6 times as effective as the 223 Remington load:

6. KEITH, ELMER – "POUNDS FEET" (K/PF)
==========

$$308 \text{ Winchester } (168 \div 7000) \times 2650 = 63.6 \quad = \mathbf{64}$$
$$12 \text{ Gauge Slug } (437.5 \div 7000) \times 1450 = 90.625 \quad = \mathbf{91}$$

This formula is not an indicator of a bullet's ability to "stop" an action or predict a "reaction" – instead, it allows comparisons of various loads to be made with regards to the probable "quickness" of a kill. Again, and for **emphasis**, any and all comparisons presuppose bullets have the same point of impact and make the same type of penetration trajectory. Any differences in the quantity of displacement/disruption will be the result of the affect of impact velocity, bullet/meplat cross sectional area and the actual depth (distance) of bullet penetration.
==========

7. MATUNAS, Edward – "**POWER INDEX RATING**" (M/PIR)
REFERENCE: Edward A. Matunas[11]

==========

Formula: M/PIR = (V²ETvBg ÷ 450240 × 269) × Dv (Original formula)
         M/PIR = (V²ETvBg ÷ 12111) × Dv   (Modified formula)

V   = Velocity in fps
ETv = Energy Transfer value
Bg = Bullet Weight in grains
Dv = Bullet Diameter value

Bullet Type	ETv Value
Bullets that actually expand	0.0100
Non-expanding flat nose bullets	0.0085
Other non-expanding bullets	0.0075

Actual Bullet Diameter	Dv Value
0.200" to 0.249"	0.80
0.250" to 0.299"	0.85
0.300" to 0.349"	0.90
0.350" to 0.399"	1.00
0.400" to 0.449"	1.10
0.450" to 0.499"	1.15

=====

Calculated Matunas' Power Index Rating (M/PIR)

9mm Luger

1) 0.355" = Original diameter

   1200² × 0.0075 × 124 ÷ 12111 = 110.577
   110.577 × 1 = 110.577 = **111**

2) 0.533" = 1.5 times original diameter

   1200² × 0.0100 × 124 ÷ 12111 = 147.436
   147.436 × 1 = 147.436 = **147**

Handgun Bullet Stopping Power

7. MATUNAS, Edward – "POWER INDEX RATING" (M/PIR)
==========

3) 0.621" = 1.75 times original diameter

$1200^2 \times 0.0100 \times 124 \div 12111 = 147.436$
$147.436 \times 1 = 147.436 = \mathbf{147}$

40 S&W

4) 0.400" = Original diameter

$1150^2 \times 0.0075 \times 155 \div 12111 = 126.942$
$126.942 \times 1.10 = 139.636 = \mathbf{140}$

5) 0.600" = 1.5 times Original diameter

$1150^2 \times 0.0100 \times 155 \div 12111 = 169.257$
$169.257 \times 1.10 = 186.182 = \mathbf{186}$

6) 0.750" = 1.75 times Original diameter

$1150^2 \times 0.0100 \times 155 \div 12111 = 169.257$
$169.257 \times 1.10 = 186.182 = \mathbf{186}$

45 ACP (45 Auto)

7) 0.451" = Original diameter

$0850^2 \times 0.0075 \times 230 \div 12111 = 102.907$
$102.907 \times 1.15 = 118.343 = \mathbf{118}$

8) 0.677" = 1.5 times Original diameter

$0850^2 \times 0.0100 \times 230 \div 12111 = 137.209$
$137.209 \times 1.15 = 157.790 = \mathbf{158}$

9) 0.789" = 1.75 times Original diameter

$0850^2 \times 0.0100 \times 230 \div 12111 = 137.209$
$137.209 \times 1.15 = 157.790 = \mathbf{158}$

==========

7. MATUNAS, Edward – "**POWER INDEX RATING**" (M/PIR)
= = = = = = = = = =

Comments:

Matunas puts forth what he calls the PIR Guidelines. He assigns levels (one through six) that purport to project the effectiveness of PIR values placed within a given level. For example, level four includes PIR values from 95 to 150, and are alleged to include cartridges (loads) that will meet the requirements of the military, are adequate for police departments and are ideal loads for personal protection.

The PIR values and recommendations are, in general, reasonable but there are two important caveats.

First and most important, no allowance is made for the type and extent of bullet penetration. With regards to reaching and disrupting vital organs or the CNS, is the bullet penetration adequate or inadequate? To illustrate how excluding or disregarding the factor of bullet penetration can result in an erroneous conclusion, Matunas asserts the 45 ACP (230 gr FMC at 0810 fps) bullet is superior to the 9mm (124 gr FMC at 1110 fps) bullet. However, he then continues by saying the 9mm (115 gr ST at 1255 fps ?) bullet is greatly superior to the 45 ACP FMJ load. Obviously this categorical statement is not correct.. In the infamous 11 April 1986 FBI firefight in Miami, Florida, one suspect, was shot with a 9mm, 115 gr ST that expanded BUT failed to reach the thorax vitals and this suspect was able to subsequently kill two FBI agents and wound five other agents before he was killed.

A comparison of the penetration potential for the 9mm (115 gr ST at 1225 fps ?) versus the 45 ACP (230 gr FMJ at 0810 fps) discloses some interesting information, one of which is the importance of the probable penetration due to variations in expansion. For example, if the 9mm bullet had expanded to 0.533", its penetration potential value is 1718, whereas, if the bullet had expanded to 0.621", its penetration potential value is about 1264. The 45 ACP bullet (230 gr FMJ at 810 fps) has a penetration potential value of about 2094 and it is generally accepted that this 45 ACP FMJ bullet at the stated impact velocity will give adequate penetration..

The 9mm bullet that expands to 0.533" should penetrate about 82% the depth or distance that the 45 ACP FMJ bullet does. By contrast, the 9mm bullet that expands to 0.621" should penetrate about 60% the depth or distance that the 45 ACP bullet does. Thus, while the 9mm bullet penetrated approximately nine inches (through Platt's right arm and into his thorax), the above 45 ACP bullet would have penetrated about fifteen inches AND had the 9mm bullet expanded to only .533" it would have penetrated about twelve inches. That additional three to four inches of penetration would have made it possible for the 9mm bullet to disrupt additional lung tissue, a major blood vessel or the heart. Quicker physiological incapacitation would have occurred. How much quicker is problematical, but it would have been quicker.

The second caveat involves the fact that no consideration is made for any variance in tissue disruption caused by differences in the degree of bullet expansion;

7. MATUNAS, Edward – "POWER INDEX RATING" (M/PIR)
==========

e.g., a .451" bullet that expands to 0.677" is given the same relative effectiveness as a .451" bullet that has a 0.789" expanded diameter. Given that both bullets penetrate ten inches, the volume of disruption for the 0.677" bullet is about 3.6 inches. The volume of disruption for the 0.789" bullet is 4.89 inches. That is a difference of more than thirty-five percent. Given that a .357" diameter bullet can cause hemorrhage incapacitation in ten seconds, then hemorrhage incapacitation will occur in about 2.8 and 2.0 seconds for the .677" and 0.789" bullets respectively. That represents about a 29% reduction in the time needed for the 0.789" bullet to achieve incapacitation. Is this time difference important? With eight-tenths (0.8) of a second of additional time to react, there is ample time for the shootee to fire at least one shot. Given your choice, would you rather the shootee have or NOT have that opportunity?

The other neglected consideration is the fact that the larger diameter bullet will also have a greater chance of impacting/tearing/severing a major blood vessel that the smaller diameter bullet just might barely miss. Regardless of the probability of this occurring, the fact remains that there is an increased chance for it to occur.

Except for the penetration factor and the volume differential due to larger diameter and/or larger meplat, this formula appears to have merit. The reader who is interested can take the time and calculate the PIR for as many "handgun" cartridges (loads) at whatever distance is of interest. The key point is to recognize and remember that bullets do NOT ALWAYS give the expansion that the manufacturer intended, and NO PERSON can say with certainty that expanding type bullet "A" will expand to diameter "X" on demand!
==========

8. MATUNAS, Edward – **"OPTIMUM GAME WEIGHTS"** (M/OGW)
REFERENCE: Edward A. Matunas[12]

===========

Formulae: For big-game bullets (and solids)

$$M/OGW \text{ (in pounds)} = V^3 \times B^2 \times 1.5 \times 10^{-12}$$

For varmint bullets:

$$M/OGW \text{ (in pounds)} = V^3 \times B^2 \times 5 \times 10^{-13}$$

=====

<u>Calculated "Optimum Game Weights" (M/OGW)</u>

Matunas' example:

30-06 Springfield

$$M/OGW \text{ (pounds)} = 2500^3 \times 180^2 \times 1.5^{-12}$$

$$1.5625^{10} \times 32400 \times 1.5^{-12} = 759.375 = \mathbf{759} \text{ lbs}$$

9mm Luger
1) M/OGW (pounds) = $1200^3 \times 124^2 \times 1.5^{-12}$
$0.1728^{10} \times 15376 \times 1.5^{-12} = 39.854 = \mathbf{40} \pm$ lbs

40 S&W
2) M/OGW (pounds) = $1150^3 \times 155^2 \times 1.5^{-12}$
$0.1521^{10} \times 24025 \times 1.5^{-12} = 54.808 = \mathbf{55} \pm$ lbs

45 ACP (45 Auto)
3) M/OGW (pounds) = $0850^3 \times 230^2 \times 1.5^{-12}$
$0.0614^{10} \times 52900 \times 1.5^{-12} = 48.731 = \mathbf{49} \pm$ lbs

----

223 Remington (5.56x45mm)

4) M/OGW (pounds) = $3200^3 \times 055^2 \times 1.5^{-12}$
$3.2768^{10} \times 03025 \times 1.5^{-12} = 148.684 = \mathbf{149}$

8. MATUNAS, Edward – **"OPTIMUM GAME WEIGHTS"** (M/OGW)
= = = = = = = = = =

308 Winchester (7.62 × 51mm)
5) M/OGW (pounds) = $2650^3 \times 168^2 \times 1.5^{-12}$
$1.8609^{10} \times 28224 \times 1.5^{-12} = 787.857 = $ **788**

12 Gauge (1 oz slug)
6) M/OGW (pounds) = $1600^3 \times 437.5^2 \times 1.5^{-12}$
$0.4096^{10} \times 191406 \times 1.5^{-12} = $ **1176**

= = = = = = = = = =

Comments:

With this formula, Matunas (unknowingly, unwittingly or perhaps capriciously) introduced a bullet performance dichotomy that would challenge a skilled dialectician. First, and using his OGW formula, the various handgun cartridges (9mm Luger, 40 S&W and 45 ACP) have optimum game weights in the area of forty (40) to about fifty-five (55) pounds. These cartridges (loads) would be suitable for taking game animals to the size of a peccary, but would exclude game animals like whitetail deer or mule deer whose adult weights can vary from somewhat less than 100 pounds to more than 300 pounds.

Second, he nonetheless maintains these handgun cartridges that are unsuitable for taking deer size game animals are appropriately chosen for self defense/personal protection, e.g., 9mm Luger, 38 Special +P and the 45 Auto, "do yeoman service for police work" or "serves admirably as a personal defense or police round." Does this mean these cartridges can be expected to reliably, although not always, stop a lethal threat action of a person who may weigh less than one hundred (<100) pounds or more than three hundred (>300) pounds?

'Tis a very strange evaluation? On the one hand, these handgun cartridges ARE NOT recommended for taking non-dangerous game animals weighing more than about fifty-five (55) pounds. This is presumably because the bullets are ineffective in quickly and humanely killing heavier game animals. On the other hand, these same handgun cartridges ARE recommended for self defense/personal protection in life threatening situations. Presumably, because the same bullets are effective in stopping a lethal threat action? At best, this is a manifestation of convoluted and disjointed reasoning with a blatant disregard for basic logic.

= = = = = = = = = =

9. PETERS, Carroll – "IMPULSE RATIO" (P/IR)
REFERENCE: Carroll Peters[13]
==========

Concept: Impulse ratio, "I". The impulse ratio for a handgun load is defined as the impulse imparted to a ballistic gelatin target divided by the impulse imparted to the same target, at point-blank range, by the 45 ACP hardball load.

Formula: P/IR = IRx ÷ IRy
 I = Impulse Ratio (Momentum)
 IRx = Impulse ratio of specific handgun load
 IRy = impulse ratio of 45 ACP hardball load; i.e., 230 gr FMJ at 812 fps = 0.830 = "1"

=====

A. <u>Impulse ratio values based on Muzzle velocity</u>

9mm Luger
I = 124 gr × 1200 fps ÷ 225000 = 0.661 ÷ 0.830 = **0.797**

40 S&W
I = 155 gr × 1150 fps ÷ 225000 = 0.792 ÷ 0.830 = **0.955**

45 ACP (45 Auto)
I = 230 gr × 0850 fps ÷ 225000 = 0.869 ÷ 0.830 = **1.047**

B. <u>Impulse ratio values based on momentum transferred to target vitals (e.g., heart) in ten (10) inches of penetration.</u>

9mm Luger
I = 124 gr × (1200 - *0550* = 0650) ÷ 225000 = **0.303**

40 S&W
I = 155 gr × (1150 - *0550* = 0600) ÷ 225000 = **0.379**

45 ACP (45 Auto)
I = 230 gr × (0850 - *0400* = 0450) ÷ 225000 = **0.409**

----

9. PETERS, Carroll – "**IMPULSE RATIO**" (P/IR)
==========

C. Impulse ratio values based on momentum transferred to target vitals (e.g., heart) in ten (10) inches of penetration and each bullet transferring about *115 to 116 foot pounds of energy*.

9mm Luger
I = 124 gr × (1200 - *0650*) ÷ 225000 = **0.358**

40 S&W
I = 155 gr × (1150 - *0570*) ÷ 225000 = **0.393**

45 ACP (45 Auto)
I = 230 gr × (0850 - *0475*) ÷ 225000 = **0.486**

==========

Comments:

Some comments made by Peters regarding the force-distance-time relationship involving kinetic energy loss and bullet momentum loss appear to be apropos, but nonetheless include unsubstantiated apriori conclusions (italicized and underlined):

"If two bullets lose the same amount of energy in a given target, the bullet with the lower impact velocity will lose more momentum and *will have the greater stopping power*. If two bullets lose the same amount of momentum in a given target, so that they have *the same stopping power*, then the bullet with the higher impact velocity will lose more energy and will cause the greater amount of damage to the target."

According to Peters (the first sentence in the previous paragraph), the 40 S&W will have greater stopping power than the 9mm Luger and the 45 Auto load will have greater stopping power than the 40 S&W. Also according to Peters (the second sentence in the previous paragraph), a 9mm Luger 115 gr bullet that impacts at 1200 fps and penetrates ten inches – it has a momentum value of 0.661 and the 45 ACP 230 gr bullet that impacts at 0647 fps and penetrates ten inches – it also has a 0.661 momentum value. Then, according to Peters, because the 9mm will lose more energy (397 ft lbs) it will do greater damage to the target than the 45 ACP that will lose less energy (214 ft lbs).

It is interesting to note that Peters, among other things, sums up this subject as of 1977 with the following:

9. PETERS, Carroll – "**IMPULSE RATIO**" (P/IR)
==========

1. The terminal-ballistic performance of a nondeforming bullet depends strongly on the product of the bullet cross sectional area and the form coefficient.
2. Expanding bullets are neither required nor desired for achieving optimum defensive handgun performance.
3. Although useful for some types of hunting, expanding bullets are poorly suited for defense because of their poor hard-target penetration characteristics and their **erratic** [emphasis added] performance.

    This *erratic* bullet performance, although not typical, was not uncommon during the late 1970s through the late 1980s. Even into the 1990s consistent and reliable handgun bullet expansion was thought to be between 60 and 70 percent; i.e., 3 to 4 out of 10 handgun bullets did NOT expand as designed. As of the middle part of the first decade of this century, consistent and reliable handgun bullet expansion is still not a one hundred (100) percent guarantee.

    Peters also addresses the subject of hard target penetration, which in general does not usually have a high priority among law enforcement. Agency by agency, the general as well as specific environs tend to indicate what amount of bullet penetration will suffice. With the notable exceptions of the FBI, the U.S. Border Patrol and perhaps the California Highway Patrol, few if any organized studies or tests have been made pertaining to the penetration problems associated with combined soft target <u>and</u> hard target bullet effectiveness.

==========

10. SMITH, Veral – "TERMINAL SECTIONAL DENSITY" (S/TSD)
REFERENCE: Smith, Veral[14]

==========

Formula: S/TSD = (BWgr ÷ grlbc) ÷ MD²
BWgr = Bullet weight in grains
grlbc = Grains to pound conversion factor = 7000
MD² = Meplat diameter squared

=====

For comparison purposes the original bullet diameter, bullet diameter expanded 1.5 times and bullet diameter expanded 1.75 times are used as the MEPLAT DIAMETERS. However, in virtually all instances the meplat diameters will be found to be smaller than the expanded bullet diameters indicate.

9mm Luger
Original bullet diameter = .355" - bullet weight = 124 grains
1) S/TSD = (124 ÷ 7000) ÷ 0.355² = **0.141**
2) S/TSD = (124 ÷ 7000) ÷ 0.533² = **0.062**
3) S/TSD = (124 ÷ 7000) ÷ 0.621² = **0.046**

40 S&W
Original bullet diameter = .400" - bullet weight = 155 grains
4) S/TSD = (155 ÷ 7000) ÷ 0.400² = **0.138**
5) S/TSD = (155 ÷ 7000) ÷ 0.600² = **0.061**
6) S/TSD = (155 ÷ 7000) ÷ 0.700² = **0.045**

45 ACP (45 Auto)
Original bullet diameter = .451" - bullet weight = 230 grains
7) S/TSD = (230 ÷ 7000) ÷ 0.451² = **0.163**
8) S/TSD = (230 ÷ 7000) ÷ 0.677² = **0.072**
9) S/TSD = (230 ÷ 7000) ÷ 0.789² = **0.053**

==========

Comments:

As has been previously mentioned, the infamous FBI firefight of 11 April 1986 wherein the 115 gr STHP 9mm bullet failed to reach the vitals can be used to illustrate the significance of terminal sectional density versus original sectional density. A non-expanding 9mm (0.355") 115 gr STHP at 1225 ± fps has a sectional density of 0.130 and a penetration potential value of about 3869. The same bullet when expanded to 0.621" has a sectional density value of about 0.043 and a penetration potential value of about 1264. This represents an approximate 3:1 ratio in penetration difference in favor of the non-expanding bullet.

Whether or not a human arm (muscle/tissue only) must first be perforated, a non-

10. SMITH, Veral – "**TERMINAL SECTIONAL DENSITY**" (S/TSD)
==========

expanding 9mm bullet (115 gr – 1225 fps) can be expected to perforate an average adult person's thorax. Yet, when expanded to 1.75 times its original diameter, the same bullet manages to penetrate approximately nine (± 1) inches – which, in the above mentioned FBI firefight, proved to be insufficient (failed to reach the vitals).

Used in conjunction with the Penetration Potential Values (**Appendix A**), this Terminal Sectional Density" formula enables one to calculate penetration values of bullets that have <u>meplats</u> of various diameters.
==========

11. SMITH, Veral – "TERMINAL DISPLACEMENT VELOCITY" (S/TDV)
REFERENCE: Smith, Veral[15]

==========

Original Formula: **S/TDV** = (Mcsa × V) ÷ MC

         Mcsa = Meplat cross sectional area (inches)
         V = Velocity in fps
         MC = Circumference of Meplat (inches)

Revised Formula: **S/TDV** = (Mdia × V) ÷ 4

         Mdia = Meplat diameter (inches)
         V = Velocity in fps

=====

For comparison purposes the original bullet diameter, the bullet diameter expanded 1.5 times and the bullet diameter expanded 1.75 times are used as the MEPLAT DIAMETERS. However, in virtually all instances the meplat diameters will be found to be smaller than the indicated diameters.

9mm Luger – Original Formula
1) Bullet diameter = 0.355" – Bullet velocity = 1200 fps
S/TDV = (0.099 × 1200) ÷ 1.115 = **106.5**

2) Bullet diameter = 0.533" = Bullet velocity = 1200 fps **?**
S/TDV = (0.224 × 1200) ÷ 1.675 = **160.5**

3) Bullet diameter = 0.621" = Bullet velocity = 1200 fps **?**
S/TDV = (0.303 × 1200) ÷ 1.951 = **186.4**

40 S&W – Original Formula
4) Bullet diameter = 0.400" – Bullet velocity = 1150 fps
S/TDV = (0.126 × 1150) ÷ 1.257 = **115.3**

5) Bullet diameter = 0.600" – Bullet velocity = 1150 **?**
S/TDV = (0.283 × 1150) ÷ 1.885 = **172.7**

6) Bullet Diameter = 0.700" – Bullet velocity = 1150 fps **?**
S/TDV = (0.385 × 1150) ÷ 2.199 = **201.3**

11. SMITH, Veral – "TERMINAL DISPLACEMENT VELOCITY" (S/TDV)
==========

45 ACP (Auto) – Original Formula
7) Bullet Diameter = 0.451" – Bullet velocity = 0850 fps
   S/TDV = (0.160 × 0850) ÷ 1.417 = **096.0**

8) Bullet Diameter = 0.677" – Bullet velocity = 0850 fps **?**
   S/TDV = (0.360 × 0850) ÷ 2.127 = **143.9**

9) Bullet Diameter = 0.789" – Bullet velocity = 0850 fps **?**
   S/TDV = (0.489 × 0850) ÷ 2.479 = **167.7**

==========
Comments:

Note that after each velocity value given for the bullets that expand to 1.5 and 1.75 times their original diameters, a question mark has been placed. These question marks are there to remind the reader that the actual remaining velocities (fps) of the bullets at the instant they attain the expanded diameters are unknown. However, the actual remaining velocities will affect the TDV as follows: The <u>rate of bullet deceleration</u> due to the increase in bullet cross sectional area, the subsequent <u>reduction in bullet momentum</u> and the <u>reduction in penetration potential values</u> are unknown but they can be determined by using calibrated 250A Ordnance Gelatin as the test medium and recording the bullet performance with chronographs and/or very high speed photography equipment.
==========

12. STOLINSKY, David, M.D. – "**STOPPING POWER**" (St/SPPR)
   REFERENCE 1: Stolinsky, David, M.D.[16]
   REFERENCE 2: Potocki, John[17]
= = = = = = = = = = =

Comments:

In his article, Dr. Stolinsky addresses the merits of Hatcher's Relative Stopping Power (RSP) concept/formula. He then considers the concept and the reasoning used by some in the Justice Department to establish the Relative Incapacitation Index (RII)

Dr. Stolinsky, begins by mentioning that "during the Philippine Insurrection, which began in 1899, complaints were received (by whom?) about its (38 Colt) lack of stopping power for men and horses." Dr. Stolinsky then writes: For a time the Army reissued the 45 "Peacemaker," but a new handgun was clearly needed.

Who was it that thought a "new handgun" was clearly needed? Was it Dr. Stolinsky? Was it the combat soldier? Was it a "Stateside" bureaucrat who rationalized an imaginary need? Was it, as is often the case, an attempt by a technocrat to resolve by technology a non-existent problem while ignoring or setting-aside the crux of the soldiers' complaints?

I refer the reader to page 4 of this book's Exordium and Captain Rowell's (a combat soldier during the Philippine Insurrection) official report of 22 October 1902 wherein he was NOT concerned with the type of available handgun (new or otherwise) BUT instead was concerned with the effectiveness of the cartridge (load) for which the handgun was chambered. He selected for combat use a .45 Colt (single action) revolver in *preference* to either the 7.65mm Luger ("automatic") pistol or the .38 Colt (double action) revolver – both of which were readily available! It appears to be a common practice that when a lethal threat is imminent and a choice of firearms (handgun/calibre) can be made, that choice will usually be made on the basis of pragmatism rather than theory.

Regarding the **Thompson-LaGarde Tests**, Dr. Stolinsky makes two assertions: The first is: "A defect of all the tests is their lack of statistical validation." The second is: "Each round should have been tested in several animals, uniform in size and sex, to show consistency."

Consider the lack of statistical validation. Regarding this assertion, Dr. Stolinsky (for statistical purposes) is correct. For each cartridge (load) to be tested, there should have been a minimum sample number of three cattle and three horses. This would have required a minimum of thirty-nine cattle and nine (?) horses. However, for whatever reason, (e.g., limited number of available animals, limited time to conduct the tests or limited finances precluding more comprehensive tests), Thompson-LaGarde conducted tests on the relatively few animals that were available – 13 cattle and several (3 ?) horses.

Consequently, for one or more of the before mentioned reasons, Thompson-LaGarde could NOT test each cartridge in several animals, uniform in size and sex to

12. STOLINSKY, David, M.D. – "**STOPPING POWER**" (St/SPPR)
==========

show consistency. It would have required a minimum of thirty-nine (39) cattle and nine (9 ?) horses ALL being uniform in size and sex. As it was the available cattle varied in size, sex and probably temperament; i.e., weights varied between about 950 and 1300 pounds. There were four cows, one steer, three bulls and five oxen. Neither the size nor the sex of the horses was mentioned. Again, a minimum total of forty-eight animals would have been needed to conduct tests that could have provided minimal required statistical data.

Dr. Stolinsky mentioned that during the quick fire tests both the 7.65mm and the 9mm pistols had malfunctions/delays that possibly caused the multiple hits to be less effective? This is a valid point, but what Dr. Stolinsky FAILED to mention was that during this same series of quick fire tests one revolver also had malfunctions/delays. A brief description is given regarding the number of shots, malfunctions, delays and animal's reaction to the handgun bullets.

First, with the Luger, semi-automatic, **7.65mm** (**92.6 gr** Jacketed Truncated Cone bullet at **1420 fps**) there was an interval of one minute between the third (3rd) and fourth (4th) shot and a short interval between the eighth (8th) and ninth (9th) shot for the insertion of another magazine.

However, even after ten (10) shots, the *animal remained standing* and had to be *killed with a hammer*. Time from the first shot (09:57:30) until ***killed with a hammer*** (10:02) was 4.5 minutes (270 seconds).

Second, with the Luger, semi-automatic, **9mm** (**123.5 gr** Jacketed Truncated Cone bullet at **1048 fps**) there was an interval of one minute between the second (2nd) and third (3rd) shot and also a short interval between the eighth (8th) and ninth (9th) shot for the insertion of another magazine. The time from the first shot (10:15) until the eighth shot (10:18:15) was 3.25 minutes (195 seconds) – the time after the eighth (8th) shot to twelfth (12th) shot was not recorded, but after the twelfth shot (10 shots into the lungs and 2 shots into the abdomen) the *animal was still standing* and had to be ***killed with a hammer***.

Third, with the Colt, revolver, **45 Colt** (**218.5 gr** Soft Lead Cupped bullet at **801 fps**) there was an interval of one-half minute between the fifth (5th) and sixth (6th) shot and an interval of one minute between the eighth (8th) and ninth (9th) shot. With the tenth (10th) shot the animal ***began to fall*** and two (2) more shots were fired into the abdomen ***while the animal was falling***. The time from the first shot until the animal's death (not when it fell) was 4.5 minutes (270 seconds). Two of the recovered bullets had expanded to about 0.70 inches and were the only bullets used in these tests that expanded while penetrating only soft (body) parts.

Reference 2, page 157: "In the Quick Firing it will be noted that the animal fell to the ground in each instance when shot with the 0?476, 0?455 and 0?45 lead bullets; and in neither instance when shot with the 9 M/M, and 7.65 M/M, jacketed bullets."

12. STOLINSKY, David, M.D. – "STOPPING POWER" (St/SPPR)
==========

While neither conclusive nor definitive, the results of the Thompson-LaGarde tests do indicate a trend; i.e., the larger calibres and heavier bullets are considered to be more effective in stopping men and dropping/dispatching large animals. At the time, (this was still the era of the horse cavalry) this was considered important (refer to the second paragraph under above comments) where the complaints were about the 38 Colt's lack of stopping power for men and **horses**. Thus, the tests conducted on large bovine and equine animals were apropos.

Regarding the **Relative Incapacitation Index (RII)**, Dr. Stolinsky makes a convincing argument that a pseudo science and theoretical bias was used to establish the RII.

Based on autopsy studies it was claimed by some that it could not be determined whether the wound (permanent cavity) had been made by a 38 Special standard velocity (158 gr RNL at 789 ± fps) or by a 357 Magnum (110 gr JHP at 1334 ± fps). Because of this alleged inability to determine what bullet had caused the permanent wound, it was asserted by some that either the calibre is more important than velocity or the permanent cavity is a poor index of incapacitation or stopping power. The second conclusion was **inferred**! This resulted from an **assumption** that the temporary cavity was of greater importance. Why? With High-speed, X-ray, pictures were taken of various bullets shot into gelatin and it was visually determined that the larger temporary cavities were caused by bullets impacting/penetrating at higher velocities.

Because the size of the temporary cavity allowed one to distinguish between faster and slower bullets of the same calibre, the temporary cavity criterion was selected. There was no supportive evidence to indicate a larger temporary cavity would provide quicker incapacitation – it was chosen because it fit those authors' preconceptions.

How then was the RII correlated with incapacitation (stopping power)? According to Dr. Stolinsky, he received information from the Army Ballistic Research Laboratory how this correlation was done. Various experts (coroners, ballisticians, etc.) were shown sample *temporary cavities* in gelatin and asked to rate them as if they were wounds. Obviously they rated the biggest ones as the most incapacitating. This is a perfect example of circular reasoning. The results were predetermined. Had these experts been shown *permanent cavities* in gelatin, they would have rated the biggest as the most incapacitating. This would have confirmed Hatcher's RSP in the same spurious way they confirmed the Justice Department's RII.

A basic question was not answered because *it was not asked*; i.e., "Is stopping power predicted better by the temporary cavity or by the permanent cavity?"
==========

13. TAYLOR, Chuck – "TAYLOR'S MODIFIED SHORT FORM" (T/MSF)
REFERENCE: Chuck Taylor[18]

Formula: **T/MSF** = W × V × BF × BSF

B = Bullet weight (nearest 10 grains)
V = Bullet velocity (nearest 100 fps)
BF = Bore factor (decimal designator, e.g. .357 = 0.1)
BSF = J. Hatcher's BSF, i.e., 9, 10, 10.5, 11 and 12.5

Calculated "Taylor Modified Short Form" (T/SMF)

9mm Luger (Parabellum)
1) 124 gr – 1200 fps – 0.355" (original diameter)
   12 × 12 × 0.099 × 1.05 = 14.9 = **15**

2) 124 gr – 1200 fps – 0.533" (1.5 × original diameter)
   12 × 12 × 0.223 × 1.05 = 33.7 = **34**

3) 124 gr – 1200 fps – 0.621" (1.75 × original diameter)
   12 × 12 × 0.303 × 1.05 = 45.8 = **46**

40 S&W
4) 155 gr – 1150 fps – 0.400" (original diameter)
   16 × 12 × 0.126 × 1.05 = 25.4 = **25**

5) 155 gr – 1150 fps – 0.600" (1.5 × original diameter)
   16 × 12 × 0.283 × 1.05 = 57.1 = **57**

6) 155 gr – 1150 fps – 0.700" (1.75 × original diameter)
   16 × 12 × 0.386 × 1.05 = 77.8 = **78**

45 ACP (45 Auto)
7) 230 gr – 0850 fps – 0.451" (original diameter)
   23 × 09 × 0.160 × 1.05 = 34.8 = **35**

8) 230 gr – 0850 fps – 0.677" (1.5 × original diameter)
   23 × 09 × 0.359 × 1.05 = 78.0 = **78**

13. TAYLOR, Chuck – "TAYLOR'S MODIFIED SHORT FORM" (T/MSF)
==========

45 ACP (45 Auto) – continued

9) 230 gr – 0850 fps – 0.789" (1.75 × original diameter)
23 × 09 × 0.489 × 1.05 = 106.3 = **106**

==========

Comments:

The bullet shape factor decimal point has been moved one digit to the left (e.g., 1.05 instead of 10.5) in order for Taylor's answers to be comparable to those obtained using Cooper's Short Form formula. Using this formula, a minimum value of approximately **30** is considered necessary for the load (bullet) to be able to provide about a 90% probability of achieving effective stopping power.

The Taylor and Cooper formulae were put forth with the idea and purpose of simplifying the Hatcher formula. Before pocket calculators became readily available, this may or may not have been achieved. However, both the Taylor and Cooper formulae lack the use of precise input data and consequently almost all answers will be less precise than the answers obtained using the Hatcher formula – which itself deals only in relative or comparative values.

==========

14. TAYLOR, John – "TAYLOR'S KNOCK OUT" (T/KO)
REFERENCE: John Taylor[19]

Formula: **T/KO** = BW ÷ CW × BV × BD

BW = Bullet weight in grains
CW = Grains to pounds conversion factor = 7000
BV = Bullet velocity in feet per second (fps)
BD = Bullet diameter in inches, e.g., 0.451"

Taylor did not explain the method he used to arrive at his "knock out" formula. Instead he only listed (reference, page 13) the KO values for several cartridges. A comparison of several of Taylor's KO values with the values obtained using the above formula indicates the formula to be basically correct:

Taylor's "Knock Out" or KO Values:

.416 Rigby – 410 gr - 2350 fps	= **57.25** KO
.375 H&H Magnum – 300 gr – 2500 fps	= **40.1** KO
.275" (bore diameter) – 173 gr – 2300 fps	= **15.6** KO

Formula KO Values: .

.416" Rigby – 410 gr – 2350 fps
410 ÷ 7000 × 2350 × .416   = **57.26** KO

.375" H&H Magnum – 300 gr – 2500 fps
300 ÷ 7000 × 2500 × .375   = **40.2** KO

.275" (7mm) – 173 gr – 2300 fps
173 ÷ 7000 × 2300 × .275   = **15.6** KO

KO Values for a few of the more popular American rifle cartridges:

270 Win – 130 gr – 3100 fps	= **16.0**
30-06 Springfield – 180 gr – 2700 fps	= **21.4**
300 Win Magnum – 180 gr – 3000 fps	= **23.8**

14. TAYLOR, John – "TAYLOR'S KNOCK OUT" (T/KO)
==========

The listed values of Taylor and the values arrived at using the above formula are in whole number agreement, with but minor differences in rounding the numbers to the nearest tenth or hundredth. However, whether or not there is a difference of one-tenth (1/10th) or one-hundredth (1/100th) in the KO values is inconsequential. How then do the three handgun calibres fare?

Calculated "Taylor Knock Out Value" (T/KO)

9mm Luger (Parabellum)

1) Original bullet diameter – no bullet expansion
124 ÷ 7000 × 1200 × 0.355" = **07.6**

2) 1.5 × Original bullet diameter
124 ÷ 7000 × 1200 × 0.533" = **11.3**

3) 1.75 × Original bullet diameter
124 ÷ 7000 × 1200 × 0.621" = **13.2**

40 S&W

4) Original bullet diameter – no bullet expansion
155 ÷ 7000 × 1150 × 0.400" = **10.2**

5) 1.5 × Original bullet diameter
155 ÷ 7000 × 1150 × 0.600" = **15.3**

6) 1.75 × Original bullet diameter
155 ÷ 7000 × 1150 × 0.700" = **17.8**

45 ACP (45 Auto)

7) Original bullet diameter – no bullet expansion
230 ÷ 7000 × 0850 × 0.451" = **12.6**

8) 1.5 × Original bullet diameter
230 ÷ 7000 × 0850 × 0.677" = **18.9**

9) 1.75 × Original bullet diameter
230 ÷ 7000 × 0850 × 0.789" = **22.0**

==========
Comments:

At first glance, it might appear that the 45 Auto load that expanded to 1.75 times its original diameter has a somewhat greater KO value (**22.0**) than the 30-06 Springfield load (**21.4**) and a somewhat lesser KO value than the 300 Winchester Magnum load (**23.8**).

However, not taken into consideration is the stated relevance of these KO values and the specific application thereof.

First, there is the matter of penetration. There is no denying that the penetration potential of the 30-06 Springfield (38,859) and the 300 Winchester Magnum (47,974) is significantly greater than the 45 Auto (2,307) and when the same bullet designs are used – in this case non-expanding bullets - there is an approximate 17:1 and 21:1 advantage for the rifle bullets respectively. It is to be understood that the bullets are such that the same type of proportional penetration tracks (paths) are made.

Second, and of greater concern is the *misuse* of the Taylor KO value method by some individuals who would use it to evaluate and rate cartridges (rifle and handgun) for general big game hunting and/or for self defense in a life threatening situation. Remember, Taylor uses (reference, page 12) the KO values for one specific purpose, to wit:

> They permit of an immediate comparison being made between any two rifles from the point of the actual punch delivered by the bullet on heavy massive-boned animals which are almost invariably shot at close quarters, and enable a sportsman to see at a glance whether or not any particular rifle is likely to prove a safe weapon for the job.

Heavy massive-boned animals as Taylor considered them include the elephant, the rhinoceros, the hippopotamus and various species of buffalo (e.g., Cape buffalo, Guar and the Wild Asiatic Water buffalo). For that purpose and under the described conditions, Taylor considered the cartridge, to be effective, needed to develop a minimum KO value of approximately forty (40). Except for those who experience severe periods of delusional fantasy or those who are vicariously experiencing the fictional endeavors of pulp magazine super heroes, it is almost inconceivable that any "normal" person would equate humans with the size and mass of these animals and thus consider the minimum cartridge that can be used to achieve Effective Stopping Power to be the 375 H&H Magnum.

Handgun Bullet Stopping Power

15. USDJ – **"RELATIVE INCAPACITATION INDEX"** (RII)
    REFERENCE 1: R. C. Dobbyn, W. J. Bruchey, Jr. and L. D. Shubin[20]
    REFERENCE 2: William J. Bruchey, Jr. and Daniel E. Frank[21]
    REFERENCE 3: Evan P. Marshall and Edwin J. Sanow[22]

= = = = = = = = = =

On page iv of Reference 2, **RII** is defined: "The product of the volume of the Maximum Temporary Cavity (MTC) produced by the interaction of a projectile and the tissue simulant (gelatin) at a given depth and the average vulnerability to incapacitation at that depth summed together for the entire penetration depth of the bullet to a maximum depth of 22 cm (8.66 inches)."

= = = = =

Formula: **RII** $= CR^2 \times VI$
CR^2 = Radius of the temporary cavity squared
VI = Vulnerability Index

The temporary cavity measurements (radial fissures emanating from the perimeter of the longitudinal axis of the permanent cavity) in properly prepared and calibrated **20%** [emphasis added] *250A Ordnance gelatin* are made at one centimeter (cm) intervals up to and including a penetration depth of 22 centimeters. The CR is squared and then multiplied by an **arbitrarily derived** [emphasis added] vulnerability index value for each cm of penetration up to 22 cm. The sum of these answers is then multiplied by Π (3.14159) which gives the RII value.

= = = = = = = = = =

Comments:

The vulnerability index values could have been listed here, but unless the interested agencies or individuals have the facilities and time to prepare and test a significant quantity of gelatin blocks, any list of vulnerability index values would have little pragmatic value. However, if the reader is interested in such values, they can be found in Reference 2, page 16.

At the onset this concept/formula was hampered by ill-conceived arbitrary parameters that ignored several factors;

First: *Incorrect gelatin/water mixture.* Twenty (20%) percent gelatin does NOT offer the same resistance to bullet penetration as does muscle/tissue – thus, the results were not only skewed but were, with regards to the determination of comparative effective stopping power, of not much more relevance than if clay, sand or an iron plate had been used as the test medium. Primarily through the efforts of Dr. Martin Fackler, it has been recognized and accepted by most law enforcement agencies and individuals that a calibrated ten (10%) percent 250A Ordnance Gelatin mixture more closely simulates muscle/tissue.

Second: *Temperature.* Nonetheless, other aspects of the gelatin preparation

15. USDJ – "**RELATIVE INCAPACITATION INDEX**" (RII)
==========

protocol continued to be incorrectly used by some well into the late 1990s; e.g., The U.S. Department of Justice, Immigration and Naturalization Service, National Firearms Unit *"Final Report" – Ammunition Barrier Penetration Tests dated August 18-29, 1997*. On page two, even though the 10% mixture is correct, the use of water heated to 180 degrees Fahrenheit did much to invalidate the test results of various cartridges – during the preparation of the 250A Ordnance Gelatin, the temperature of the gelatin/water mixture should NOT exceed 104 degrees Fahrenheit.

Third: *Bullet Point of Entry*. All RII calculations are predicated on an assumed forward torso entry point (Reference 2, page 8). This is with little doubt, one of the more serious faults of the RII concept. Unfortunately, it took the results of the tragic FBI, Miami firefight of 11 April 1986 to reveal this erroneous predication. The RII value for the 115 gr ST bullet is given at 27.5 whereas 230 gr FMJ 45 Auto bullets have RII values of 3+ to 4+? This absurd disregard for bullet penetration beyond 22 cm (8.66") was exemplified by that 9mm STHP bullet penetrating about 9 (± 1) inches – which included first the penetration of the right arm. To seriously think that all lethal threat confrontations will be face to face and there will not be intervening media (e.g., arm) that must first be penetrated is unconscionable – and when such thinking reflects official policy it can cause an officer to be shot and wounded/killed EVEN though the officer's bullet hit the intended external point of aim.

Fourth: As was mentioned within the Dr. Stolinsky section of this chapter (page 112) the selection of the temporary cavity (TC) as the main criterion to use in determining RII is a classic example of implementing a predetermined bias. If one uses the comparative sizes of the TC to establish RII values – then obviously the TC of larger size would rank higher, BUT if one had instead decided to use the comparative sizes of the permanent cavity to establish RII values – then obviously the PC of larger size would rank higher. If the latter was used, it would also be an example of implementing a predetermined bias.

Fifth. *Smoke and Mirror plus Spin*. The RII concept also included other considerations such as the "average" police officer's marksmanship and the relative value of hits in different locations on a human target. It should be stressed that whether or not an officer, or for that matter anyone else involved in a lethal threat confrontation, is a tyro or an expert marksman; it has no bearing on the inherent efficacy of the load (bullet). To evaluate any cartridge based on how a theoretical "average" police officer can shoot is a sophism and ignores an apriori condition; i.e., the bullet hits or misses – the bullet stops or does not stop the lethal threat action. There is no such thing as an "average" lethal threat confrontation; i.e., one cannot call "time-out" and redo the incident until the "intended" results are the "actual" results.
==========

16. WALKER, Louise – **"DEFENSIVE AMMO PERFORMANCE"** (WL/DAP)
   REFERENCE: Louise Walker[23]
==========
Comments:

Some information from this article is included as examples to describe just how pervasive the supercilious attitude has become that considers the relative size of the "temporary cavity" in gelatin as the primary criterion to use in determining a <u>handgun</u> bullet's probable effectiveness in stopping a lethal threat action.

Almost at the onset, Walker (reference, page 83) claims:

> Because of its outstanding performance in real-life shootouts, the 125 grain semi-jacketed hollowpoint 357 load was fired into the gelatin without a barrier as a control to measure the other loads against. It expanded to .50 inch and penetrated 10 inches.

Walker appears to have accepted (without question) the promulgated written views of some writers (e.g., Evan Marshall) that allege the above mentioned load to be superior in incapacitating animated targets. How was "superior" determined? Ecce! It was determined by measuring the width of the "temporary" cavity in gelatin and <u>allegedly</u> correlating it with "unavailable" source material consisting of <u>allegedly</u> reported "field" performances of the load used in lethal threat confrontations.

Walker then describes the performance of various cartridges (loads) fired into gelatin after first being fired through drywall, glass and plywood. Again, another statement of Walker reveals either a naivety or a willingness to be duped, to wit:

> Rounding out the 357s is the 125 gr JHP that works so well without a barrier. Its characteristics change dramatically when that light little bullet has to negotiate an obstacle. It held together through the plywood, but it was slowed enough to lose a full inch off the <u>temporary</u> cavitation damage. The <u>massive damage</u> is apparently a large part of the reason why this round has worked so well. Its performance is questionable through drywall and glass. All the slugs fragmented heavily in the gelatin and did not penetrate more than 5 inches. The <u>maximum damage</u> width, however, was well over 3 inches.

From the forgoing two quotes, it is evident that Walker appears not to understand what is meant by temporary. <u>Temporary:</u> "lasting only for a time." In the situations involving muscle/tissue, the <u>temporary</u> cavitation lasts only a few milliseconds. After the descending magnitude of the **tissue** oscillation subsides and without high speed photography there remains no visually discernible evidence for the existence of a temporary cavity. This is because the <u>impact velocities of most handgun bullets</u> do

16. WALKER, Louise – "**DEFENSIVE AMMO PERFORMANCE**" (WL/DAP)
==========

not cause the elasticity limits of most muscle/tissue to be exceeded. With **gelatin**, the temporary cavitation is manifested by fissures extending laterally away from the longitudinal permanent cavity. The length of these fissures indicates the size of the temporary cavitation <u>in gelatin</u>. The primary reason the fissures exist is the elasticity limits of 250A Ordnance gelatin are relatively small and easily exceeded.

Again, Walker (reference, page 85) unequivocally and without reservation considers the temporary cavity to be *<u>the</u>* wound channel, to wit:

> For the purpose of comparison only, the "wound" channel widths are measured across the widest area of gelatin damage. This was at the point where <u>temporary cavitation</u> occurred. The gelatin fractured extensively for a few inches and then narrowed down to the bullet path.

Ergo, those who attach primary importance to temporary cavitation believe and will not be dissuaded that the temporary cavity <u>in gelatin</u> does NOT reflect the condition or affect of the temporary cavity in most muscle/tissue. Such opinion can be considered surrealistic.
==========

17. WALTERS, Kenneth – "**HANDGUN STOPPING POWER**" (WK/CSPF)
   REFERENCE: Kenneth L. Walters[24]
==========
Comments:
   Walters describes the RSP formula of J. S. Hatcher and then describes, compares and contrasts the formulae given by M. H. Josserand and J. A. Stevenson; Jeff Cooper; John Taylor and Elmer Keith.
   With all due respect to Walters, this material – for the most part – represents a combination of unnecessary complications and obfuscation. To compound the unnecessary complications and obfuscation, there are also statements given as fact when the reality is that they are false, as follows:
   First. <u>Unnecessary complications and obfuscation</u>. Julian S. Hatcher's RSP is an uncomplicated concept and his formula while written in prose, is easily put to numbers and there does not appear to be a deliberate attempt to obscure his own calculations.
   Even though Walters mentioned ". . . his (Hatcher's) error is of no real consequence. Its net effect is to simply halve an arbitrary multiplier used in his bullet shape factors." The Hatcher "error" pertains to the calculation of momentum and has absolutely nothing to do with "bullet shape factors" – the shape of the bullet does not and cannot affect the initially developed momentum. Whether halved, doubled or tripled, when all momentum calculations are done using the same method, the RSP values will still be relative.
   <u>Second</u>. Josserand's determination of the missing constant (0.00000221 ?) is an interesting but unnecessary consideration. The important point to remember is that no where in Hatcher's writings was a direct reference made to a constant. It is therefore presumptuous of Josserand and Walters to categorically state (without supporting evidence) that Hatcher used a constant. He may have, but to my knowledge there is no written evidence that he did. Consequently, any assertion is merely an inference based on speculation. He is also mistaken when it is asserted that "those who endeavor to work a given cartridge through the Hatcher formula and arrive at a figure for RSP which will correspond to those Hatcher gives in his tables are foredoomed to disappointment. . . ." As the reader may recall, Hatcher's formula multiplies the <u>bullet momentum</u> by the <u>bullet cross sectional area</u> by the <u>bullet shape factor</u>.
   On page 434 of Hatcher's "Textbook of Pistols and Revolvers" Hatcher lists seven cartridges and their relative stopping power values; e.g., the 455 Man Stopper (218.5 gr at 801 fps) with a RSP value of **73**. Now using the appropriate numbers for the prose method of Hatcher, the following is the result: *Momentum* (288 ft lbs ÷ 801 fps) = **0.360** × *Cross Sectional Area* (0.455 ÷ 2 = 0.227 then 0.227^2 × 3.14159) = **0.163** × *Bullet Shape Factor* = **1.25** (page 431) for the 455 Man Stopper 218.5 gr bullet = **0.07335** but changing the value of the bullet shape factor by moving the

17. WALTERS, Kenneth L. – "HANDGUN STOPPING POWER" (WK/CSPF)
==========

decimal three places to the right as suggested by Hatcher on page 433 gives a RSP of **73.35** which when rounded to the nearest whole number is **73** and that is in complete agreement with Hatcher!

Third. The subject of Cooper's Short Form RSP has been described on pages 82 through 84 of this work. Note that Cooper himself did not suggest that his formula should replace Hatcher's RSP formula; only that "you can do my 'short form' in your head, while the General's are too cumbersome for that."

Fourth. As mentioned on page 115 of this work, John Taylor's formula is intended to provide a comparison between the actual punch of bullets used against "heavy massive-boned animals" – e.g., elephant, rhinoceros, or the large bovines (Cape buffalo, Guar and Wild Asiatic Water buffalo). There is little if any relevance for his formula if applied to the ESP of humans.

Fifth. Keith's pounds feet method has been described on pages 95 and 96 of this work and it is primarily concerned with the comparative terminal (wound) effects of carbine/rifle cartridges used to take big game. Keith qualified his formula's application by stating it might not give the best indication of probable <u>wound</u> effectiveness on light, thin skinned big game. Thus, as with John Taylor's formula, persons are mistaken if they believe either or both of these formulae can or should be used to determine the comparative or relative stopping power effectiveness of handgun cartridges. Neither formula was developed for that purpose. There are other errors in Walters' article – some probably typographical and others may be due perhaps to the results of hasty and limited research.

Walters (reference, page 262) lists the cross sectional area values for several cartridges (bullets), e.g.:

Cartridge	Diameter	Claimed Cross Sectional Area	Actual (nearest 0.001") Cross Sectional Area
38 Super	0.355"	0.102"	0.099" (0.09897")
9mm Luger and	0.355"	0.102"	0.099" (0.09897")
9mm Luger	0.355"	0.100"	0.099" (0.09897")
38 Special and	0.356"	0.102"	0.100" (0.09953")
38 Special	0.3564"	0.100"	0.100" (0.09976")
357 Magnum and	0.356"	0.100"	0.100" (0.09953")
357 Magnum	0.3564"	0.102"	0.100" (0.09976")

- - - - -

17. WALTERS, Kenneth L. – "HANDGUN STOPPING POWER" (WK/CSPF)
==========

The main errors are with regards to the cross sectional areas (csa) for the 38 Super and the 9mm Luger where they are listed as 0.102" and somewhat less egregious errors for the 38 Special and 357 Magnum where they are listed as 0.102" – it is mathematically impossible for a smaller diameter to have a larger csa. The next error involves claiming the same csa for different diameters, e.g., how can a 0.356" and a 0.3564" both have a csa of 0.100" and 0.102"? For the csa to equal 0.102" (0.10178") a diameter of 0.360" is required.

Finally, Walters' comment that "*As such handgun projectiles (expanding bullets) were not even dreamed of in the 1930's, ...*" is patently and incontrovertibly false. On page 111 of this work, the second complete paragraph where it is mentioned that the two soft lead cupped bullets fired into the abdomen **expanded** to about **0.70 inches** – only soft body parts were penetrated – this occurred during the first decade of the 1900s.
==========

18. WOOTTERS, John – **"WOOTTERS' LETHALITY"** (W/L)
   REFERENCE: George Bredsten & John Hillegass[25]
   Note: Original reference describing this formula was inadvertently lost.
===========

Formula: W/L = D × KE × SD

   D   = Diameter (inches)
   KE   = Kinetic energy (foot pounds)
   SD   = Sectional Density
=====

9mm Luger (124 gr at 1200 fps)
1) .355" – 397 ft lbs – 0.141 SD
   W/L = .355 × 397 × 0.141 = 19.87 = **20**

2) .533" – 397 ft lbs – 0.062 SD
   W/L = .533 × 397 × 0.062 = 13.12 = **13**

3) .621" – 397 ft lbs – 0.046 SD
   W/L = .621 × 397 × 0.046 = 11.34 = **11**

40 S&W (155 gr at 1150 fps)
4) .400" – 455 ft lbs – 0.134 SD
   W/L = .400 × 455 × 0.134 = 24.39 = **24**

5) .600" – 455 ft lbs – 0.060 SD
   W/L = .600 × 455 × 0.060 = 16.38 = **16**

6) .700" – 455 ft lbs – 0.044 SD
   W/L = .700 × 455 × 0.044 = 14.01 = **14**

45 ACP (230 gr at 0850 fps)
7) .451" – 369 ft lbs – 0.162 SD
   W/L = .451 × 369 × 0.162 = 26.96 = **27**

8) .677" – 369 ft lbs – 0.072 SD
   W/L = .677 × 369 × 0.072 = 17.99 = **18**

9) .789" – 369 ft lbs – 0.053 SD
   W/L = .789 × 369 × 0.053 = 15.43 = **15**
=====

18. WOOTTERS, John – "WOOTTERS' LETHALITY" (W/L)
==========

For comparison purposes, the W/L of three popular rifle cartridges used to take big game and one very common cartridge used during World War II are given:

30-30 Winchester (170 gr at 2200 fps)

1) .308" – 1827 ft lbs – 0.256 SD
W/L = 0.308 × 1827 × 0.256 = 144.06 = **144**

270 Winchester (130 gr at 3060 fps)

2) .277" – 2704 ft lbs – 0.242 SD
W/L = 0.277 × 2704 × 0.242 = 181.26 = **181**

30-06 Springfield (180 gr at 2700 fps)

3) .308" – 2915 ft lbs – 0.271 SD
W/L = 0.308 × 2915 × 0.271 = 243.31 = **243**

30 Carbine (110 gr at 1990 fps)

4) .308" – 0968 ft lbs – 0.166 SD
W/L = 0.308 × 0968 × 0.166 = 049.49 = **050**

==========
Comments:

At first glance this formula seems to provide answers that reflect the relative lethality of various cartridges. With similar bullet placement, few rational individuals would opine that any of the mentioned carbine/rifle cartridges are less effective than the three handgun cartridges. However, all is not as it may first appear.

When a <u>non-expanding</u> and/or <u>non-fragmenting</u> bullet also penetrates <u>without noticeable yawing</u>, it can be relatively ineffective (excluding the bullet that penetrates the brain or the cervical/thoracic spinal cord). The wound may prove lethal BUT the effect of the wound is often delayed for some time – from several seconds to several minutes. This less than desirable performance characteristic (i.e., delayed effect) has been known to occur from at least the time of the Philippine–Insurrection where the U.S.A. military's 30-40 Krag cartridge with its round nose, full metal jacket bullet would often fail to stop a Moro intent on killing the soldier – even though the wound would eventually prove to be fatal.

18. WOOTTERS, John – "**WOOTTERS' LETHALITY**" (W/L)
==========

Now for another misleading effect of this formula. Consider the four previously mentioned rifle/carbine cartridges (loads) where the bullets now expand to 1.75 times their original diameter:

<u>30-30 Winchester (170 gr at 2200 fps)</u>

1) .539" – 1827 ft lbs – 0.084 SD
W/L = 0.539 × 1827 × 0.084 = 082.72 = **083**

<u>270 Winchester (130 gr at 3060 fps)</u>

2) .485" – 2704 ft lbs – 0.079 SD
W/L = 0.485 × 2704 × 0.079 = 103.60 = **103**

<u>30-06 Springfield (180 gr at 2700 fps)</u>

3) .539" – 2915 ft lbs – 0.089 SD
W/L = 0.539 × 2915 × 0.089 = 139.84 = **140**

<u>30 Carbine (110 gr at 1990 fps)</u>

4) .539" – 0968 ft lbs – 0.054 SD
W/L = 0.539" × 0968 × 0.054 = 028.18 = **028**

Is it reasonable to conclude, e.g., a 30-06, 180 gr bullet that expands to .539" is going to be less effective than that same bullet that does not expand? Yet according to this formula, the non-expanding bullet has a W/L value of <u>243</u> versus a W/L value of <u>140</u> if it expands. The non-expanding bullet by this formula is supposed to be about 74% more effective?

Another example, while multiple thousands of firearms chambered for the 30 Carbine were issued and used during World War Two, the Korean and the Viet Nam conflicts; a common complaint regarding this cartridge (<u>W/L 50</u>) was its reported failure to reliably stop enemy combatants (unless <u>multiple hits</u> to the abdomen/thorax were made in <u>rapid succession</u>).

Yet preliminary comparison discloses the 30 Carbine <u>expanding</u> bullet has a Wootters' Lethality value that is now comparable to the 45 Auto **AND** at the same time still has a significantly greater penetration potential.

18. WOOTTERS, John – "**WOOTTERS' LETHALITY**" (W/L)
==========

Cartridge	Wootters' Lethality	Penetration Potential
30 Carbine (0.539" expanded diameter)	**028**	**04246**
45 Auto (0.451" no expansion)	027	02306

    Except for agenda driven radical revisionists, there is virtually no disagreement regarding the reliable fight stopping ability of the 45 Auto, military ball cartridge; i.e., 230 gr JRN at 850 ± fps. How can it be that the 30 Carbine with a non-expanding bullet (W/L value of **50**) is generally recognized to be a relatively ineffective fight-stopper while the 45 Auto with a non-expanding bullet (W/L value of **27**) is considered to be an effective fight stopper? Yet when the 30 Carbine bullet (e.g., 110 gr SP) expands to 0.539" its lower W/L value of **28** makes it comparable to the W/L value of **27** for the 45 Auto military ball load?

    It is apparent that this formula is basically flawed and can only have a meaningful relevance where (by inference) penetration is the primary consideration. This is another formula that endeavors to rank or rate various cartridges according to their comparative effectiveness in producing a <u>lethal</u> wound in a big game animal. As has been mentioned before in this book, both killing and wounding power <u>should not be considered</u> synonymous with stopping power.
==========

CHAPTER SEVEN ENDNOTES

[1] 2004 Handguns Annual, pp. 109-114.

[2] Kenneth L Walters, "Handgun Stopping Power," *Gun Digest* 1976 Edition (Northfield, Illinois: DBI Books, 1975) pp. 260-263.

[3] Chuck Taylor, "Combat Corner," *Combat Handguns*, Vol. 3 (June 1988), p. 71.

[4] V. J. M. DiMaio, M.D. et al. *A Comparison of the Wounding Effects of Commercially Available Handgun Ammunition Suitable for Police Use*, FBI Law Enforcement Bulletin, December 1974, pp. 3-8.

[5] V. J. M. DiMaio, M.D. *Gunshot Wounds* (New York: Elsevier Science, 1985), p. 25.

[6] E. Marshall & E. Sanow. *Handgun Stopping Power: The Definitive Study* (Boulder, Colorado: Paladin Press, 1992), pp. 43, 44.

[7] E. Marshall & E. Sanow, *Street Stoppers: The Latest Handgun Stopping Power Street Results* (Boulder, Colorado: Paladin Press, 1996), pp. 337-349.

[8] E. Marshall & E. Sanow, *Stopping Power: A Practical Analysis of the Latest Handgun Ammunition* (Boulder, Colorado: Paladin Press, 2001).

[9] Julian S. Hatcher, *Textbook of Pistols & Revolvers* (Small Arms Technical Publishing Co., 1935 – Reprinted by Wolfe Publishing Company, 1985), p. 433.

[10] Elmer Keith, *Big Game Rifles and Cartridges* (Plantersville, South Carolina: Thomas Samworth Small Arms Technical Publishing Company, 1936), p.4.

[11] E. Matunas, "Power Index Rating," *Gun Digest* 1984 Edition (Northfield, Illinois: DBI Books, 1983, pp. 6-14.

[12] E. Matunas, *American Ammo: Selection, Use, Ballistics* (Outdoor Life Books, Grolier Book Clubs Inc., 1989), pp. 139, 140.

[13] C. Peters, *Defensive Handgun Effectiveness* (Manchester, Tennessee: Carroll Peters, 1977), p. 43.

[14] Veral Smith, *Jacketed Performance with Cast Bullets* (Moyie Springs, Idaho: LBT, 1984 – Third Edition 1990), p. 96

[15] Ibid., pp. 99-101.

[16] D. Stolinsky, M.D. "Stopping Power – A Physicians Report," *Guns & Ammo 1986 Handgun Annual* (Los Angels, California: Petersen Publishing Company, 1986), pp. 61-67.

[17] John. Potocki, *The Colt Model 1905 Automatic Pistol* (Lincoln, R.I.: Mowbray, Inc., 1998) pp. 122-164.

[18] C. Taylor, "Combat Corner," Combat Handguns, Vol. 2, No. 3 (June 1988), pp. 12, 13, 71.

[19] J. Taylor, *African Rifles and Cartridges* (Harrisburg, Pennsylvania: The Stackpole Company, 1948), pp. 12, 13.

[20] R. C. Dobbyn, W. J. Bruchey, Jr. and L. D. Shubin. *An Evaluation of Police Handgun Ammunition: Summary Report*, October 1975 (Washington, D.C.: U.S. Government Printing Office, 1976).

[21] W. J. Bruchey, Jr. and Daniel E. Frank. *Police Handgun Ammunition: Incapacitation Effects Volume 1: Evaluation* (Boulder, Colorado: Paladin Press, post 1981?).

[22] Marshall and Sanow, *Street Stoppers*, op. cit., pp. 15, 16.

[23] Louise Walker. "Defensive Ammo Performance" *Guns & Ammo* 1992 Annual (Los Angeles, California: Petersen Publishing Company, 1991), pp. 82-88.

[24] Kenneth L. Walters, loc. cit.

[25] G. Bredsten and J. Hillegass. Ballistics Workbook and Calculator (Glynco, Georgia: Federal Law Enforcement Training Center, Firearms Division, 1998), Calculator Line 41.

CHAPTER EIGHT

FORMULAE/CONCEPTS COMPARISONS

While the reader can and is encouraged to peruse and evaluate each formula/concept in order to obtain a more detailed and comprehensive understanding; this chapter attempts to provide a format that enables the reader to make quick comparisons. It is important for the reader NOT to confuse, equate or otherwise mistake either "killing" or "wounding" power for "stopping" power. The essential difference to remember is that neither killing nor wounding power includes a definite or specific *time frame* whereas effective stopping power always does.

All but one formula/concept have at least one graph. The exception pertains to the material comparing/describing "Handgun Stopping Power" of Kenneth Walters. His material, page 122, while interesting, introduced complications and unnecessary obfuscation. It is mentioned here again to illustrate how an otherwise well-qualified individual can:

1. Assert *incorrectly* that the shape of a bullet is a factor affecting *initial* momentum.
2. Include an *irrelevant* and *nonessential* bit of datum – the so-called "missing constant" of Hatcher.
3. Contend *erroneously* that a person is doomed to disappointment if an attempt is made to work a given cartridge through the Hatcher formula.

The following graphs (Various formulae) illustrate the cartridges' relative performance values. Most graphs for a particular formula, e.g., Archibald, show direct comparisons of the three cartridges (9mm Luger, 40 S&W and 45 ACP). The comparisons begin with the original diameters (no expansion). Subsequent graphs for the same formula then compare these three cartridges with the bullets 1.5 times and 1.75 times their original diameters. A few graphs, for increased elucidatory purposes, also contain the relative performance values of other cartridges (calibres).

In the following graphs, I have indicated by one or more asterisk marks whether or not the specific formula/concept relates primarily to stopping power (*), lethality (**) or wounding power (***).

Handgun Bullet Stopping Power

* Archibald: "One Shot Stop Ratio"

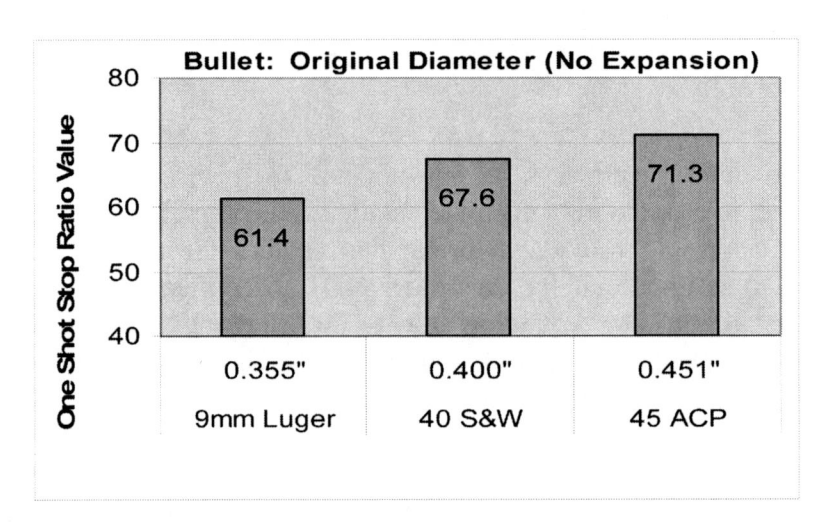

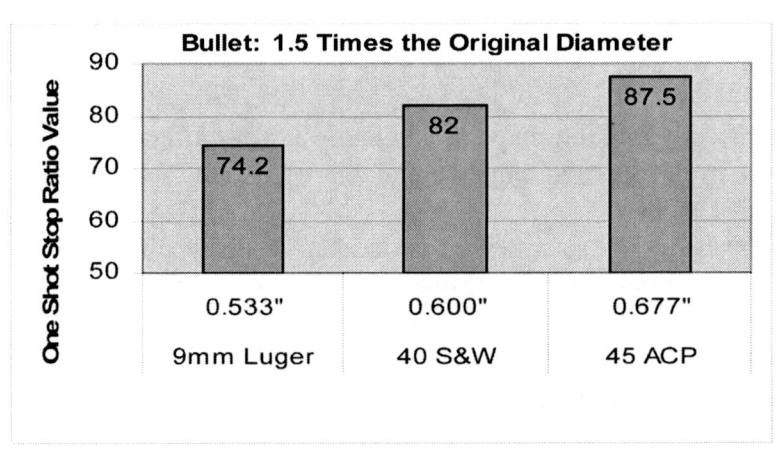

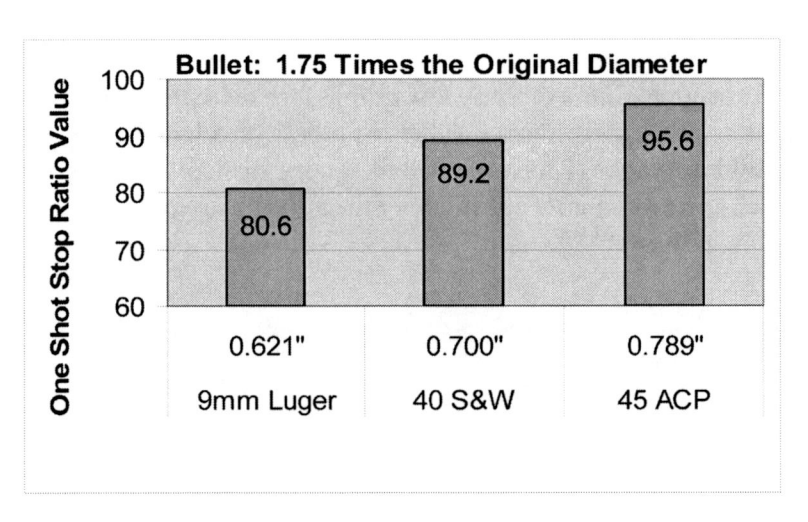

Bullet: Original Diameter (No Expansion)

	0.355" 9mm Luger	0.400" 40 S&W	0.451" 45 ACP
One Shot Stop Ratio Value	61.4	67.6	71.3

Bullet: 1.5 Times the Original Diameter

	0.533" 9mm Luger	0.600" 40 S&W	0.677" 45 ACP
One Shot Stop Ratio Value	74.2	82	87.5

Bullet: 1.75 Times the Original Diameter

	0.621" 9mm Luger	0.700" 40 S&W	0.789" 45 ACP
One Shot Stop Ratio Value	80.6	89.2	95.6

* J. Cooper: "RSP Short Form" (1ˢᵗ Formula)

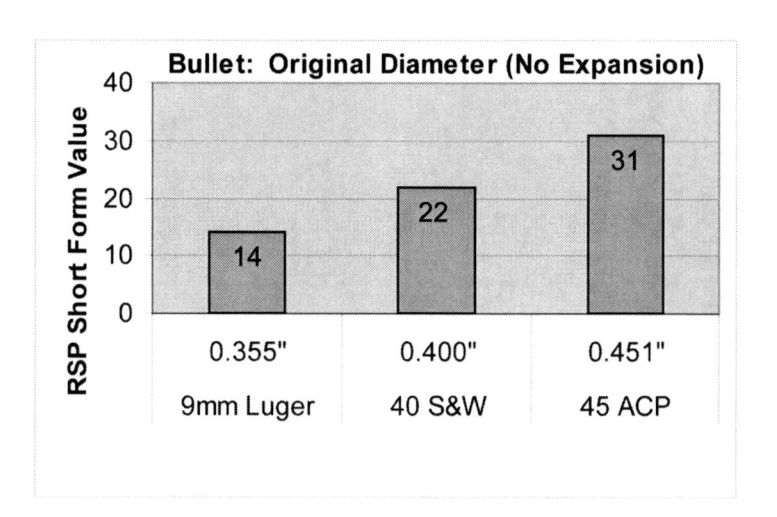

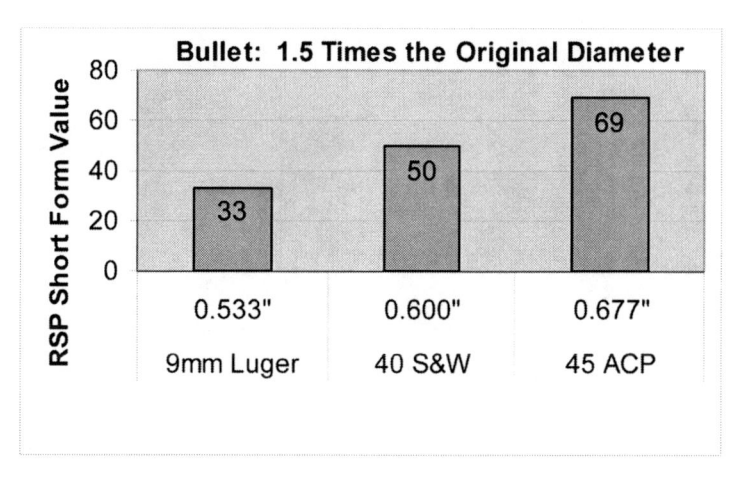

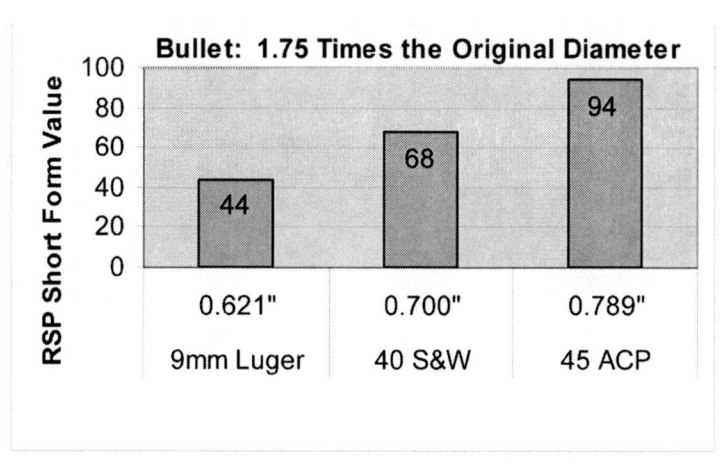

Bullet: Original Diameter (No Expansion)

	0.355"	0.400"	0.451"
	9mm Luger	40 S&W	45 ACP
RSP Short Form Value	14	22	31

Bullet: 1.5 Times the Original Diameter

	0.533"	0.600"	0.677"
	9mm Luger	40 S&W	45 ACP
RSP Short Form Value	33	50	69

Bullet: 1.75 Times the Original Diameter

	0.621"	0.700"	0.789"
	9mm Luger	40 S&W	45 ACP
RSP Short Form Value	44	68	94

* J. Cooper: "RSP Short Form" (2nd Formula)

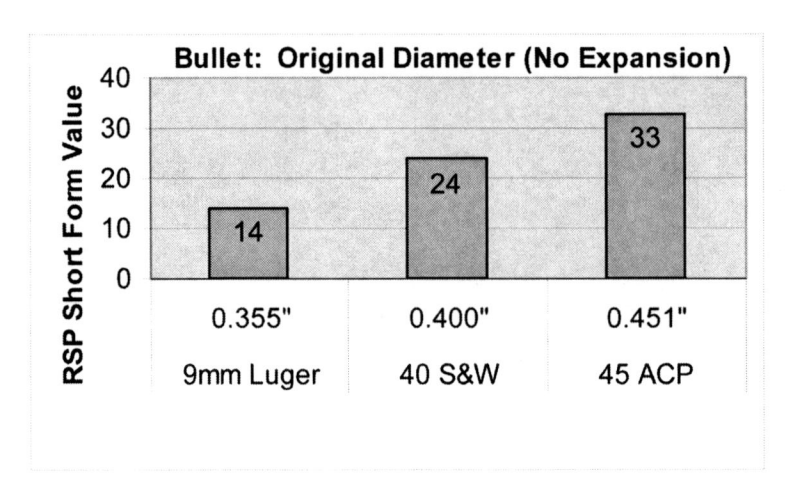

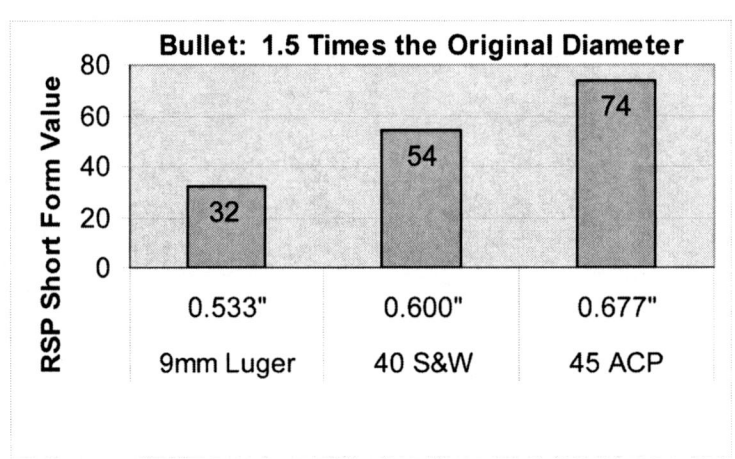

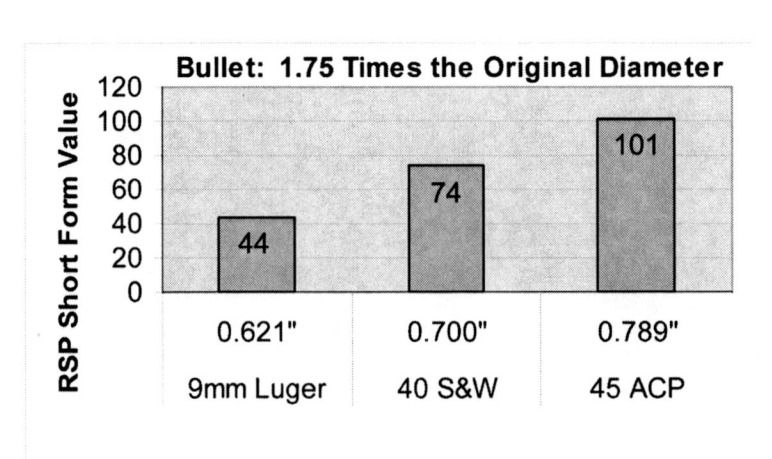

Bullet: Original Diameter (No Expansion)

Caliber	Diameter	RSP Short Form Value
9mm Luger	0.355"	14
40 S&W	0.400"	24
45 ACP	0.451"	33

Bullet: 1.5 Times the Original Diameter

Caliber	Diameter	RSP Short Form Value
9mm Luger	0.533"	32
40 S&W	0.600"	54
45 ACP	0.677"	74

Bullet: 1.75 Times the Original Diameter

Caliber	Diameter	RSP Short Form Value
9mm Luger	0.621"	44
40 S&W	0.700"	74
45 ACP	0.789"	101

George B. Bredsten

*** V. DiMaio: "Energy Loss/Transfer"

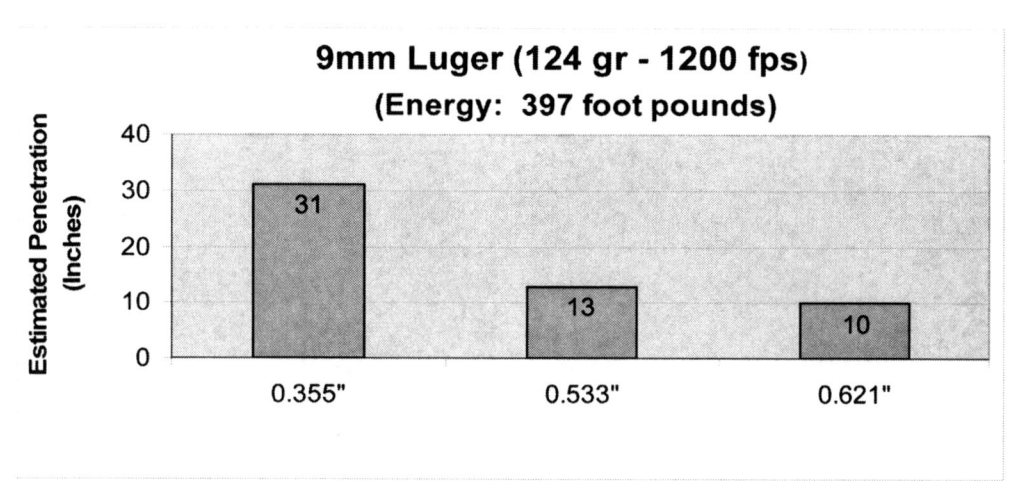

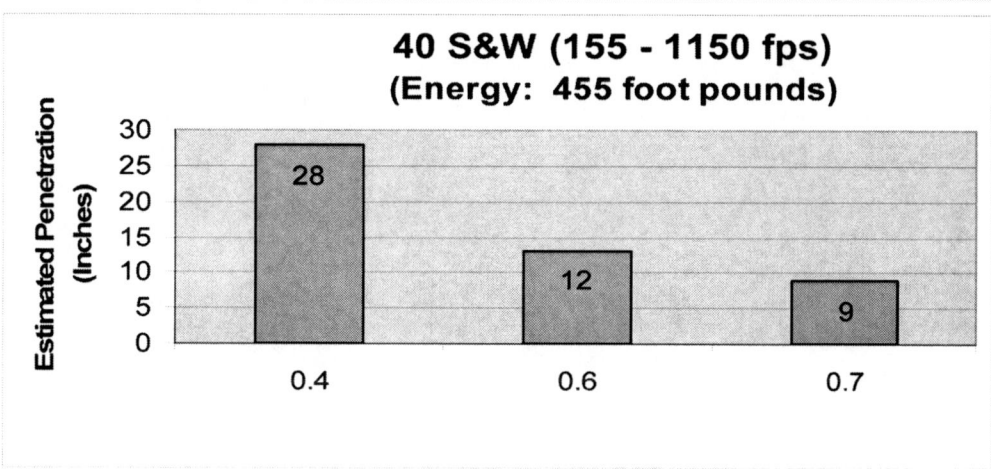

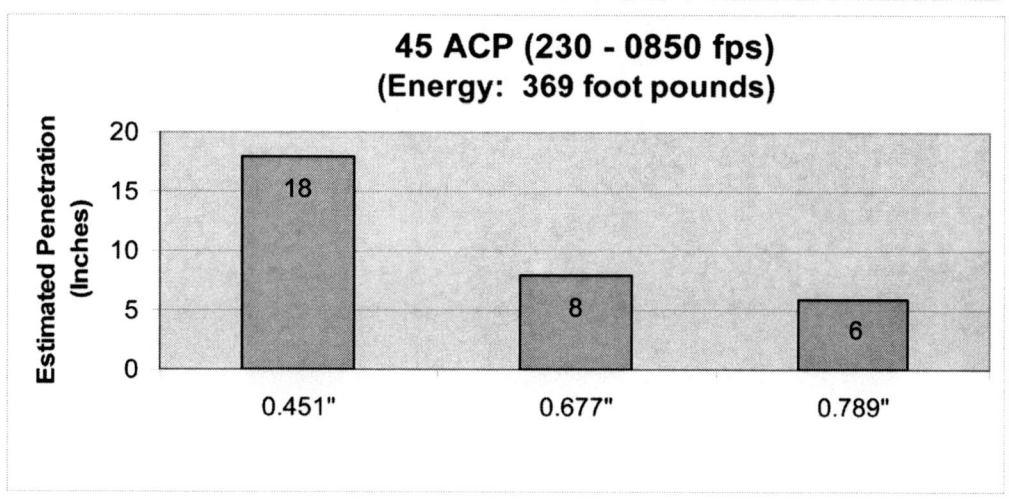

9mm Luger (124 gr - 1200 fps)
(Energy: 397 foot pounds)

0.355"	0.533"	0.621"
31	13	10

40 S&W (155 - 1150 fps)
(Energy: 455 foot pounds)

0.4	0.6	0.7
28	12	9

45 ACP (230 - 0850 fps)
(Energy: 369 foot pounds)

0.451"	0.677"	0.789"
18	8	6

Estimated Penetration (Inches)

* S. Fuller: "Fuller Index Technique"

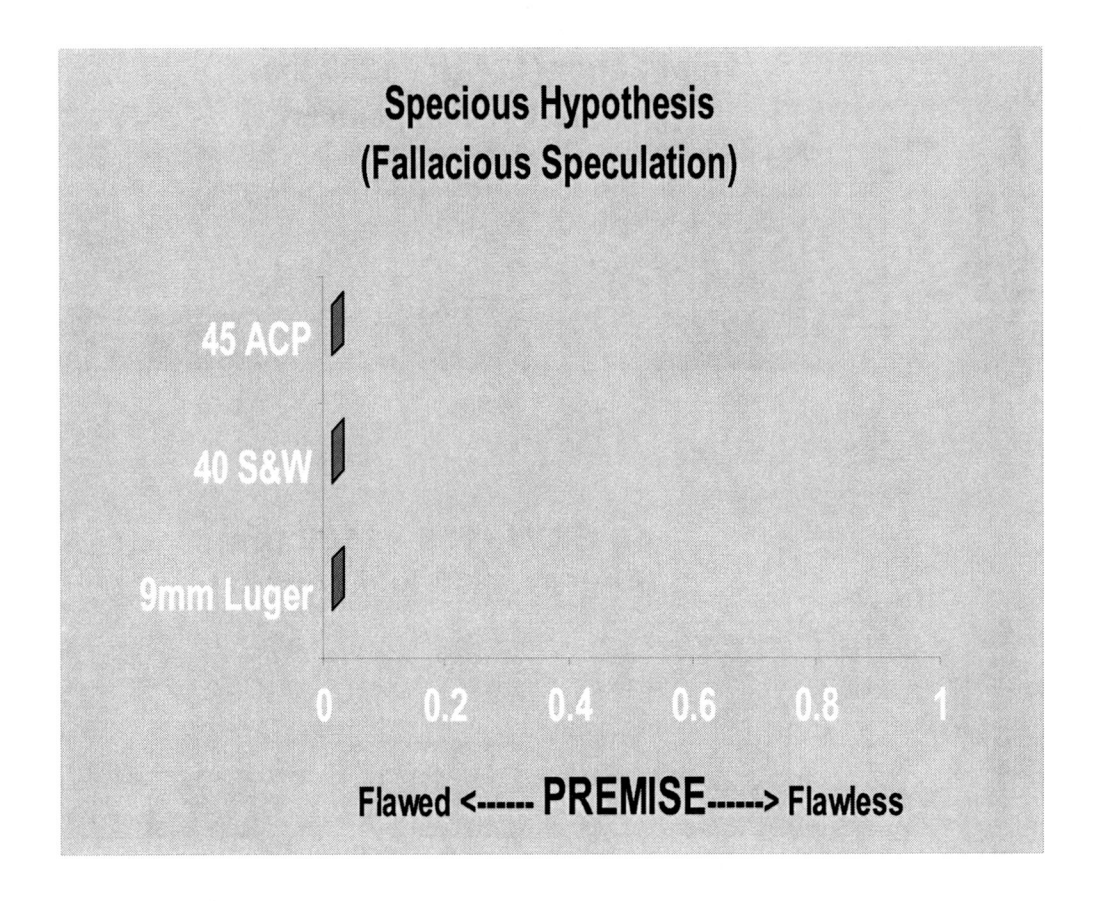

**Specious Hypothesis
(Fallacious Speculation)**

- 45 ACP
- 40 S&W
- 9mm Luger

0   0.2   0.4   0.6   0.8   1

Flawed <------ PREMISE ------> Flawless

* Hatcher: "Relative Stopping Power"

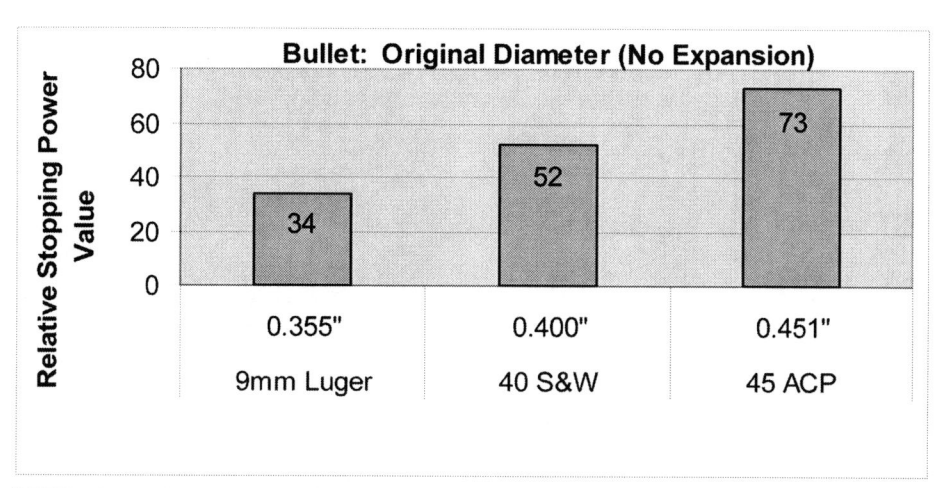

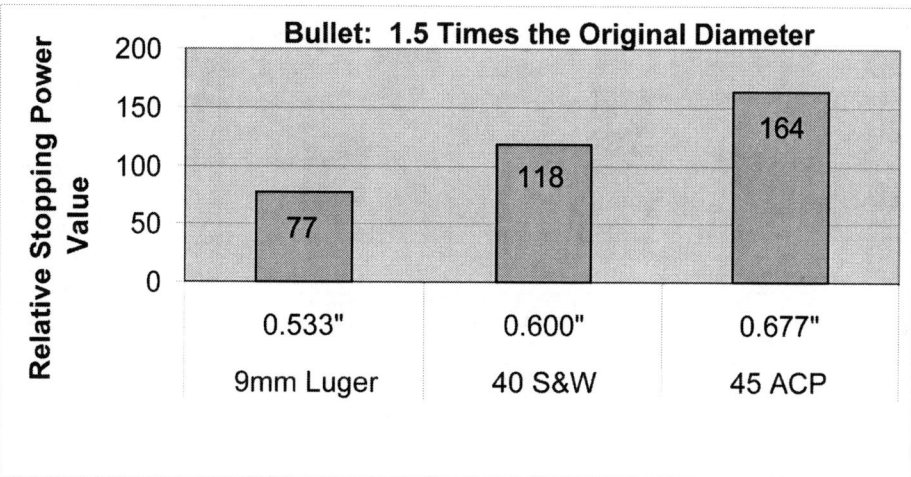

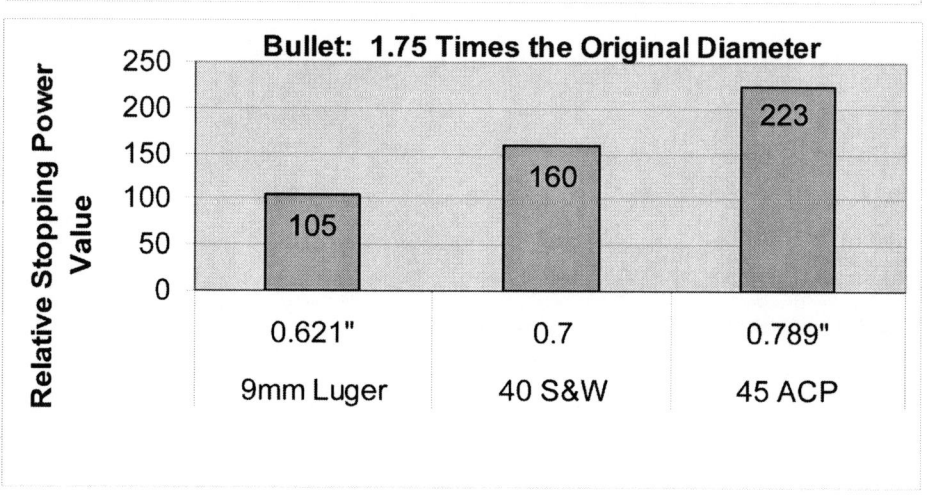

Bullet: Original Diameter (No Expansion)

	0.355"	0.400"	0.451"
	9mm Luger	40 S&W	45 ACP
Relative Stopping Power Value	34	52	73

Bullet: 1.5 Times the Original Diameter

	0.533"	0.600"	0.677"
	9mm Luger	40 S&W	45 ACP
Relative Stopping Power Value	77	118	164

Bullet: 1.75 Times the Original Diameter

	0.621"	0.7	0.789"
	9mm Luger	40 S&W	45 ACP
Relative Stopping Power Value	105	160	223

** E. Keith: "Pounds Feet"

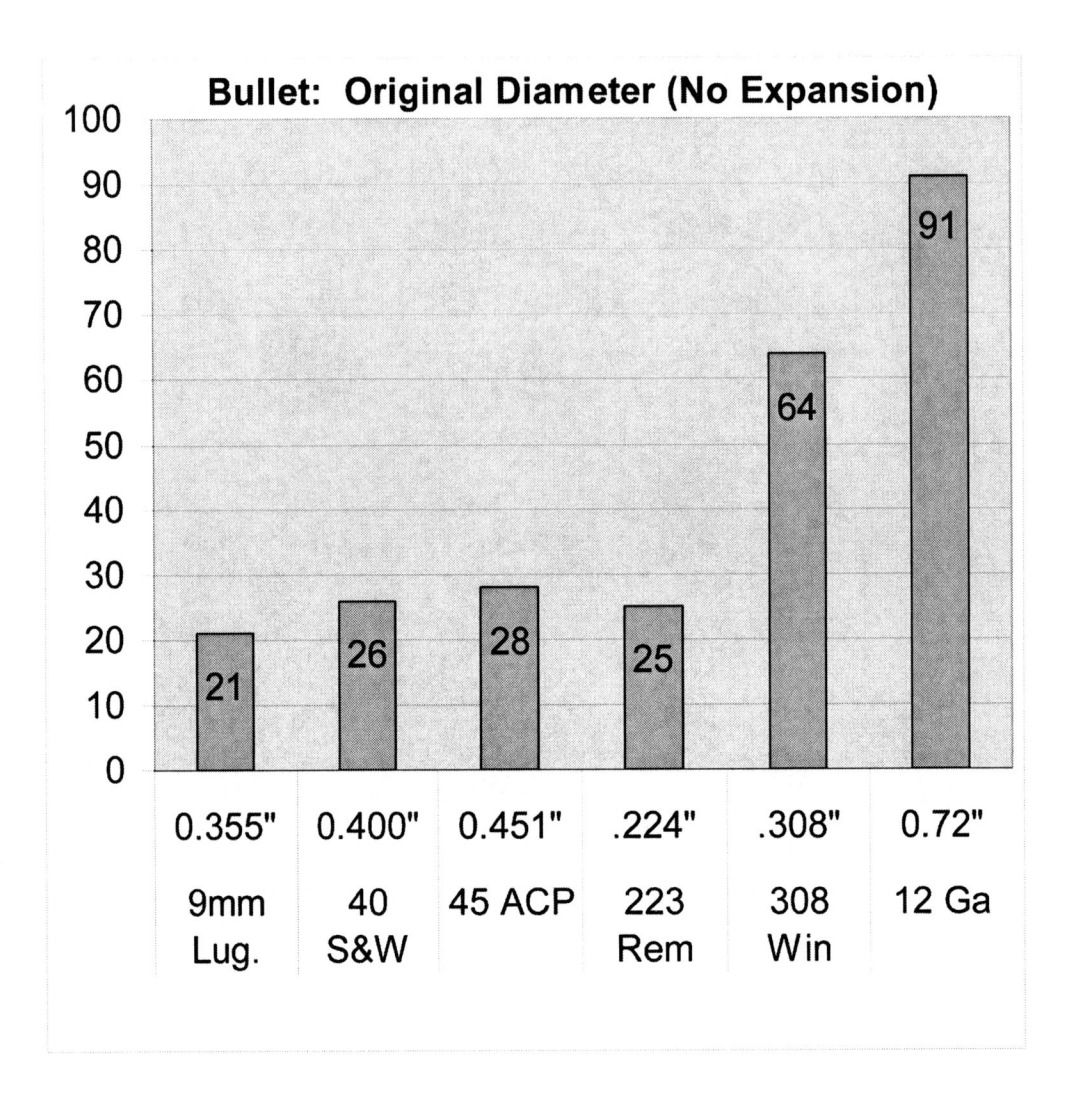

Bullet: Original Diameter (No Expansion)

	0.355"	0.400"	0.451"	.224"	.308"	0.72"
	9mm Lug.	40 S&W	45 ACP	223 Rem	308 Win	12 Ga
Pounds Feet	21	26	28	25	64	91

* Matunas: "Power Index Rating"

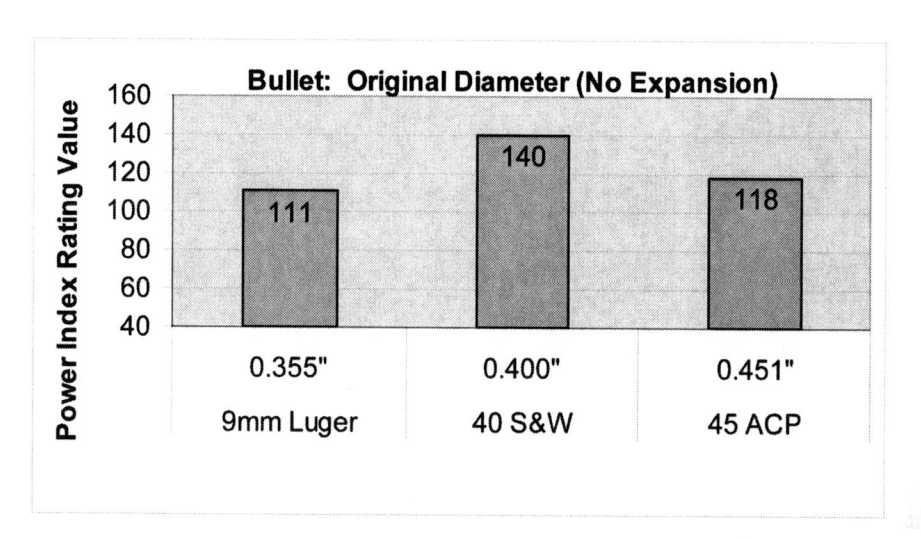

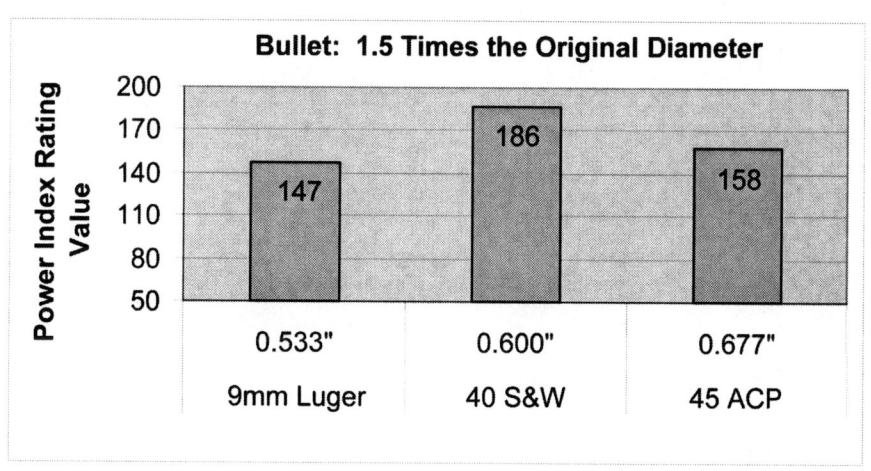

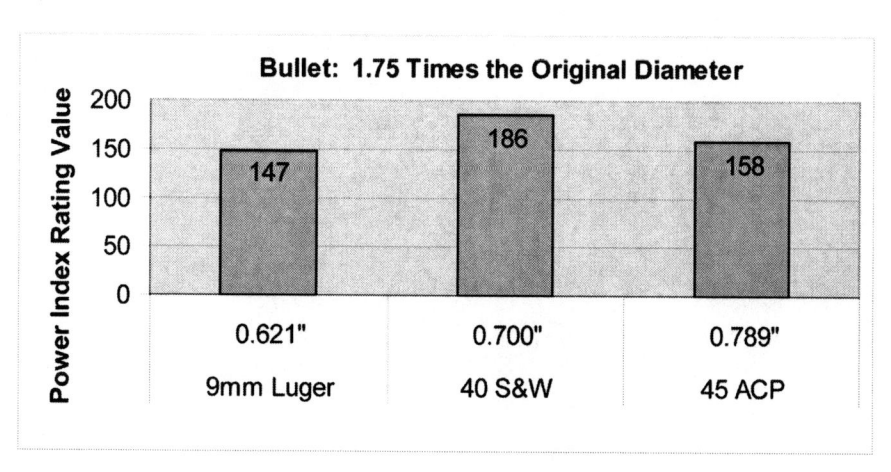

Bullet: Original Diameter (No Expansion)

Caliber	Diameter	Power Index Rating Value
9mm Luger	0.355"	111
40 S&W	0.400"	140
45 ACP	0.451"	118

Bullet: 1.5 Times the Original Diameter

Caliber	Diameter	Power Index Rating Value
9mm Luger	0.533"	147
40 S&W	0.600"	186
45 ACP	0.677"	158

Bullet: 1.75 Times the Original Diameter

Caliber	Diameter	Power Index Rating Value
9mm Luger	0.621"	147
40 S&W	0.700"	186
45 ACP	0.789"	158

Handgun Bullet Stopping Power

** Matunas: "Optimum Game Weights"

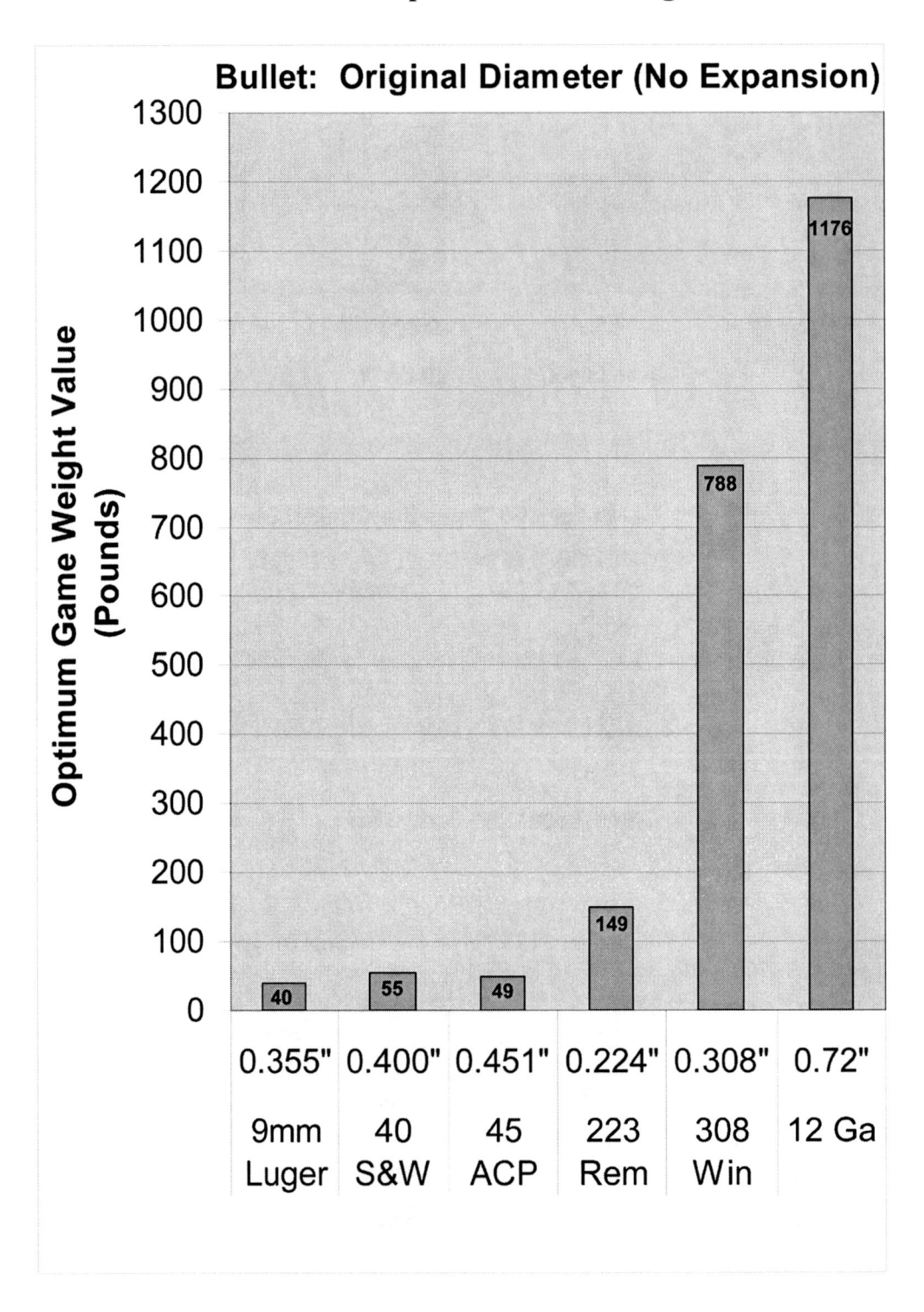

Bullet: Original Diameter (No Expansion)

Diameter	Cartridge	Optimum Game Weight Value (Pounds)
0.355"	9mm Luger	40
0.400"	40 S&W	55
0.451"	45 ACP	49
0.224"	223 Rem	149
0.308"	308 Win	788
0.72"	12 Ga	1176

* C. Peters: "Impulse Ratio"

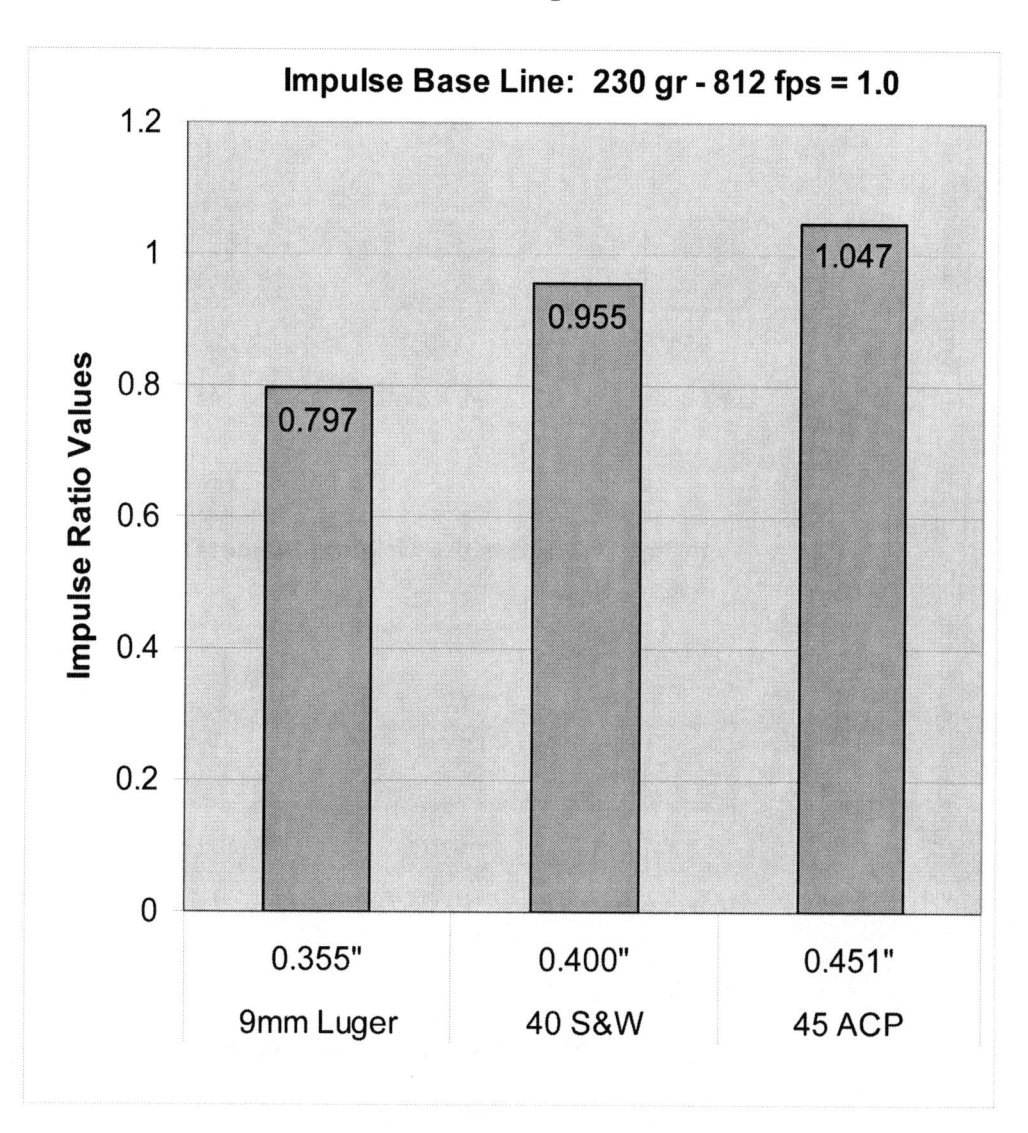

Impulse Base Line: 230 gr - 812 fps = 1.0

Caliber	Diameter	Impulse Ratio
9mm Luger	0.355"	0.797
40 S&W	0.400"	0.955
45 ACP	0.451"	1.047

** V. Smith: "Terminal Sectional Density"

Bullet: Original Diameter (No Expansion)

	9mm Luger	40 S&W	45 ACP
Diameter	0.355"	0.400"	0.451"
Terminal Sectional Density Value	0.141	0.138	0.163

Bullet: 1.5 Times the Original Diameter

	9mm Luger	40 S&W	45 ACP
Diameter	0.533"	0.600"	0.677"
Terminal Sectional Density Value	0.062	0.061	0.072

Bullet: 1.75 Times the Original Diameter

	9mm Luger	40 S&W	45 ACP
Diameter	0.621"	0.700"	0.789"
Terminal Sectional Density Value	0.046	0.045	0.053

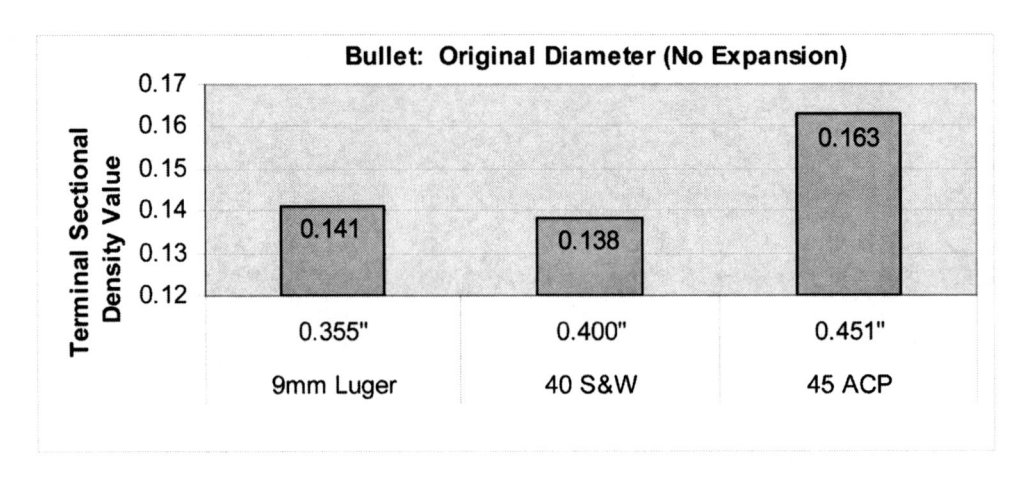

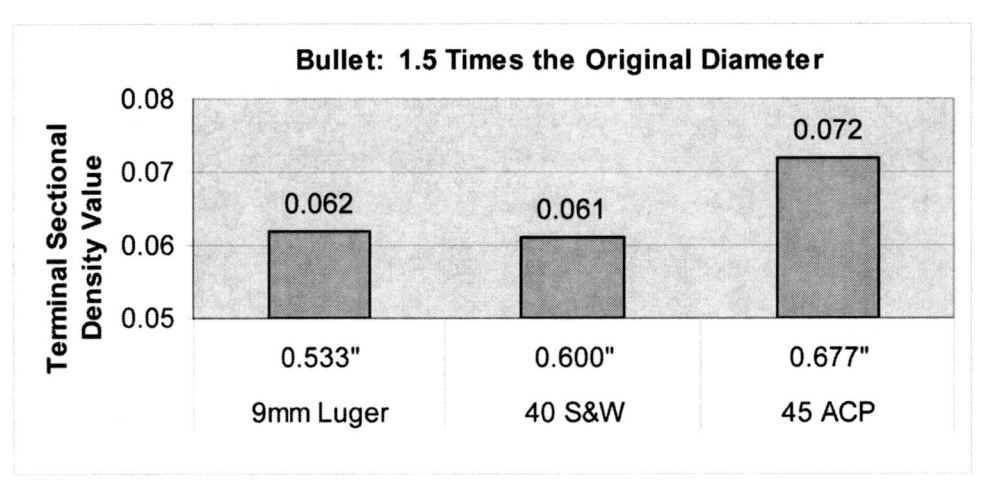

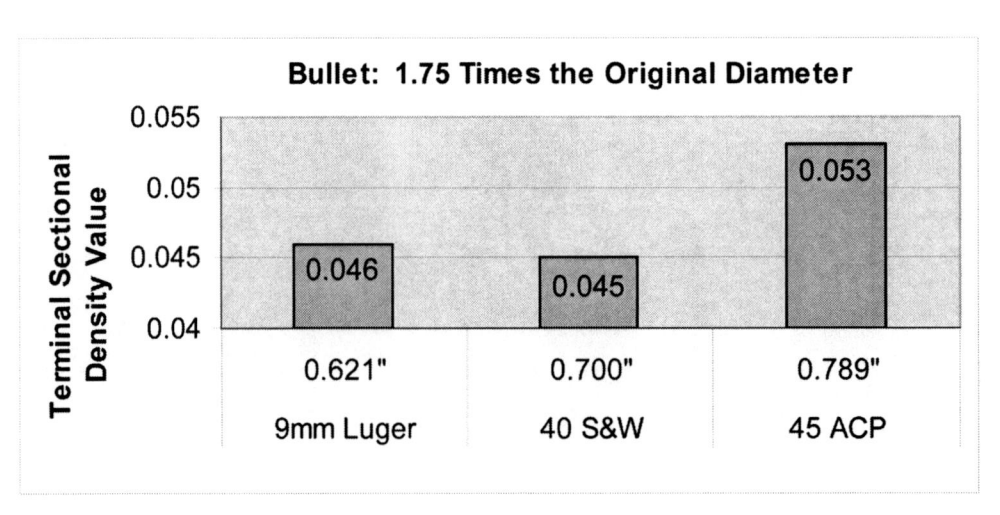

*** V. Smith: "Terminal Displacement Velocity"

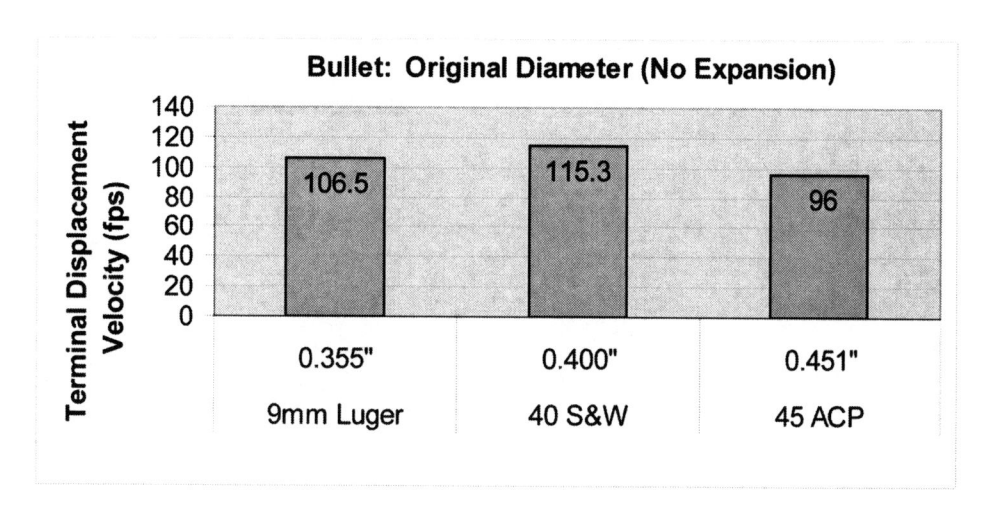

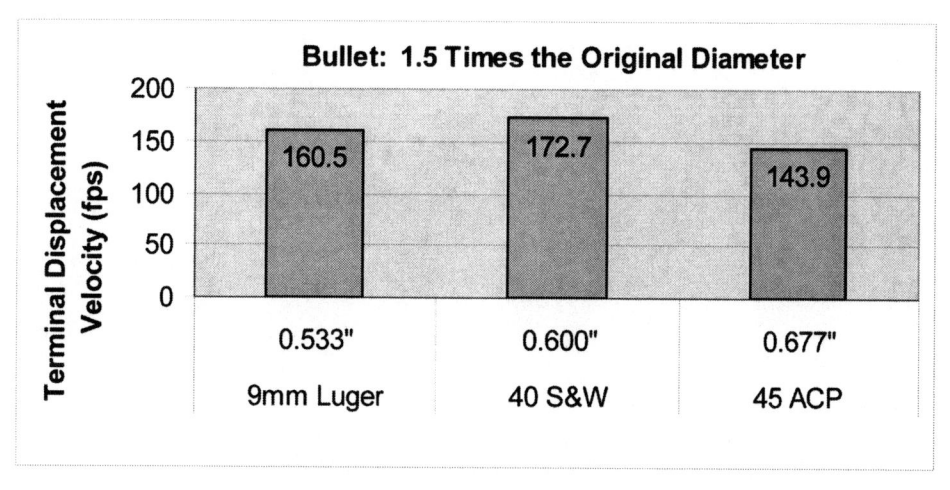

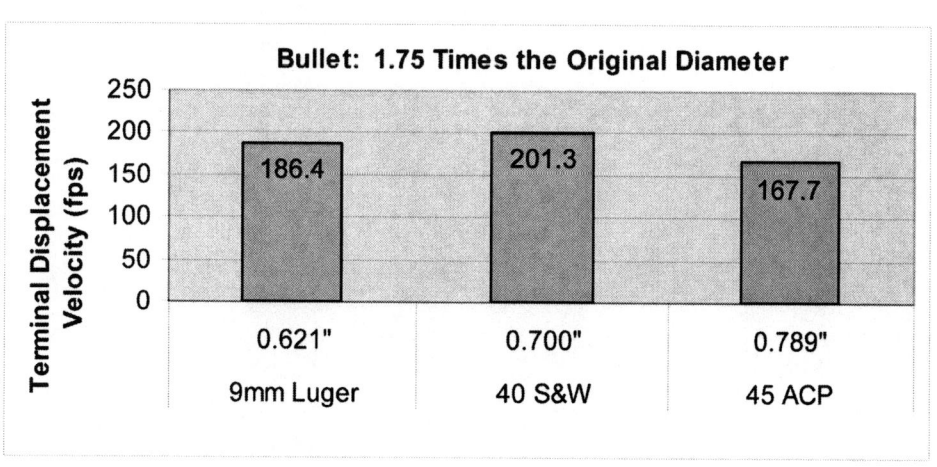

Bullet: Original Diameter (No Expansion)

	0.355" 9mm Luger	0.400" 40 S&W	0.451" 45 ACP
Terminal Displacement Velocity (fps)	106.5	115.3	96

Bullet: 1.5 Times the Original Diameter

	0.533" 9mm Luger	0.600" 40 S&W	0.677" 45 ACP
Terminal Displacement Velocity (fps)	160.5	172.7	143.9

Bullet: 1.75 Times the Original Diameter

	0.621" 9mm Luger	0.700" 40 S&W	0.789" 45 ACP
Terminal Displacement Velocity (fps)	186.4	201.3	167.7

* S. Stolinsky: "Stopping Power a Physicians Report"

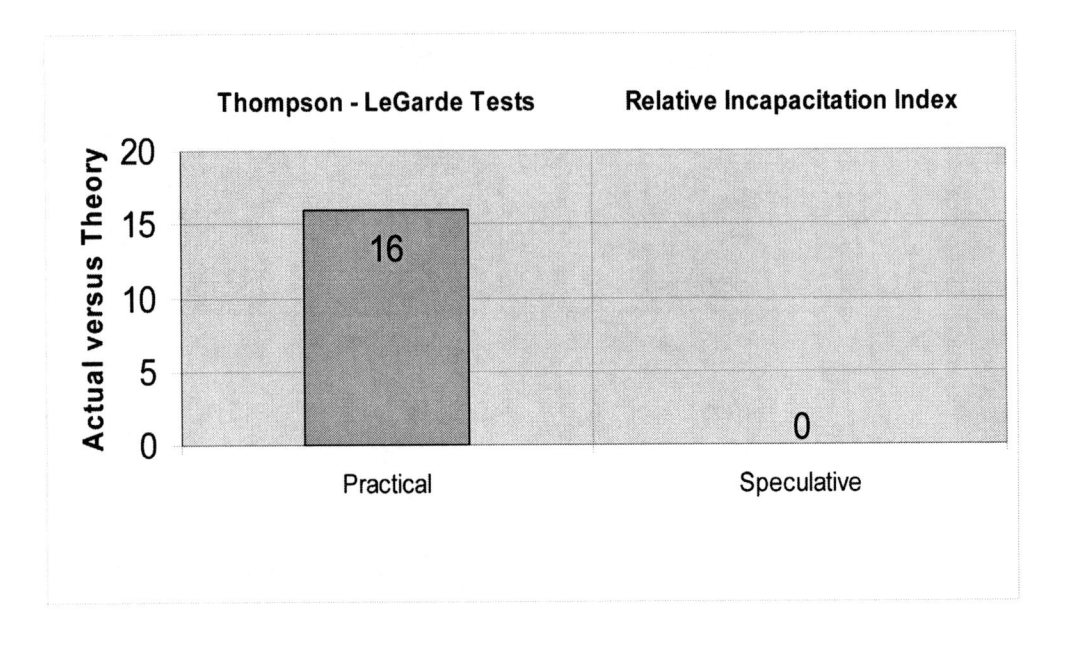

Thompson - LeGarde Tests — Practical: 16

Relative Incapacitation Index — Speculative: 0

Y-axis: Actual versus Theory (0–20)

* C. Taylor: "Modified Short Form RSP"

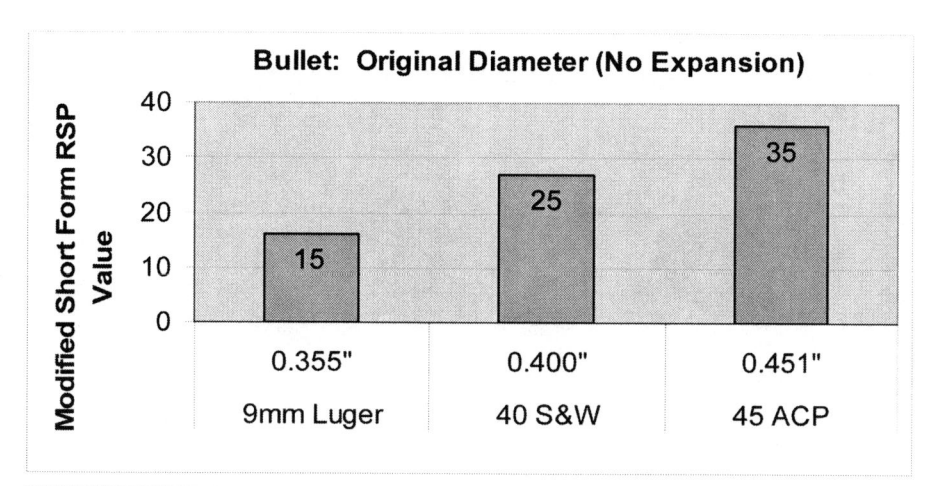

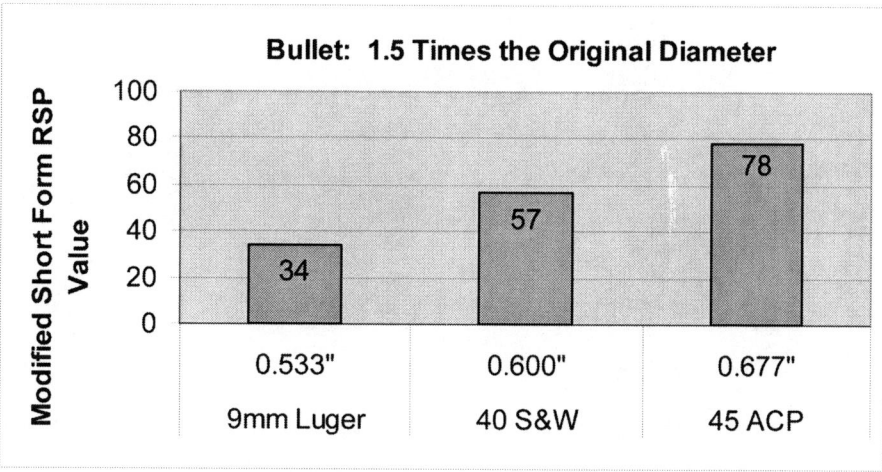

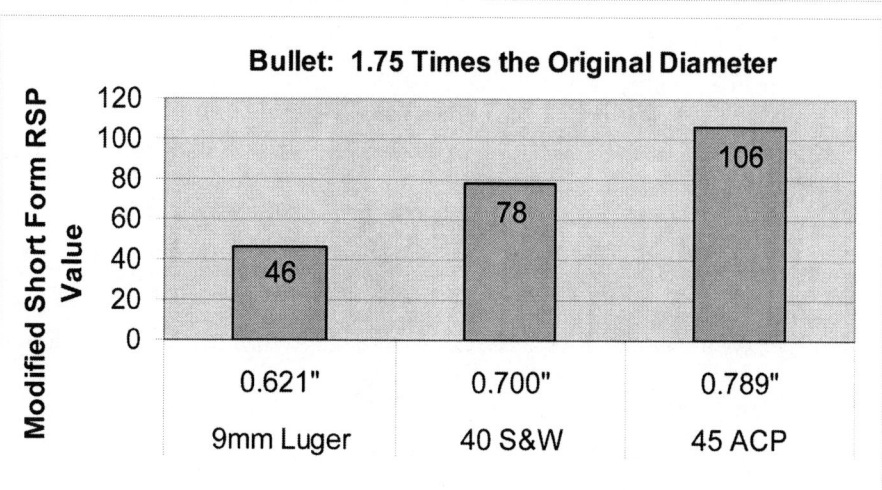

Bullet: Original Diameter (No Expansion)

Caliber	Diameter	Modified Short Form RSP Value
9mm Luger	0.355"	15
40 S&W	0.400"	25
45 ACP	0.451"	35

Bullet: 1.5 Times the Original Diameter

Caliber	Diameter	Modified Short Form RSP Value
9mm Luger	0.533"	34
40 S&W	0.600"	57
45 ACP	0.677"	78

Bullet: 1.75 Times the Original Diameter

Caliber	Diameter	Modified Short Form RSP Value
9mm Luger	0.621"	46
40 S&W	0.700"	78
45 ACP	0.789"	106

* J. Taylor: "Taylor's Knock Out (KO)"

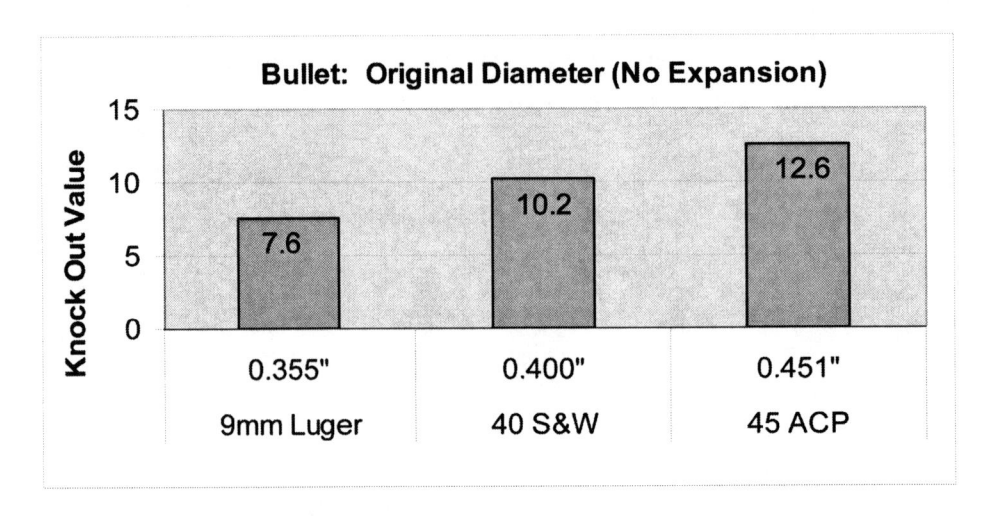

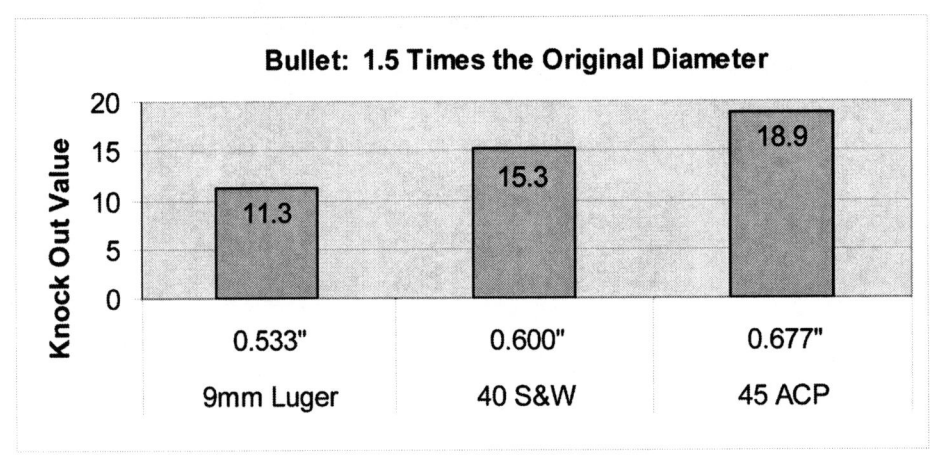

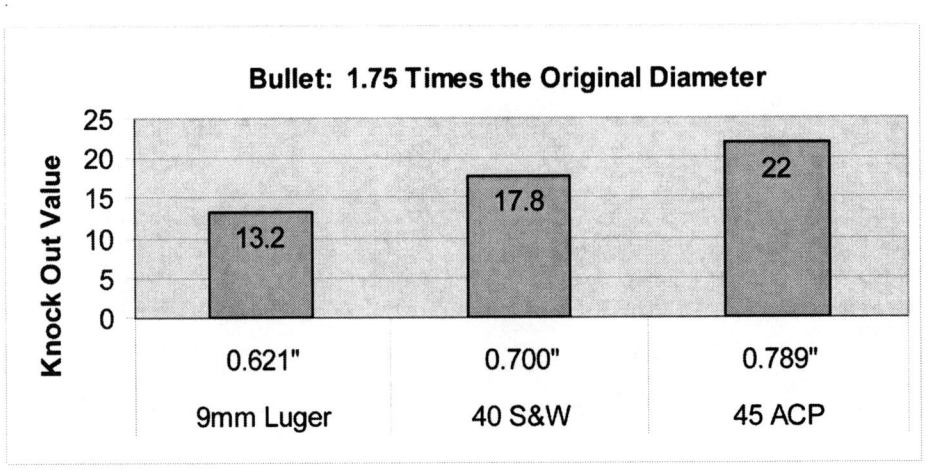

Bullet: Original Diameter (No Expansion)

Caliber	Diameter	Knock Out Value
9mm Luger	0.355"	7.6
40 S&W	0.400"	10.2
45 ACP	0.451"	12.6

Bullet: 1.5 Times the Original Diameter

Caliber	Diameter	Knock Out Value
9mm Luger	0.533"	11.3
40 S&W	0.600"	15.3
45 ACP	0.677"	18.9

Bullet: 1.75 Times the Original Diameter

Caliber	Diameter	Knock Out Value
9mm Luger	0.621"	13.2
40 S&W	0.700"	17.8
45 ACP	0.789"	22

* USDJ Protocol (RII)

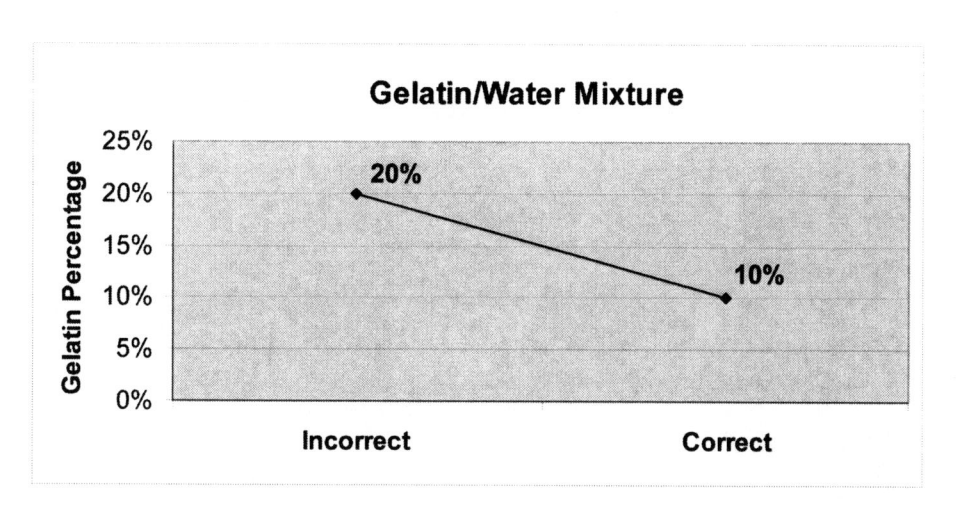

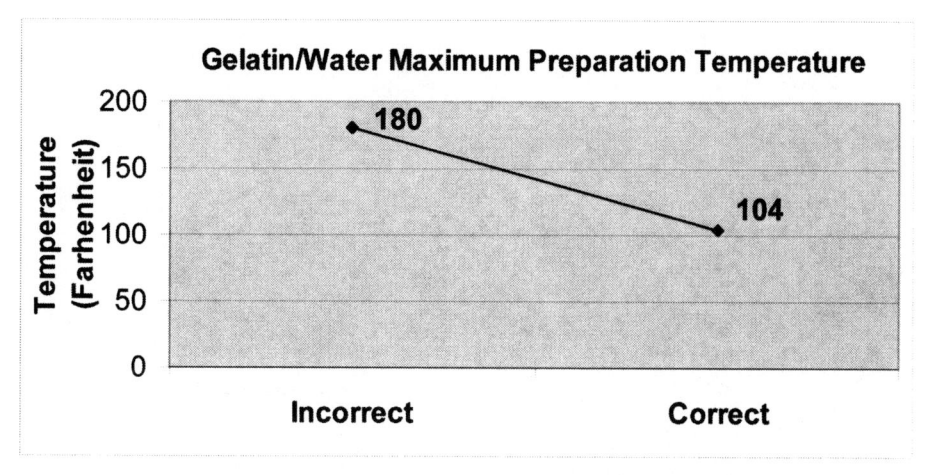

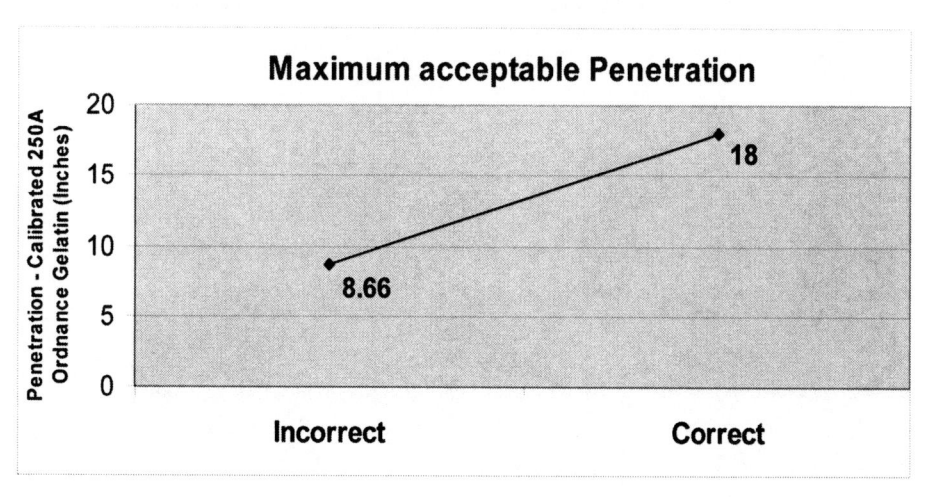

Gelatin/Water Mixture

- Incorrect: 20%
- Correct: 10%

Gelatin/Water Maximum Preparation Temperature

- Incorrect: 180 °F
- Correct: 104 °F

Maximum acceptable Penetration (Penetration - Calibrated 250A Ordnance Gelatin (Inches))

- Incorrect: 8.66
- Correct: 18

* L. Walker: "Defensive Ammo Performance"

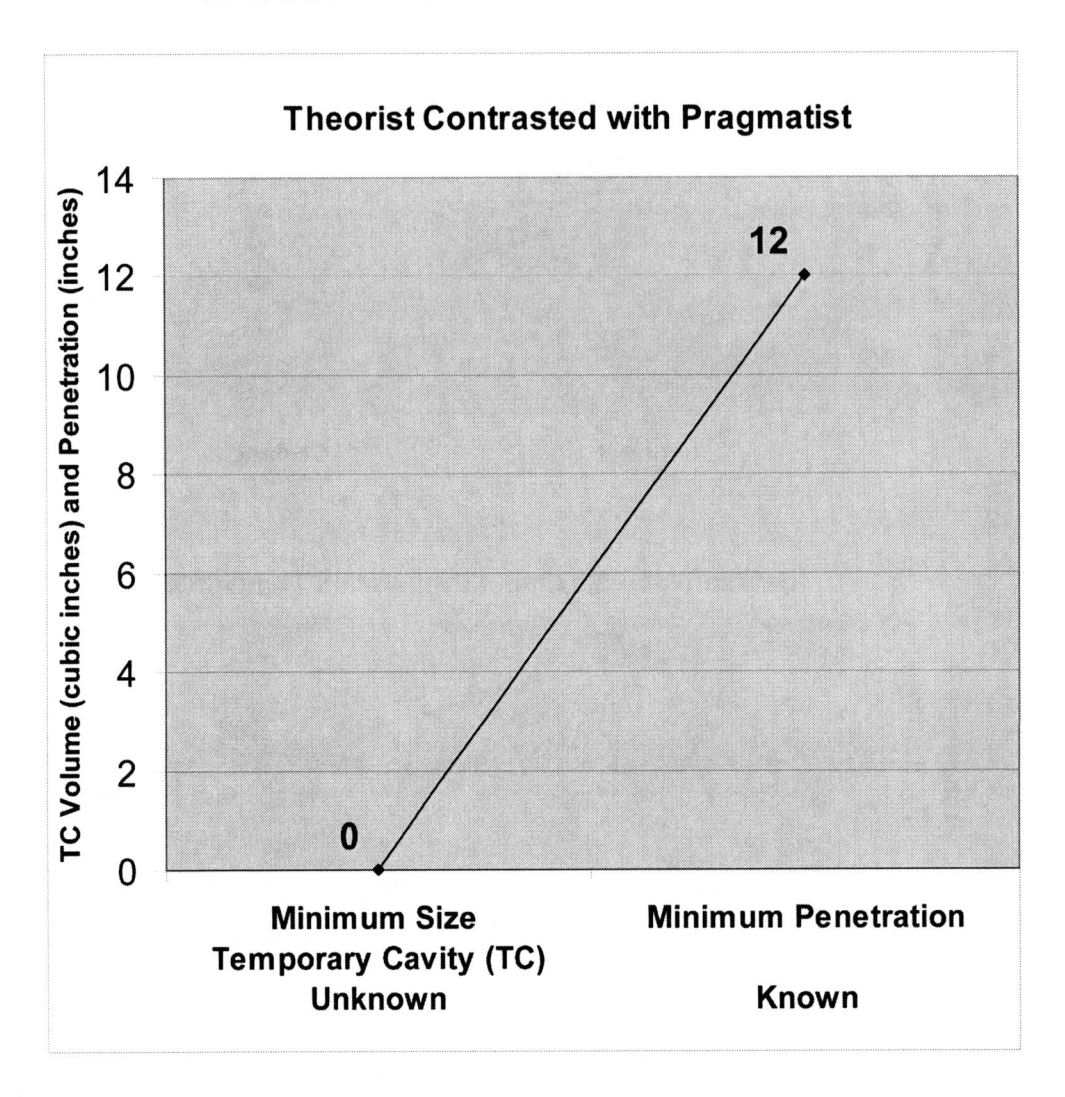

Theorist Contrasted with Pragmatist

TC Volume (cubic inches) and Penetration (inches)

- Minimum Size Temporary Cavity (TC) Unknown: 0
- Minimum Penetration Known: 12

George B. Bredsten

** J. Wootters: "Wootters' Lethality"

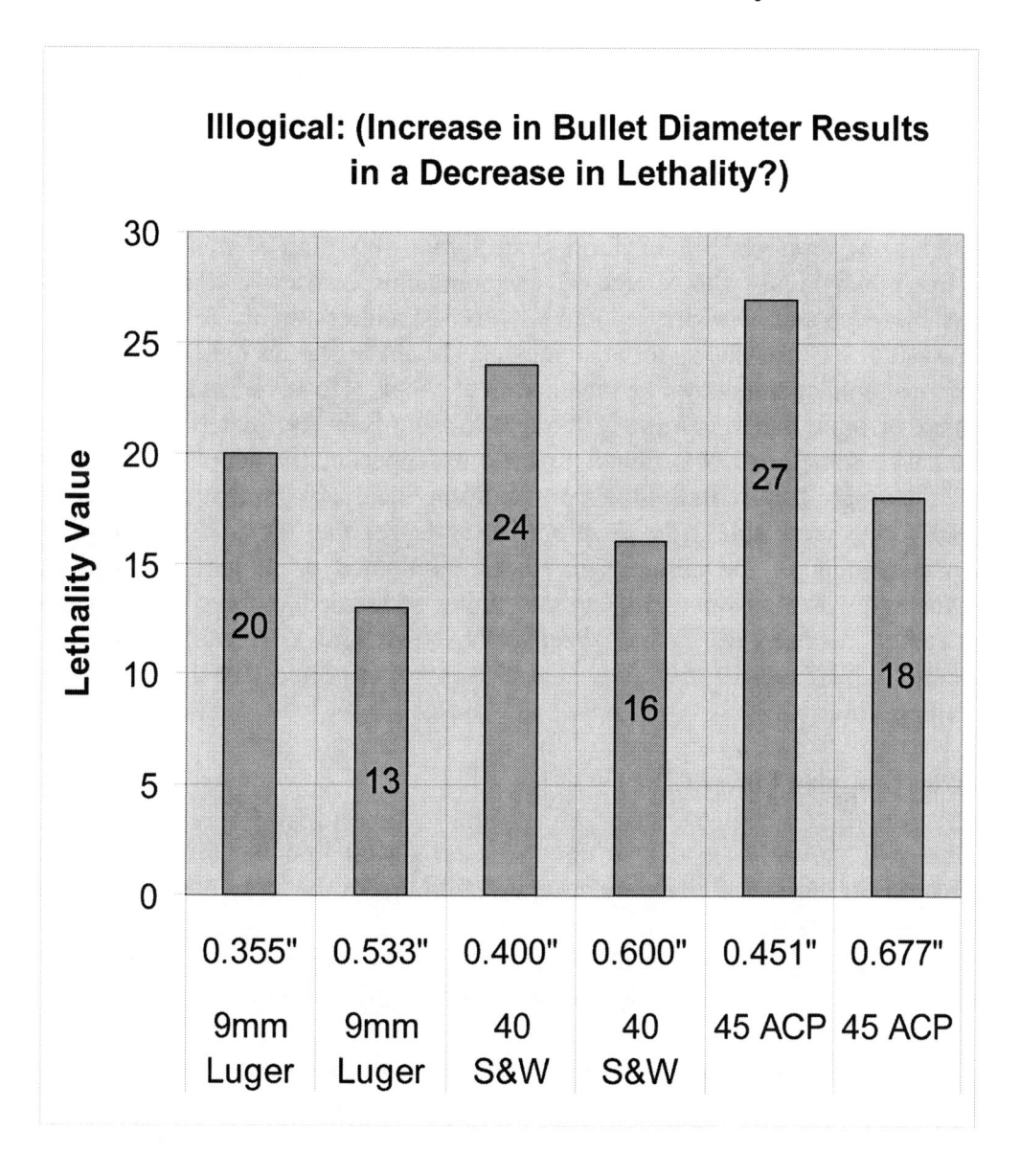

Illogical: (Increase in Bullet Diameter Results in a Decrease in Lethality?)

	0.355"	0.533"	0.400"	0.600"	0.451"	0.677"
Lethality Value	20	13	24	16	27	18
	9mm Luger	9mm Luger	40 S&W	40 S&W	45 ACP	45 ACP

CHAPTER NINE

RECAPITULATION AND CONCLUSION

RECAPITULATION

During the research, organization, drafting and rewriting of this opuscule, there were many individuals who offered advice, comments, remarks and suggestions as to what subjects should be addressed and how to best address them. Among this group, there was not a consensus as to what subjects should or should not be addressed and therefore should or should not be included in the book. However, as is often the case, a subject or topic that was initially thought to have been adequately researched and drafted was sometimes determined to be only superficially addressed. This was where the input of those individuals proved to be invaluable in that numerous topics and sub-topics were able to be developed to a degree that most, if not all, possible misunderstanding of the contents has been eliminated or at least reduced to an acceptable low level. Nonetheless, to this author's knowledge, there has not yet been any author whose work has been UNANIMOUSLY reader approved or UNANIMOUSLY reader disapproved, and it is not expected that this work will be the exception.

Effective Stopping Power (ESP)

This will probably remain an enigmatic term well into the foreseeable future. One reason for this is that there are several definitions of the term in general use BUT there is not a single one that is recognized and accepted as ***the*** standard definition. The author has no illusion that his definition will become the standard, but it is the definition that was used within the confines of this work – to wit:

> The ability of a bullet to immediately stop a lethal threat action that, if not immediately stopped, COULD result in the death or grievous bodily injury to the person at risk.

The primary factors contributing the reality of any "stopping" phenomenon within the term ESP are the Physiological Response, the Psychological Response, the Time-Frame Parameter and Bullet Efficacy. All are important, but in the final analysis it is, most often, bullet efficacy (the impacting/penetrating bullet) that determines whether or not ESP occurs.

Determinants

What degree of bullet efficacy is achieved depends on what are considered to be the determinants and what significance is assigned to each one. These determinants are usually considered to be bullet calibre (diameter), bullet cross sectional area, bullet design, bullet meplat, bullet penetration, bullet shape, bullet velocity and bullet weight. The differences in opinions as to which of these determinants are more important and the order of importance are what make for the perceived and real schisms between the advocates of one or another stopping power concept and/or formula used to rank or grade various cartridges (loads) as to their probability of achieving ESP.

Bullet Performance Characteristics (BPC)

Many methods have been used to identify and explain (quantify) how the application of the determinants contributes to ESP. These are usually considered to be various Bullet_Performance Characteristic(s) (BPC) and include Energy, Momentum, Anatomical Disruption, Hemorrhage and Neural Dysfunction. Here too, those who study the "effective stopping power" facet of wound ballistics are not in accord as to what BPC is more important or even in what order the BPC should be graded.

There are many concepts and formulae that purport to correctly explain and then predict the relative killing, *stopping* and/or wounding power of various cartridges (loads). However, It is extremely important to differentiate between *killing*, *stopping* and *wounding* power – realizing and recognizing they are not synonymous. The law enforcement officer or civilian involved in a lethal threat confrontation is not nor should not be primarily concerned with either the killing or the wounding efficacy of the cartridge (load). Instead, the vital concern and question should be: How efficient is the cartridge (load) in immediately stopping a lethal threat action?

Stopping Power Concepts/Formulae

A serious effort was made to name and give a detailed description of those Stopping Power Concepts/Formulae that the readers might consider to be contentious, controversial, pragmatic, theoretical or even apropos. Included within the description of most of these formulae are examples that offered the comparative values of three common handgun cartridges; i.e., the 9mm Luger, the 40 S&W and the 45 ACP. The author did not include any of the more esoteric formulae nor did he include concepts/formulae that are merely poorly concealed attempts to promote what at the time is/was considered to be politically correct.

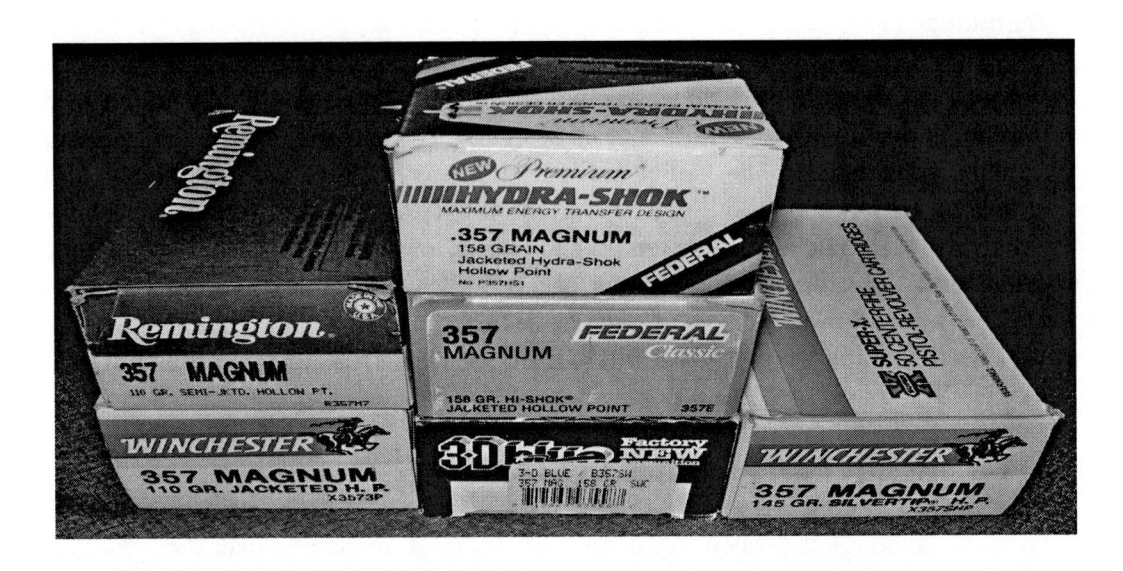

While not discussed in the text, the .357 Magnum is also a popular handgun cartridge.

CONCLUSION

How then can an objective (pragmatic) evaluation of these various concepts/formulae be determined? The **first step** is to identify and then exclude from additional consideration those concepts/formulae that address other subject(s), e.g., *killing* and/or *wounding* power but do NOT address the subject of stopping power:

Name	Concept/Formula	Reason(s) for Exclusion
DiMAIO, Vincent	D/EL – page 85	Different subject
KEITH, Elmer	K/PF – page 95	Different subject
MATUNAS, Edward	M/OGW – page 101	Different subject
SMITH, Veral	S/TSD – page 106	Different subject
SMITH, Veral	S/TDV – page 108	Different subject
TAYLOR, John	T/KO – page 115	Different subject
WOOTTERS, John	W/L – page 125	Different subject

The **second step** is to discard those concepts/formulae that rely on subjective reasoning and to support their conclusion(s) only parrot the unproven/unsubstantiated or even refuted opinions of others:

Name	Concept/Formula	Reason(s) for Rejection
WALKER, Louise	WL/DAP – page 120	Unsupported conjecture

The **third step** is to eliminate those concepts/formulae that utilize *erroneous, faulty, fabricated, flawed* and/or *inexact* (*vague*) data as the basis for establishing the method of evaluation. In the author's opinion the following concepts/formulae can be eliminated from consideration due to the use of one or more of the preceding questionable types of data:

Name	Concept/Formula	Reason(s) for Elimination
ARCHIBALD, Bob	A/OSSR – page 80	Flawed/inexact results
FULLER, Steve	F/FIT – page 87	Flawed data base

The **fourth step** is to differentiate between those concepts/formulae that address the question in a similar but more general manner, and reject those that provide methods that are less precise. In the author's opinion the following concepts/formulae fit into this group and should be considered as an expediency to determine temporary values until a more precise method can be used:

Name	Concept/Formula	Reason(s) for Temporary Use
COOPER, Jeff	C/SF – page 82	Less precise
TAYLOR, Chuck	T/MSF – page 113	Less precise

The **fifth step** is to assess the significance (if any) of comments made by authors regarding some of the negative and positive aspects pertaining to the Thompson-LaGarde Tests, the Relative Incapacitation Index theory; Hatcher's RSP with comparisons and contrasts of the comments/formulae of E. Keith, J. Cooper, M. Josserand, J. Stevenson and J. Taylor:

Name	Concept/Formula	Reasons to Peruse
STOLINSKY, David	St/SPPR – page 110	Elucidation
WALTERS, Kenneth	WK/CSPF – page 122	Comparison/Contrasts

The **sixth step** is to carefully work through each of the remaining four stopping power formulae and evaluate the results relative to the particular cartridges (loads) being compared and to factor out that data which tends to skew values unrealistically:

Name	Concept/Formula	Evaluation
USDJ	RII – page 118	Flawed
MATUNAS, Ed	M/PIR – page 97	Conditionally Acceptable
PETERS, Carroll	P/IR – page 103	Acceptable
HATCHER, Julian	RSP – page 91	Best Available

Handgun Bullet Stopping Power

The **USDJ (RII)** concept is tied to arbitrarily established criteria that posits all shooting incidents will have the bullet entering the combatant <u>directly into the frontal thorax</u>, and thus established a grading system based on the maximum size of the temporary cavity and measurements limited to a maximum penetration of about 8.66 inches – penetration in excess of 8.66 inches was disregarded. Consequently, and as a result of such convoluted and disjointed logic, cartridges (loads) receive values that do not reflect reality. For example, three 38 Special cartridges, using the 158 gr LRN at <u>measured</u> velocities of 855 fps are assigned RII values varying from <u>3.8 to 7.2</u> - compare this with a 45 ACP (45 Auto) cartridge, using the 230 gr FMJ at a measured velocity of 800 fps that is assigned a <u>3.6</u> RII value. The various 38 Special loads (using the 158 gr LRN bullets) have been categorically criticized for being unreliable in stopping a lethal threat action? Contrast this with the almost universally recognized fight stopping ability of the 45 ACP using the 230 gr FMJ and one should question the method used, the data recorded and most important the *relevance* of the RII concept. Laboratory theory is just that – theory – but fortunately for law enforcement officers and/or civilians at risk, reality eventually dictates that pragmatism will prevail over ill-conceived theory.

The **Ed MATUNAS Power Index Rating** utilizes a formula that includes consideration of the bullet velocity, the bullet weight, the energy transfer (?) and the bullet diameter. Calculated power index ratings generally are a mix with values that can agree with the Peter's Impulse Ratio values and Hatcher's Relative Stopping Power values. However, because there is a provision for factoring in alleged energy transfer values, there appears to be occasional anomalies in the Power Index Rating values. This is primarily due to Matunas not making allowances for the type and extent of bullet penetration and for no consideration being made for any variance in tissue disruption caused by differences in the degree of bullet diameter (expansion). This variance in the degree of tissue disruption is an especially important factor when hemorrhage is the primary cause for the cessation of the lethal threat action.

The **Carroll PETERS Impulse Ratio** formula uses as a <u>standard</u> the impulse ratio value of the 45 ACP hardball load; i.e., 230 gr FMJ at 812 fps and to it assigns a value of one (1). This is a formula that is not greatly affected by the calibre (diameter) and consequently there are a number of cartridges that can or do have loads the *smaller diameter bullets* of which produce impulse ratio values greater than one (1). Peters does emphasize that an impulse ratio value of one should be the acceptable minimum, because it (45 ACP, 230 gr FMJ, impact velocity of 812 fps) is generally considered to be about 90 percent effective in achieving a one shot stop!

The **Julian HATCHER Relative Stopping Power** formula uses a combination of the bullet shape, the bullet momentum and the cross sectional area to arrive at a Relative Stopping Power value. I know of no source that criticizes the RSP values when applied to non-expanding bullets. In fact many consider it to be the most reliable indicator of the relative effectiveness of a bullet in achieving effective stopping power. Criticism arises when the subject is expanding bullets. Since Hatcher did not include a bullet shape factor (value) for expanding bullets, there are those who contend the RSP formula cannot be used? Apparently these individuals have not thought about using the diameter (cross sectional area) of the expanded bullet in the formula in order to calculate RSP? **See Appendix G**. On the surface this seems reasonable and it IS. The complaint sometimes heard/read usually contains the question: When/where in the penetration track did the expanded bullet attain its final or largest diameter? This appears to be a reasonable question, but it is actually specious. In order to be objective in any effort to establish relative stopping power values, it is presumed that all expanding bullets reach their largest diameter at a specific depth of penetration. This insures that the comparisons will be "apples with apples" and prevents bias (intentional or unintentional) from occurring.

It is understood that not all expanding type handgun bullets will expand uniformly, nor will they reach their largest diameter at the same depth of penetration. These are important considerations and should be addressed – but to ascertain when and where requires sophisticated equipment that is generally unavailable to most individuals. Thus, that facet of wound ballistics remains in the purview of the ballistics engineer or ballistics technician.

There continues to be development regarding the modification of current bullet designs and/or the introduction of new bullet designs. Consequently, expanding handgun bullet designs can be considered to be in a continuous state of flux regarding the rate (time frame) for and the degree (extent) of bullet expansion; i.e., what may currently be a bullet design that expands either too fast or too slow could be in the process of being modified (redesigned) or replaced by a new design by the manufacturer to change the specifics regarding the rate and extent of expansion.

Nonetheless, regarding the Hatcher RSP formula (or other relevant formulae), to remain objective, all expanding type handgun bullets should be considered to have reached their largest diameter at the same depth of penetration.

In only one way is the Hatcher RSP formula *possibly* deficient and that is with regards to the subject of handgun bullet penetration. It is not known, but Hatcher may have presumed that with any cartridge (load) being considered, its bullet would give adequate penetration. Unfortunately, the problem of *consistently* adequate bullet expansion combined with *consistently* adequate bullet penetration under *varied* conditions is still (2008) unresolved. Some, many and perhaps most expanding type handgun bullets (at one time or another) will expand to the final diameter too soon and/or the final expanded diameter will be excessively large. Consequently a bullet may EITHER expand too much and/or too soon and the result can be inadequate penetration (i.e., the bullet fails to reach and disrupt critical/vital body parts) OR a bullet may not expand significantly (if at all) and the result might be excessive penetration

Finally, in this author's opinion nothing to date, with respect to concepts or

Handgun Bullet Stopping Power

formulae, has been proffered that provides as reliable an ***indication*** of the probability of achieving Effective Stopping Power than does the Relative Stopping Power formula of Julian S. Hatcher.

George B. Bredsten

Appendix A

PENETRATION POTENTIAL

VARIOUS HANDGUN LOADS

Cartridge	Bullet/Weight Velocity & Energy	Bullet Diameter	CSA Inches	Penetration Value
25 Auto	050 – 0760 – 0065	1.0 (.251")	0.049	**1327**
		1.5 (.376")	0.111	0585
		1.75 (.439")	0.151	0431
30 Carbine	110 – 1400 – 0479	1.0 (.308")	0.075	**6387**
		1.5 (.462")	0.168	2851
		1.75 (.539")	0.228	2101
32 Auto	065 – 0950 – 0130	1.0 (.312")	0.076	**1710**
		1.5 (.468")	0.172	0755
		1.75 (.546")	0.234	0556
380 Auto	090 – 1000 – 0200	1.0 (.355")	0.099	**2020**
		1.5 (.533")	0.223	0897
		1.75 (.621")	0.303	0660
9mm Luger	115 – 1225 – 0383	1.0 (.355")	0.099	**3869**
		1.5 (.533")	0.223	1718
		1.75 (.621")	0.303	1264
9mm Luger	147 – 1010 – 0333	1.0 (.355")	0.099	**3364**
		1.5 (.533")	0.223	1493
		1.75 (.621")	0.303	1099
38 Super +P	125 – 1240 – 0427	1.0 (.355")	0.099	**4313**
		1.5 (.533")	0.223	1915
		1.75 (.621")	0.303	1409

Appendix A

PENETRATION POTENTIAL

VARIOUS HANDGUN LOADS

Cartridge	Bullet/Weight Velocity & Energy	Bullet Diameter	CSA Inches	Penetration Value
357 SIG	125 – 1350 – 0506	1.0 (.355")	0.099	**5111**
		1.5 (.533")	0.223	2269
		1.75 (.621")	0.303	1670
38 Special	148 – 0710 – 0166	1.0 (.357")	0.100	**1660**
		1.5 (.536")	0.226	0735
		1.75 (.625")	0.307	0541
38 Special	158 – 0755 – 0200	1.0 (.357")	0.100	**2000**
		1.5 (.536")	0.226	0885
		1.75 (.625")	0.307	0652
38 Special	+P158 – 0890 – 0278	1.0 (.357")	0.100	**2780**
		1.5 (.536")	0.226	1230
		1.75 (.625")	0.307	0906
357 Magnum	125 – 1450 – 0584	1.0 (.357")	0.100	**5840**
		1.5 (.536")	0.226	2584
		1.75 (.625")	0.307	1902
357 Magnum	145 – 1290 – 0535	1.0 (.357")	0.100	**5350**
		1.5 (.536")	0.226	2367
		1.75 (.625")	0.307	1743
357 Magnum	158 – 1235 – 0535	1.0 (.357")	0.100	**5350**
		1.5 (.536")	0.226	2367
		1.75 (.625")	0.307	1743

George B. Bredsten

Appendix A

PENETRATION POTENTIAL

VARIOUS HANDGUN LOADS

Cartridge	Bullet/Weight Velocity & Energy	Bullet Diameter	CSA Inches	Penetration Value
40 S&W	155 – 1205 – 0500	1.0 (.400")	0.126	**3968**
		1.5 (.600")	0.283	1767
		1.75 (.700")	0.385	1295
40 S&W	165 – 1130 – 0468	1.0 (.400")	0.126	**3714**
		1.5 (.600")	0.283	1654
		1.75 (.700")	0.385	1216
40 S&W	180 – 1010 – 0408	1.0 (.400")	0.126	**3238**
		1.5 (.600")	0.283	1442
		1.75 (.700")	0.385	1060
10mm Auto	175 – 1290 – 0649	1.0 (.400")	0.126	**5151**
		1.5 (.600")	0.283	2293
		1.75 (.700")	0.385	1686
41 Rem Mag	175 – 1250 – 0607	1.0 (.410")	0.132	**4599**
		1.5 (.615")	0.297	2044
		1.75 (.718")	0.404	1503
41 Rem Mag	240 – 1250 – 0833	1.0 (.410")	0.132	**6311**
		1.5 (.615")	0.297	2805
		1.75 (.718")	0.404	2062
44-40 Winchester	225 – 0750 – 0281	1.0 (.426")	0.142	**1979**
		1.5 (.639")	0.320	0878
		1.75 (.746")	0.437	0643

Appendix A

PENETRATION POTENTIAL

VARIOUS HANDGUN LOADS

Cartridge	Bullet/Weight Velocity & Energy	Bullet Diameter	CSA Inches	Penetration Value
44 S&W Special	200 – 0900 – 0360	1.0 (.429")	0.145	**2483**
		1.5 (.643")	0.324	1111
		1.75 (.751")	0.443	0813
44 S&W Special	246 – 0755 – 0310	1.0 (.429")	0.145	**2138**
		1.5 (.643")	0.324	0957
		1.75 (.751")	0.443	0700
44 Rem Magnum	210 – 1250 – 0729	1.0 (.429")	0.145	**5028**
		1.5 (.643")	0.324	2250
		1.75 (.751")	0.443	1646
44 Rem Magnum	240 – 1180 – 0741	1.0 (.429")	0.145	**5110**
		1.5 (.643")	0.324	2287
		1.75 (.751")	0.443	1673
44 Rem Magnum	250 – 1250 – 0867	1.0 (.429")	0.145	**5979**
		1.5 (.643")	0.324	2676
		1.75 (.751")	0.443	1957
44 Rem Magnum	300 – 1250 – 1040	1.0 (.429")	0.145	**7172**
		1.5 (.643")	0.324	3210
		1.75 (.751")	0.443	2348
45 G.A.P.	230 – 0880 – 0396	1.0 (.451")	0.160	**2475**
		1.5 (.677")	0.358	1106
		1.75 (.789")	0.489	0810

Appendix A

PENETRATION POTENTIAL

VARIOUS HANDGUN LOADS

Cartridge	Bullet/Weight Velocity & Energy	Bullet Diameter	CSA Inches	Penetration Value
45 Auto	185 – 1000 – 0411	1.0 (.451")	0.160	**2568**
		1.5 (.677")	0.358	1148
		1.75 (.789")	0.489	0841
45 Auto	**230 – 0812 – 0337**	1.0 (.451")	0.160	**2106**
		1.5 (.677")	0.358	0941
		1.75 (.789")	0.489	0689
45 Auto +P	185 – 1140 – 0534	1.0 (.451")	0.160	**3338**
		1.5 (.677")	0.358	1492
		1.75 (.789")	0.489	1092
45 Colt	250 – 0750 – 0312	1.0 (.451")	0.160	**1950**
		1.5 (.677")	0.358	0872
		1.75 (.789")	0.489	0638
45 Colt	255 – 0860 – 0420	1.0 (.451")	0.160	**2625**
		1.5 (.677")	0.358	1173
		1.75 (.789")	0.489	0859
454 Casull	260 – 1800 – 1871	1.0 (.451")	0.160	**11694**
		1.5 (.677")	0.358	5226
		1.75 (.789")	0.489	3826
454 Casull	300 – 1625 – 1759	1.0 (.451")	0.160	**10993**
		1.5 (.677")	0.358	4913
		1.75 (.789")	0.489	3597

Appendix A

PENETRATION POTENTIAL

VARIOUS HANDGUN LOADS

Cartridge	Bullet/Weight Velocity & Energy	Bullet Diameter	CSA Inches	Penetration Value
480 Ruger	325 – 1350 – 1315	1.0 (.475")	0.177	**7429**
		1.5 (.7125")	0.399	3295
		1.75 (.83125")	0.543	2422
50 Action Express	300 – 1550 – 1600	1.0 (.500")	0.196	**8163**
		1.5 (.750")	0.442	3620
		1.75 (.875")	0.601	2662
500 S&W	400 – 1800 – 2877	1.0 (.500")	0.196	**14679**
		1.5 (.750")	0.442	6509
		1.75 (.875")	0.601	4787

Appendix B

INCAPACITATION DUE TO HEMORRHAGE (BLOOD LOSS)

(Ten [10] Seconds)

Diameter Bullet (Meplat)	Volume (Inches) 10-inches Penetration	Hemorrhage Seconds (± 0.1)
.224"	0.40	25.0
.251"	0.50	20.0
.312"	0.77	13.0
.355"	0.99	10.1
.357"	**1.00**	**10.0 (Given)**
.36"	1.02	09.8
.37"	1.08	09.3
.38"	1.13	08.9
.39"	1.20	08.3
.40"	1.28	07.9
.41"	1.32	07.6
.42"	1.39	07.2
.43"	1.45	06.9
.44"	1.52	06.6
.451"	1.60	06.3

Appendix B

INCAPACITATION DUE TO HEMORRHAGE (BLOOD LOSS)

(Ten [10] Seconds)

Diameter Bullet (Meplat)	Volume (Inches) 10-inches Penetration	Hemorrhage Seconds (± 0.1)
.46"	1.66	06.0
.47"	1.74	05.8
.48"	1.81	05.5
.49"	1.89	05.3
.50"	1.95	05.1
.51"	2.04	04.9
.52"	2.12	04.7
.53"	2.21	04.5
.54"	2.29	04.4
.55"	2.38	04.2
.56"	2.46	04.1
.57"	2.55	03.9
.58"	2.64	03.8
.59"	2.73	03.7
.60"	2.83	03.5

Appendix B

INCAPACITATION DUE TO HEMORRHAGE (BLOOD LOSS)

(Ten [10] Seconds)

Diameter Bullet (Meplat)	Volume (Inches) 10-inches Penetration	Hemorrhage Seconds (± 0.1)
.61"	2.92	03.4
.62"	3.02	03.3
.63"	3.12	03.2
.64"	3.22	03.1
.65"	3.32	03.0
.66"	3.42	02.9
.67"	3.53	02.8
.68"	3.63	02.8
.69"	3.74	02.7
.70"	3.85	02.6
.714"	4.00	02.5
.72"	4.07	02.5
.73"	4.19	02.4
.74"	4.30	02.3
.75"	4.42	02.3

Appendix B

INCAPACITATION DUE TO HEMORRHAGE (BLOOD LOSS)

(Ten [10] Seconds)

Diameter Bullet (Meplat)	Volume (Inches) 10-inches Penetration	Hemorrhage Seconds (± 0.1)
.76"	4.54	02.2
.77"	4.66	02.2
.78"	4.78	02.1
.79"	4.90	02.0
.80"	5.03	02.0
.81"	5.15	01.9
.82"	5.28	01.9
.83"	5.41	01.9
.84"	5.54	01.8
.85"	5.68	01.8
.86"	5.81	01.7
.87"	5.95	01.7
.88"	6.08	01.7
.89"	6.22	01.6
.90"	6.36	01.6

Appendix C

INCAPACITATION DUE TO HEMORRHAGE (BLOOD LOSS)

(Twenty [20] Seconds)

Diameter Bullet (Meplat)	Volume (Inches) 10-inches Penetration	Hemorrhage Seconds (± 0.1)
.224"	0.40	50.0
.251"	0.50	40.0
.312"	0.77	26.0
.355"	0.99	20.2
.357"	**1.00**	**20.0 (Given)**
.36"	1.02	19.6
.37"	1.08	18.5
.38"	1.13	17.7
.39"	1.20	16.7
.40"	1.26	15.9
.41"	1.32	15.2
.42"	1.39	14.4
.43"	1.45	13.8
.44"	1.52	13.2
.451"	1.60	12.5

Appendix C

INCAPACITATION DUE TO HEMORRHAGE (BLOOD LOSS)

(Twenty [20] Seconds)

Diameter Bullet (Meplat)	Volume (Inches) 10-inches Penetration	Hemorrhage Seconds (± 0.1)
.46"	1.66	12.1
.47"	1.74	11.5
.48"	1.81	11.1
.49"	1.89	10.6
.50"	1.95	10.3
.51"	2.04	09.8
.52"	2.12	09.4
.53"	2.21	09.1
.54"	2.29	08.7
.55"	2.38	08.4
.56"	2.48	08.1
.57"	2.55	07.8
.58"	2.64	07.6
.59"	2.73	07.3
.60"	2.83	07.1

Appendix C

INCAPACITATION DUE TO HEMORRHAGE (BLOOD LOSS)

(Twenty [20] Seconds)

Diameter Bullet (Meplat)	Volume (Inches) 10-inches Penetration	Hemorrhage Seconds (± 0.1)
.61"	2.92	06.9
.62"	3.02	06.6
.63"	3.12	06.4
.64"	3.22	06.2
.65"	3.32	06.0
.66"	3.42	05.9
.67"	3.53	05.7
.68"	3.63	05.5
.69"	3.74	05.4
.70"	3.85	05.2
.714"	4.00	05.0
.72"	4.07	04.9
.73"	4.19	04.8
.74"	4.30	04.7
.75"	4.42	04.5

Appendix C

INCAPACITATION DUE TO HEMORRHAGE (BLOOD LOSS)

(Twenty [20] Seconds)

Diameter Bullet (Meplat)	Volume (Inches) 10-inches Penetration	Hemorrhage Seconds (± 0.1)
.76"	4.52	04.4
.77"	4.66	04.3
.78"	4.78	04.2
.79"	4.90	04.1
.80"	5.03	04.0
.81"	5.15	03.9
.82"	5.28	03.8
.83"	5.41	03.7
.84"	5.54	03.6
.85"	5.68	03.5
.86"	5.81	03.4
.87"	5.95	03.4
.88"	6.08	03.3
.89"	6.22	03.2
.90"	6.36	03.2

Appendix D

INCAPACITATION DUE TO HEMORRHAGE (BLOOD LOSS)

(Thirty [30] Seconds)

Diameter Bullet (Meplat)	Volume (Inches) 10-inches Penetration	Hemorrhage Seconds (± 0.1)
.224"	0.40	75.0
.251"	0.50	60.0
.312"	0.77	40.0
.355"	0.99	30.3
.357"	**1.00**	**30.0 (Given)**
.36"	1.02	29.4
.37"	1.08	27.8
.38"	1.13	26.6
.39"	1.20	25.0
.40"	1.26	23.8
.41"	1.32	22.7
.42"	1.39	21.6
.43"	1.45	20.7
.44"	1.52	19.7
.451"	1.60	18.8

Appendix D

INCAPACITATION DUE TO HEMORRHAGE (BLOOD LOSS)

(Thirty [30] Seconds)

Diameter Bullet (Meplat)	Volume (Inches) 10-inches Penetration	Hemorrhage Seconds (± 0.1)
.46"	1.66	18.1
.47"	1.74	17.2
.48"	1.81	16.6
.49"	1.89	15.9
.50"	1.95	15.4
.51"	2.04	14.7
.52"	2.12	14.2
.53"	2.21	13.6
.54"	2.29	13.1
.55"	2.38	12.6
.56"	2.46	12.2
.57"	2.55	11.8
.58"	2.64	11.4
.59"	2.73	11.0
.60"	2.83	10.6

Appendix D

INCAPACITATION DUE TO HEMORRHAGE (BLOOD LOSS)

(Thirty [30] Seconds)

Diameter Bullet (Meplat)	Volume (Inches) 10-inches Penetration	Hemorrhage Seconds (± 0.1)
.61"	2.92	10.3
.62"	3.02	09.9
.63"	3.12	09.6
.64"	3.22	09.3
.65"	3.32	09.0
.66"	3.42"	08.8
.67"	3.53	08.5
.68"	3.63	08.3
.69"	3.74	08.0
.70"	3.85	07.8
.714"	4.00	07.5
.72"	4.07	07.4
.73"	4.19	07.2
.74"	4.30	07.0
.75"	4.42	06.8

Appendix D

INCAPACITATION DUE TO HEMORRHAGE (BLOOD LOSS)

(Thirty [30] Seconds)

Diameter Bullet (Meplat)	Volume (Inches) 10-inches Penetration	Hemorrhage Seconds (± 0.1)
.76"	4.54	06.6
.77"	4.66	06.4
.78"	4.78	06.3
.79"	4.90	06.1
.80"	5.03	06.0
.81"	5.15	05.8
.82"	5.28	05.7
.83"	5.41	05.6
.84"	5.54	05.4
.85"	5.68	05.3
.86"	5.81	05.2
.87"	5.95	05.0
.88"	6.08	04.9
.89"	6.22	04.8
.90"	6.36	04.7

Appendix E

INCAPACITATION DUE TO HEMORRHAGE (BLOOD LOSS)

(Two Hundred Forty [240] Seconds)

Diameter Bullet (Meplat)	Volume (Inches) 10-inches Penetration	Hemorrhage Seconds (± 0.1)
.224"	0.40	1812.3
.251"	0.50	1449.8
.312"	0.77	941.4
.355"	0.99	732.2
.357"	1.00	724.9
.36"	1.02	710.7
.37"	1.08	671.2
.38"	1.13"	641.5
.39"	1.20"	604.1
.40"	1.26"	575.3
.41"	1.32"	549.2
.42"	1.39"	521.5
.43"	1.45"	499.9
.44"	1.52"	476.9
.451"	1.60"	453.1

Appendix E

INCAPACITATION DUE TO HEMORRHAGE (BLOOD LOSS)

(Two Hundred Forty [240] Seconds)

Diameter Bullet (Meplat)	Volume (Inches) 10-inches Penetration	Hemorrhage Seconds (± 0.1)
.46"	1.66"	436.7
.47"	1.74"	416.6
.48"	1.81"	400.5
.49"	1.89"	383.6
.50"	1.95"	371.7
.51"	2.05"	353.6
.52"	2.12"	341.9
.53"	2.21"	328.0
.54"	2.29	316.6
.55"	2.38	304.6
.56"	2.46	294.7
.57"	2.55	284.3
.58"	2.64	274.6
.59"	2.73	265.5
.60"	2.83	256.2

George B. Bredsten

Appendix E

INCAPACITATION DUE TO HEMORRHAGE (BLOOD LOSS)

(Two Hundred Forty [240] Seconds)

Diameter Bullet (Meplat)	Volume (Inches) 10-inches Penetration	Hemorrhage Seconds (± 0.1)
.61"	2.92	248.3
.62"	**3.02**	**240.0 (Given)**
.63"	3.12	232.3
.64"	3.22	225.1
.65"	3.32	218.3
.66"	3.42	212.0
.67"	3.53	205.4
.68"	3.63	199.7
.69"	3.74	193.8
.70"	3.85	188.3
.714"	4.00	181.2
.72"	4.07	178.1
.73"	4.19	173.0
.74"	4.30	168.6
.75"	4.42	164.0

Appendix E

INCAPACITATION DUE TO HEMORRHAGE (BLOOD LOSS)

(Two Hundred Forty [240] Seconds)

Diameter Bullet (Meplat)	Volume (Inches) 10-inches Penetration	Hemorrhage Seconds (± 0.1)
.76"	4.52	160.4
.77"	4.66	155.6
.78"	4.78	151.7
.79"	4.90	147.9
.80"	5.03	144.1
.81"	5.15	140.8
.82"	5.28	137.3
.83"	5.41	134.0
.84"	5.54	130.9
.85"	5.68	127.6
.86"	5.81	124.8
.87"	5.95	121.8
.88"	6.08	119.2
.89"	6.22	116.5
.90"	6.36	114.0

George B. Bredsten

Appendix F

INCAPACITATION DUE TO HEMORRHAGE (BLOOD LOSS)

(Three Hundred [300] Seconds)

Diameter Bullet (Meplat)	Volume (Inches) 10-inches Penetration	Hemorrhage Seconds (± 0.1)
.224"	0.40	2265.0
.251"	0.50	1812.0
.312"	0.77	1176.6
.355"	0.99	915.2
.357"	1.00	906.0
.36"	1.02	888.2
.37"	1.08	838.9
.38"	1.13	801.8
.39"	1.20	755.0
.40"	1.26	719.1
.41"	1.32	686.4
.42"	1.39	651.8
.43"	1.45	624.8
.44"	1.52	596.1
.451"	1.60	566.3

Appendix F

INCAPACITATION DUE TO HEMORRHAGE (BLOOD LOSS)

(Three Hundred [300] Seconds)

Diameter Bullet (Meplat)	Volume (Inches) 10-inches Penetration	Hemorrhage Seconds (± 0.1)
.46"	1.66	545.8
.47"	1.74	520.7
.48"	1.81	500.6
.49"	1.89	479.4
.50"	1.95	464.6
.51"	2.05	442.0
.52"	2.12	427.4
.53"	2.21	410.0
.54"	2.29	395.6
.55"	2.38	380.7
.56"	2.46	368.3
.57"	2.55	355.3
.58"	2.64	343.2
.59"	2.73	331.9
.60"	2.83	320.1

Appendix F

INCAPACITATION DUE TO HEMORRHAGE (BLOOD LOSS)

(Three Hundred [300] Seconds)

Diameter Bullet (Meplat)	Volume (Inches) 10-inches Penetration	Hemorrhage Seconds (± 0.1)
.61"	2.92	310.3
.62"	**3.02**	**300.0 (Given)**
.63"	3.12	290.4
.64"	3.22	281.4
.65"	3.32	272.9
.66"	3.42	264.9
.67"	3.53	256.7
.68"	3.63	249.6
.69"	3.74	242.3
.70"	3.85	235.3
.714"	4.00	226.5
.72"	4.07	222.6
.73"	4.19	216.2
.74"	4.30	210.7
.75"	4.42	205.0

Appendix F

INCAPACITATION DUE TO HEMORRHAGE (BLOOD LOSS)

(Three Hundred [300] Seconds)

Diameter Bullet (Meplat)	Volume (Inches) 10-inches Penetration	Hemorrhage Seconds (± 0.1)
.76"	4.52	200.4
.77"	4.66	194.4
.78"	4.78	189.5
.79"	4.90	184.9
.80"	5.03	180.1
.81"	5.15	175.9
.82"	5.28	171.6
.83"	5.41	167.5
.84"	5.54	163.5
.85"	5.68	159.5
.86"	5.81	155.9
.87"	5.95	152.3
.88"	6.08	149.0
.89"	6.22	145.7
.90"	6.36	142.5

Appendix G

HATCHER'S RELATIVE STOPPING POWER (RSP)

VARIOUS HANDGUN LOADS

Before the reader begins to assess, compare and/or possibly select a cartridge (load) from among the various RSP values that follow, it is important to realize:

1. RSP values are NOT values that indicate the percentage probability of a particular bullet achieving a one-shot stop. The RSP values are relative; e.g., a RSP value of 50 is one-half of a RSP value of 100 or a RSP value of 100 is twice that of a RSP value of 50. Those numbers, by themselves, reveal little as to the PROBABLE relative percentages of achieved effective stopping power.

   However, the vast majority of researched material that evaluated cartridges AND cited numerous incidents as evidence, indicated the 45 ACP (military hard ball load) achieves about <u>ninety (90) percent</u> one-shot stops with <u>proper</u> shot (bullet) placement. That load rates a RSP value of about **sixty (60)**. By comparison, the 38 Spl (158 gr RNL) loads used for many years by law enforcement personnel and the 9mm Luger (military/civilian 115/124 gr FMJ) loads achieve one-shot stops about <u>fifty (50) percent</u> of the time. Both of these cartridges have RSP values of approximately **thirty (30)**.

2. It is important for the reader to ALSO consider the comparative penetration potential of the various loads (bullets). **See Appendix A.** But, whatever load is chosen and whatever degree of expansion occurs – a penetration potential value of about 1700 (± 50) should be considered to be a realistic minimum. This minimum penetration potential value is considered to be sufficient in that adequate bullet penetration should occur not only from a direct frontal shot, but also if the penetration angle is oblique or if an intervening object (e.g., arm) must first be perforated. Finally, a prudent choice would be a handgun cartridge (load) that has a RSP value of at least <u>sixty (60)</u> and a penetration potential value of <u>1700 (± 50)</u>. This would provide the maximum allowable bullet expansion *combined* with an acceptable minimum depth of bullet penetration

Appendix G

HATCHER'S RELATIVE STOPPING POWER (RSP)

VARIOUS HANDGUN LOADS

Cartridge	Bullet Weight Velocity & Energy	Bullet Diameter	CSA Inches	Bullet Momentum	BSF	RSP Value
25 Auto	050 – 0760 – 0065 (JRN)	1.0 (.251")	0.049	0.086	0900	**003.8**
		1.5 (.376")	0.111	0.086	0900	008.6
		1.75 (.439")	0.151	0.086	0900	011.7
30 Carbine	110 – 1400 – 0479 (JRN)	1.0 (.308")	0.075	0.342	0900	**023.1**
		1.5 (.462")	0.168	0.342	0900	051.7
		1.75 (.539")	0.228	0.342	0900	070.2
32 Auto	067 – 0950 – 0130 (JLFN)	1.0 (.312")	0.076	0.137	1050	**010.9**
		1.5 (.468")	0.172	0.137	1050	024.7
		1.75 (.546")	0.234	0.137	1050	033.7
380 Auto	090 – 1000 – 0200 (JLFN)	1.0 (.355")	0.099	0.200	1050	**020.8**
		1.5 (.533")	0.223	0.200	1050	046.8
		1.75 (.621")	0.303	0.200	1050	063.6
9mm Luger	115 – 1225 – 0383 (JLFN)	1.0 (.355")	0.099	0.313	1050	**032.5**
		1.5 (.533")	0.223	0.313	1050	073.3
		1.75 (.621")	0.303	0.313	1050	099.6
9mm Luger	147 – 1010 – 0333 (JLFN)	1.0 (.355")	0.099	0.330	1050	**034.3**
		1.5 (.533")	0.223	0.330	1050	077.3
		1.75 (.621")	0.303	0.330	1050	105.0
38 Super +P	125 – 1240 – 0427 (JLFN)	1.0 (.355")	0.099	0.344	1050	**035.8**
		1.5 (.533")	0.223	0.344	1050	080.6
		1.75 (.621")	0.303	0.344	1050	109.4

George B. Bredsten

Appendix G

HATCHER'S RELATIVE STOPPING POWER (RSP)

VARIOUS HANDGUN LOADS

Cartridge	Bullet Weight Velocity & Energy	Bullet Diameter	CSA Inches	Bullet Momentum	BSF	**RSP Value**
357 SIG	125 – 1350 – 0510 (JLFN)	1.0 (.355")	0.099	0.378	1050	**039.3**
		1.5 (.533")	0.223	0.378	1050	088.5
		1.75 (.621")	0.303	0.378	1050	120.3
38 Spl	148 – 0710 – 0166 (LWC)	1.0 (.357")	0.100	0.234	1250	**029.3**
		1.5 (.536")	0.226	0.234	1250	066.1
		1.75 (.625")	0.307	0.234	1250	089.8
38 Spl	158 – 0755 – 0200 (LRN)	1.0 (.357")	0.100	0.265	1000	**026.5**
		1.5 (.536")	0.226	0.265	1000	059.9
		1.75 (.625")	0.307	0.265	1000	081.4
38 Spl +P	158 – 0890 – 0270 (LSWC)	1.0 (.357")	0.100	0.303	1250	**037.9**
		1.5 (.536")	0.226	0.303	1250	085.6
		1.75 (.625")	0.307	0.303	1250	116.3
357 Magnum	125 – 1450 – 0584 (JLFN)	1.0 (.357")	0.100	0.403	1050	**042.3**
		1.5 (.536")	0.226	0.403	1050	095.6
		1.75 (.625")	0.307	0.403	1050	129.9
357 Magnum	145 – 1290 – 0535 (JLFN)	1.0 (.357")	0.100	0.415	1050	**043.6**
		1.5 (.536")	0.226	0.415	1050	098.5
		1.75 (.625")	0.307	0.415	1050	133.8
357 Magnum	158 – 1235 – 0535 (JLFN)	1.0 (.357")	0.100	0.433	1050	**045.5**
		1.5 (.536")	0.226	0.433	1050	102.8
		1.75 (.625")	0.307	0.433	1050	139.6

Appendix G

HATCHER'S RELATIVE STOPPING POWER (RSP)

VARIOUS HANDGUN LOADS

Cartridge	Bullet Weight Velocity & Energy	Bullet Diameter	CSA Inches	Bullet Momentum	BSF	RSP Value
40 S&W	155 – 1205 – 0500 (JLFN)	1.0 (.400")	0.126	0.415	1050	**054.9**
		1.5 (.600")	0.282	0.415	1050	122.9
		1.75 (.700")	0.385	0.415	1050	167.8
40 S&W	165 – 1130 – 0468 (JLFN)	1.0 (.400")	0.126	0.414	1050	**054.8**
		1.5 (.600")	0.282	0.414	1050	122.6
		1.75 (.700")	0.385	0.414	1050	167.4
40 S&W	180 – 1010 – 0408 (JLFN)	1.0 (.400")	0.126	0.404	1050	**053.5**
		1.5 (.600")	0.282	0.404	1050	119.6
		1.75 (.700")	0.385	0.404	1050	163.3
10mm Auto	175 – 1290 – 0649 (JLFN)	1.0 (.400")	0.126	0.503	1050	**066.6**
		1.5 (.600")	0.282	0.503	1050	148.9
		1.75 (.700")	0.385	0.503	1050	203.3
41 Rem Mag	175 – 1250 – 0607 (JLFN)	1.0 (.410")	0.132	0.486	1050	**067.4**
		1.5 (.615")	0.297	0.486	1050	151.6
		1.75 (.738")	0.428	0.486	1050	218.4
41 Rem Mag	240 – 1250 – 0833 (LLFN)	1.0 (.410")	0.132	0.666	1100	**096.7**
		1.5 (.615")	0.297	0.666	1100	217.6
		1.75 (.738")	0.428	0.666	1100	313.6
44-40 Win	225 – 0750 – 0281 (LLFN)	1.0 (.426")	0.143	0.375	1100	**059.0**
		1.5 (.639")	0.321	0.375	1100	132.4
		1.75 (.746")	0.437	0.375	1100	180.3

George B. Bredsten

Appendix G

HATCHER'S RELATIVE STOPPING POWER (RSP)

VARIOUS HANDGUN LOADS

Cartridge	Bullet Weight Velocity & Energy	Bullet Diameter	CSA Inches	Bullet Momentum	BSF	**RSP Value**
44 S&W Spl	200 – 0900 – 0360 (JLFN)	1.0 (.429")	0.145	0.400	1050	**060.9**
		1.5 (.644")	0.326	0.400	1050	136.9
		1.75 (.751")	0.443	0.400	1050	186.1
44 S&W Spl	246 – 0755 – 0310 (LRN)	1.0 (.429")	0.145	0.411	1000	**059.6**
		1.5 (.644")	0.326	0.411	1000	134.0
		1.75 (.751")	0.443	0.411	1000	182.1
44 Rem Mag	210 – 1250 – 0729 (JLFN)	1.0 (.429")	0.145	0.583	1050	**088.8**
		1.5 (.644")	0.326	0.583	1050	199.6
		1.75 (.751")	0.443	0.583	1050	271.2
44 Rem Mag	240 – 1180 – 0741 (JLFN)	1.0 (.429")	0.145	0.628	1050	**095.6**
		1.5 (.644")	0.326	0.628	1050	215.0
		1.75 (.751")	0.443	0.628	1050	291.1
44 Rem Mag	250 – 1250 – 0867 (JLFN)	1.0 (.429")	0.145	0.694	1050	**105.7**
		1.5 (.644")	0.326	0.694	1050	237.6
		1.75 (.751")	0.443	0.694	1050	322.8
44 Rem Mag	300 – 1250 – 1040 (LLFN)	1.0 (.429")	0.145	0.832	1100	**132.7**
		1.5 (.644")	0.326	0.832	1100	298.4
		1.75 (.751")	0.443	0.832	1100	405.4
45 GAP	230 – 0880 – 0396 (JLFN)	1.0 (.451")	0.160	0.450	1050	**075.6**
		1.5 (.677")	0.360	0.450	1050	170.1
		1.75 (.789")	0.489	0.450	1050	231.1

Appendix G

HATCHER'S RELATIVE STOPPING POWER (RSP)

VARIOUS HANDGUN LOADS

Cartridge	Bullet Weight Velocity & Energy	Bullet Diameter	CSA Inches	Bullet Momentum	BSF	RSP Value
45 Auto	185 – 1000 – 0411 (JLFN)	1.0 (.451")	0.160	0.411	1050	**069.1**
		1.5 (.677")	0.360	0.411	1050	155.4
		1.75 (.789")	0.489	0.411	1050	211.0
45 Auto	**230 – 0812 – 0337** (JRN)	1.0 (.451")	0.160	0.415	0900	**059.8**
		1.5 (.677")	0.360	0.415	0900	134.5
		1.75 (.789")	0.489	0.415	0900	182.6
45 Auto +P	185 – 1140 – 0534 (JLFN)	1.0 (.451")	0.160	0.468	1050	**078.6**
		1.5 (.677")	0.360	0.468	1050	176.9
		1.75 (.789")	0.489	0.468	1050	240.1
45 Colt	250 – 0750 – 0312 (LSFN)	1.0 (.451")	0.160	0.416	1050	**069.9**
		1.5 (.677")	0.360	0.416	1050	157.3
		1.75 (.789")	0.489	0.416	1050	213.6
45 Colt	255 – 0860 – 0420 (LSFN)	1.0 (.451")	0.160	0.488	1050	**082.0**
		1.5 (.677")	0.360	0.488	1050	184.5
		1.75 (.789")	0.489	0.488	1050	250.6
454 Casull	260 – 1800 – 1871 (JLFN)	1.0 (.451")	0.160	1.039	1050	**174.5**
		1.5 (.677")	0.360	1.039	1050	392.7
		1.75 (.789")	0.489	1.039	1050	533.5
454 Casull	300 – 1625 – 1759 (JLFN)	1.0 (.451")	0.160	1.083	1050	**181.9**
		1.5 (.677")	0.360	1.083	1050	409.4
		1.75 (.789")	0.489	1.083	1050	556.1

George B. Bredsten

Appendix G

HATCHER'S RELATIVE STOPPING POWER (RSP)

VARIOUS HANDGUN LOADS

Cartridge	Bullet Weight Velocity & Energy	Bullet Diameter	CSA Inches	Bullet Momentum	BSF	**RSP Value**
480 Ruger	325 – 1350 – 1315 (JLFN)	1.0 (.475")	0.177	0.974	1050	**181.0**
		1.5 (.713")	0.399	0.974	1050	408.1
		1.75 (.831")	0.542	0.974	1050	554.3
50 AE	300 – 1550 – 1600 (JLFN)	1.0 (.500")	0.196	1.032	1050	**212.4**
		1.5 (.750")	0.442	1.032	1050	479.0
		1.75 (.875")	0.601	1.032	1050	651.2
500 S&W	400 – 1800 – 2877 (JLFN)	1.0 (.500")	0.196	1.598	1050	**328.9**
		1.5 (.750")	0.442	1.598	1050	741.6
		1.75 (.875")	0.601	1.598	1050	1008.4
500 S&W	500 – 1425 – 2254 (JLFN)	1.0 (.500")	0.196	1.582	1050	**325.6**
		1.5 (.750")	0.442	1.582	1050	734.2
		1.75 (.875")	0.601	1.582	1050	998.3

Handgun Bullet Stopping Power

BIBLIOGRAPHY

BOOKS and MANUALS

ACKLEY, P. O. *Handbook for Shooters And Reloaders*. Salt Lake City, Utah: Ackley, Spiral Bound, No date of publication but from dated material within the handbook probably between 1955 and 1962?

ACKLEY, P. O. *Handbook for Shooters and Reloaders, Volume I*. Salt Lake City, Utah: Publishers Press, 1962.

ACKELY, P. O. *Handbook for Shooters and Reloaders, Volume II*. Salt Lake City, Utah: Publisher Press, 1966.

ADAMS, R. J., McTERNAN, T. M. and REMSBERG, C. *Street Survival*. Northbrook, Illinois: Calibre Press, 1989.

ANDERSON, W.F., M.D. *Forensic Analysis of the April 11, 1986 FBI Firefight*. Los Angeles, California: University of Southern California School of Medicine, 1996 – 2nd printing 1997.

APPLEGATE, Rex. *Kill or Get Killed*. Boulder, Colorado: Paladin Press, 1976.

ASKINS, Charles. *The Pistol Shooter's Book*. Harrisburg, Pennsylvania: The Stackpole Company, 1953 – Second printing, 1957.

BAILLIE, W. L. *Averages, Means and the Theory of Errors*. Philadelphia, Pennsylvania: Lefax Leaf + Facts Publishing Co., Order No. 14-120, Dewey 519, undated.

BAIN, David Haward. *Sitting In Darkness – Americans in the Philippines*. Boston, Massachusetts: Houghton Mifflin Company, 1984.

BAKER, Samuel W. *Wild Beasts and Their Ways*. London, England: MacMillan and Co., 1890 – Reprinted Prescott, Arizona: Wolfe Publishing Company (limited edition of 1000), 1988.

BOWDEN, Mark. *Black Hawk Down*. NYC, New York: Published by New American Library, a division of Penguin Putnam Inc., 2001.

BREDSTEN, George, HILLEGASS, John and DEMPSEY, Ron. *Semiautomatic Pistol Ammunition and Ballistics, Lesson Plan 6093.02, rev. ed.* Glynco, Georgia: Federal Law Enforcement Training Center/Firearms Division, 1994.

BREDSTEN, George and HILLEGASS, John. *Ballistics Workbook & Calculator*. Glynco, Georgia: Federal Law Enforcement Training Center/Firearms Division, 1998.

BREDSTEN, George, et al. *Handgun Ammunition Test Number: HG/DEP/1999*. Glynco, Georgia: Federal Law Enforcement Training Center/Firearms Division, 1999.

BREDSTEN, George, et al. *Handgun Ammunition (Non-Toxic, Lead Free and/or Frangible) Test Number: NT/DEP/2000.* Glynco, Georgia: Federal Law Enforcement Training Center/Firearms Division, 2000.

BRISTOW, Allen P. *The Search for an Effective Police Handgun.* Springfield, Illinois: Charles C. Thomas Publisher, 1973.

BROWNLEE, Richard S. – *Gray Ghosts of the Confederacy – Guerrilla Warfare in the West 1861-1865.* Baton Rouge, Louisiana: Louisiana State University Press, 1958 – 6th printing 1990.

BRUCHEY, William J. Jr. and FRANK, Daniel E. *Police Handgun Ammunition: Incapacitation Effects.* Boulder Colorado, Paladin Press, Undated (post 1981).

BURCH, John P. *A True Story of Chas. W. Quantrell.* Vega, Texas: J. P. Burch, 1923.

CASSIDY, William L. *Quick or Dead.* Boulder, Colorado: Paladin Press, 1976.

CASTEL, Albert and GOODRICH, Thomas. *Bloody Bill Anderson, The Short, Savage Life of a Civil War Guerrilla.* Mechanicsburg, Pennsylvania: Stackpole Books, 1998.

CHAPEL, Charles E. *Guns of the Old West.* New York: Coward-McCann, Inc., 1961 – Special Edition privately printed by Odysseus Editions, Inc. for the National Rifle Association, 1995.

CHAPUT, Donald. *Virgil Earp, Western Peace Officer.* Norman, Oklahoma: University of Oklahoma Press, 1994 – First Oklahoma Press printing, 1996.

COOPER, Jeff, et al. *The Complete Book of Modern Handgunning*. Englewood Cliffs, New Jersey: Prentice-Hall, 1961.

COOPER, Jeff, *To Ride, Shoot Straight, and Speak the Truth*. Paulden, Arizona: Gunsite Press, 1988.

CUNNINGHAM, Eugene. *Triggernometry: A Gallery of Gunfighters*. Caldwell, Idaho: The Caxton Printers, Ltd., 1941 – Sixth printing, 1952.

DAVIS, Richard C. *Now Over 550 Second Chance "Saves."* Central Lake, Michigan: Second Chance Body Armor Co., Undated.

DiMAIO, Vincent J., M.D. *Gunshot Wounds*. New York: Elsevier Science, 1985.

DOBBYN, R. C. and BRUCHEY, W. J. *An Evaluation of Police Handgun Ammunition: Summary Report (LESP-RPT-0101.01 October 1975)*. Washington, DC.: U.S. Government Printing Office, 1976.

DOBSON, Christopher and PAYNE, R. *The Terrorists: Their Weapons, Leaders and Tactics*. NYC, New York: Facts on File, Inc., 1982.

FACKLER, M. L., M.D. *What's Wrong with the Wound Ballistics Literature?* San Francisco, California: Letterman Institute, Report Number 239, 1987.

FAIRBAIRN, W. E. and SYKES, E. A. *Shooting to Live*. Boulder, Colorado: Paladin Press (originally published 1942?), Undated.

FINCEL, E. *Wound Ballistics Workshop Presentations*. FBI Academy, January 19-22, 1993.

FIREARMS DIVISION/FEDERAL LAW ENFORCEMENT TRAINING CENTER. *Ammunition Glossary*. Glynco, Georgia: Federal Law Enforcement Training Center/Firearms Division, undated.

FITZGERALD, J. Henry. *Shooting*. Harford, Connecticut: G. F. Book Company, 1930.

FORD, Roger and Ripley, Tim. *The White of Their Eyes: Close-Quarter Combat*. Dulles, Virginia: Brassey's Inc., 2001.

FROMM, Erich. *The Anatomy of Human Destructiveness*. New York: Holt, Rinehart and Winston, 1973.

GAYLORD, Chic. *Handgunner's Guide*. NYC, New York: Hastings House, 1960.

GRANT, Matt and GRANT, Bruce. *The Sharp Shooter*. Wellington, Sydney, London: A. H. & A. W. Reed, Ltd., 1972.

GROSSMAN, Dave, Lt. Col. *On Killing: The Psychological Cost of Learning to Kill in War and Society*. New York: Back Bay Books – Little Brown and Company, 1996.

HATCHER, Julian S. Textbook of Pistols and Revolvers. Small Arms Technical Publishing Company, 1935 – Reprinted Prescott, Arizona: Wolfe Publishing, 1985.

___. *Hatcher's Notebook*. Harrisburg, Pennsylvania: The Stackpole Company, 1962.

HERNON, Peter. *A Terrible Thunder*. Garden City, New York: Doubleday & Co., Inc. 1978

JORDAN, William H. *No Second Place Winner*. Copyright 1965 by W. H. Jordon, 3840 Creswell Avenue, Shreveport, Louisiana, 71106.

JOSSERAND, M. H. and STEVENSON, Jan A. *Pistols, Revolvers and Ammunition*. NYC. New York: Crown Publishers Inc., 1972.

KAUFFMAN, Michael W. *American Brutus*. New York: Random House, 2004.

KEITH, Elmer. Sixgun Cartridges and Loads. Plantersville, South Carolina: Samworth, 1936.

___. *Big Game Rifles and Cartridges*. Plantersville, South Carolina: Samworth, 1936.

___. *Keith's Rifles for Large Game*. Huntington, West Virginia: Standard Publications, 1946.

___. ***Sixguns*. Harrisburg, Pennsylvania: Stackpole, 1955.**

KUHN, Karl F. *Basic Physics*. New York: John Wiley and Sons, Inc., 1979.

LaGARDE, Louis A., Col. *Gunshot Injuries.* **New York: Wm. Wood & Co., 1916 – Second Edition, Mt. Ida., Arkansas: Lancer Militaria, 1991.**

LEE, Wayne C. *Bad Men & Bad Towns.* Caldwell, Idaho: Caxton Printers, Ltd., 1993.

MacPherson, Duncan. *Bullet Penetration: Modeling the Dynamics and the Incapacitation Resulting from Wound Trauma.* **El Segundo, California: Ballistic Publications, 1994.**

MANGOLD, Tom and PENYCATE, John. *The Tunnels of Cu Chi.* New York: Random House, 1985.

MARCINKO, Richard with WEISMAN, John. *Rogue Warrior.* NYC, New York: Pocket Books, a Division of Simon & Schuster, Inc., 1992.

MARSHALL, Evan P. and SANOW, Edwin J. *Handgun Stopping Power.* Boulder, Colorado: Paladin Press, 1992.

___. *Street Stoppers.* Boulder, Colorado: Paladin Press, 1996.

___. *Stopping Power: A Practical Analysis of the Latest Handgun Ammunition.* Boulder Colorado: Paladin Press, 2001.

MARTIN, Douglas D. *The Earps of Tombstone.* Tombstone, Arizona: Tombstone Epitaph, 1959.

MASON, James D. *Combat Handgun Shooting.* Springfield, Illinois: Thomas, 1976.

MATUNAS, Edward. *American Ammunition and Ballistics.* Tulsa, Oklahoma: Winchester Press, 1979.

___. *American Ammo: Selection, Use, Ballistics.* Danbury, Connecticut: Grolier Book Clubs, 1989.

McLOUGHLIN, D. *Wild and Woolly – An Encyclopedia of the Old West.* New York: Barnes & Noble Books, 1995.

MENNINGER, Bonar. *Mortal Error: The Shot That Killed JFK.* New York: St Martin's Press, 1992.

MULLIN, Timothy John. *Training the Gunfighter*. Boulder, Colorado: Paladin Press, 1981.

MURRAY, I. MacKay, M.D. *Human Anatomy Made Simple*. Garden City, New York: Doubleday & Company, 1969.

MYERS, JOHN Myers. *Doc Holliday*. Boston, Massachusetts: Little Brown & Co., 1955.

McGIVERN, Ed. *Fast & Fancy Revolver Shooting*. Chicago, Illinois: Follett Publishing Co., Anniversary Edition, 1975.

McHENRY, Roy C. and ROPER, Walter F. *Smith & Wesson Hand Guns*. Huntington, West Virginia: Standard Publications Incorporated, 1945.

NOGUCHI, Thomas T., M.D. *Coroner at Large*. NYC, New York: Simon & Schuster, 1985.

NONTE, George. *Combat Handguns*. Harrisburg, Pennsylvania: Stackpole Books, 1980.

O'BRIEN, C. Smith, Dr. *Position Paper, Incapacitation Effectiveness 9mm vs. 45 ACP*. Wound Ballistics Workshop, FBI Academy, 1987.

O'NEAL, Bill. *Encyclopedia of Western Gunfighters*. Norman, Oklahoma: University of Oklahoma Press, 1979 – Third printing, 1983.

PATRICK, Urey W. *Handgun Wounding Factors and Effectiveness*. Quantico, Virginia: FBI Academy, Firearms Training Unit, 1989.

PATTERSON, Richard. *Historical Atlas of the Outlaw West*. Boulder, Colorado: Johnson, 1985.

PETERS, Carroll E. *Defensive Handgun Effectiveness*. Copyright 1977 by Carroll Peters, Manchester, Tennessee 37355.

POTOCKI, John. *The Colt Model 1905 Automatic Pistol*. Lincoln, R.I.: Andrew Mowbray Publishers, 1998.

PRASSEL, Frank, Richard. *The Western Peace Officer*. Norman, Oklahoma: University of Oklahoma Press, 1972 – Third printing, 1981.

RAINE, William MacLeod. *Guns of the Frontier*. Boston, Massachusetts: Houghton Mifflin Company (The Riverside Press Cambridge), 1940.

REESE II, Michael. *1900 Luger U.S. Test Trials*. Union City, Tennessee: Pioneer Press, rev. ed., 1976.

REMSBERG, Charles. *The Tactical Edge*. Northbrook, Illinois: Calibre Press, 1986.

RINKER, Robert A. *Understanding Ballistics*. Corydon, Indiana: Mulberry House Publishing House Co., 1995 – Second revised edition, 1998.

ROBERTSON, Frank G. and HARRIS, Beth K. *Soapy Smith – King of the Frontier Con Men*. NYC, New York: Hastings House, 1961.

ROOSEVELT, Kermit. *The Happy Hunting-Grounds (1920)*. New York: Barnes and Noble Publishing, 2004.

ROOSEVELT, Theodore. *Hunting Trips of A Ranchman (1885) & The Wilderness Hunter (1893)*. New York, New York: Modern Library, 1998.

ROSA, JOSEPH G. *The Gunfighter: Man or Myth*. Norman, Oklahoma: University of Oklahoma Press, 1969.

SHIDELER, Dan, ed., *The Gun Digest of Semi-Auto Pistols*. Iola, Wisconsin: KP Books, 2005.

SCHOENBERGER, Dale T. *The Gunfighters*. Caldwell, Idaho: Caxton Printers, Ltd., 1971.

SCHULTZ, Duane. *Quantrill's War: The Life and Times of William Clarke Quantrill*. New York, New York: St. Martin's Press, 1996.

SIMMONS, Marc. *When Six-Guns Ruled*. Santa Fe, New Mexico: Ancient City Press, 1990.

SMITH, Veral. *Jacketed Performance with Cast Bullets*. Moyie Springs, Idaho: LBT, 1984 – Third Edition, 1990.

SPURR, Russell. *Enter the Dragon*. New York: Newmarket Press, 1988.

STEBBINS, HENRY M., et al. *Pistols a Modern Encyclopedia*. Harrisburg, Pennsylvania: Stackpole Books, 1961.

STEVENSON, R. Scott, ed., *The Universal Home Doctor*. Englewood Cliffs, New Jersey: Prentice-Hall, Inc., 1965 – Second printing 1968.

TAYLOR, John. *African Rifles and Cartridges*. Harrisburg, Pennsylvania: The Stackpole Company, 1948.

TANNER, Karen Holliday. *Doc Holliday A Family Portrait*. Norman, Oklahoma: University of Oklahoma, 1998.

TEIXEIRA, Bernardo. *The Fabric of Terror: Three Days in Angola*. New York: Devin-Adair Co., 1965.

TORREY, E. Fuller, M.D. *Frontier Justice: The Rise and Fall of the Loomis Gang*. Utica, New York: North Country Books, Inc., 1992.

TOWLAND, John. *In Mortal Combat*. NYC, New York: William Morrow and Company, Inc., 1991.

TRAHTMAN, Paul. *The Gunfighters*. Alexandria, Virginia: Time-Life Books, 1974 – Fifth Printing, Revised, 1977.

TRAYWICK, Ben T. *John Henry Holliday Tombstone's Deadliest Gun*. Tombstone, Arizona: Red Marie's, 1984.

___. *Tombstone Outlaw Album*. Tombstone, Arizona: Red Marie's, 1984.

___. *The Residents of Tombstone's Boothill*. Tombstone, Arizona: Red Marie's, 1st Edition, 1971.

TROTTER, William R. *Bushwhackers: The Civil War in North Carolina The Mountains*. Winston-Salem, North Carolina: John F. Blair Publisher, 1988.

TRZONIEC, Stanley W. *Modern American Centerfire Handguns*. Tulsa, Oklahoma: Winchester Press, 1981.

TURNER, Alford E., ed., *The Earps Talk*. College Station, Texas: Creative Publishing Company, 1980.

U.S. DEPARTMENT OF JUSTICE. *Law Enforcement Officers Killed and Assaulted*. U.S. Department of Justice, Federal Bureau of Investigation, Uniform Crime Reports (annual publication), 1982 – 1995.

WALLACK, L. R. *American Pistol & Revolver Design and Performance*. NYC, New York: Winchester Press, 1978.

WELLS, Peter S. *The Battle that Stopped Rome*. New York, New York: W. W. Norton Company, 2003.

WESTON, Paul B. *Combat Shooting for Police*. Springfield, Illinois: Thomas Press, 1960.

WHELEN, Townsend. *Small Arms Design and Ballistics, Volume II – Ballistics*. Georgetown, South Carolina: Thomas G. Samworth (Small Arms Technical Publishing Company), 1946.

WINTON, F. R., M.D. and BAYLISS, L. E., PhD. *Human Physiology*. Boston, Massachusetts: Little Brown and Co., Fifth Edition, 1962.

JOURNALS or OTHER PERIODICALS

"Anglers Kill Bear, Then Swear Off Night Fishing." ALASKA 69, No. 10 (December/January 2003): p. 56.

"The Armed Citizen." AMERICAN RIFLEMAN. June 1995, 143(5):8

Associated Press, "Across the Nation, Georgia: Fort Valley." USA TODAY, December 2, 2004.

Associated Press, "Deming man, teen-ager kill each other." *SILVER CITY HERALD* (Silver City, New Mexico), 17 July 2002, pp. 1, 9.

Campbell, S. and Dunlap, M., "9mm 147 Sub-Sonic Is Alive and Well." *GUNS & WEAPONS FOR LAW ENFORCEMENT*, September 1993, 5(5):14-16.

Carman, Roderick C., "Guns of the Real Indiana Jones." GUN DIGEST 2005. Iola, Wisconsin: Krause Publications, 2004, pp. 29, 32.

DiMaio, Vincent J., M.D., et al. "A comparison of the Wounding Effects of Commercially Available Handgun Ammunition Suitable for Police Use." FBI LAW ENFORCEMENT BULLETIN, December 1974, pp. 3-8.

Fairburn, D., "Ammo Tests, Part II: You Bet Your Life." *SWAT MAGAZINE*, September 1993, 12(6):24-27, 82.

Farnam, John. "Combat Weaponcraft." SOLDIER OF FORTUNE, August 2004, p. 20.

Hackworth, D., Col., "Sound Off." SOLDIER OF FORTUNE, November 2002, p. 82.

Libourel, J., "Handgun Stopping Power." *GUNS & AMMO*, October 1992, 36(10):40-45, 97.

MacPherson, Duncan, "Relative Incapacitation BULListics." *WOUND BALLISTICS REVIEW*, Winter 1992, 1(2):12-15.

Matunas, E. A., "Loading for Maximum PIR." HANDLOADER'S DIGEST, Tenth Edition, 1984, pp. 144-152.

Miller, R., "Tales of the 45 Auto." GUNS PLUS HUNTING, May 1972, 1(6):14-17, 56.

The Reader's Digest Association, ABC's of the Human Body. Pleasantville, New York: Reader's Digest Association, Inc. 1987, pp. 92, 93.

Rutledge, L. A., "That Remarkable GI 45 Auto." *1985 HANDGUN ANNUAL*, March 1985, 2:29-37.

___. "Trial by Fire: 38s vs. Moros." 1985 HANDGUN ANNUAL, March 1985, 2:138-143.

Seyfried, Ross. "Bone-Bashing Big Game Bullets." GUNS & AMMO, January 1990, p.41.

Shulman, Terry. "Struck Down: Shock, Trauma and the Truth About Civil War Wounds." CIVIL WAR, April 1997, Issue 61, pp. 36-41.

Siemon, E., "Ammo & Stopping Power." COMBAT HANDGUNS, December 1987, pp. 52-53, 72.

___. "Ammo & Stopping Power." COMBAT HANDGUNS, February 1988, pp. 50-51, 67-68.

___. "Ammo & Stopping Power." COMBAT HANDGUNS, April 1988, pp. 56-57, 64-65.

Stolinsky, D., M.D. "Stopping Power." HANDGUN ANNUAL, Volume 3, March 1986, pp. 61-67.

Tarwacki, R., "In Defense of the 38 Special." THE NARCOFFICER, August 1990, 6(8):29, 31.

Taylor, Chuck. "Combat Corner." COMBAT HANDGUNS, June 1988. pp. 12, 13, 71.

Tobin, Ernest J. and Fackler, Martin L., M.D. "Officer Reaction-Response Times in Firing a Handgun." WOUND BALLISTICS REVIEW, 1997, 3(1):7, 8.

Walker, L., "Defense Ammo Performance." GUNS & AMMO *1992 ANNUAL*, pp. 82-88.

Walters, K., "Handgun Stopping Power." GUN DIGEST 1976 EDITION, pp. 260-263.

CHARTS and MAPS

Coxe, Wallace H. and Beugless, Edgar. EXTERIOR BALLISTIC CHARTS (Wilmington, Delaware: E. I. du Pont de Nemours & Company, Inc.), 1936.

Map Ink. OKLAHOMA OUTLAW AND LAWMAN MAP (Oklahoma City: Oklahoma Heritage Association, 1989).

UNPUBLISHED

Keith, Elmer. *Letters to the author.* Various dates: from 20 November 1961 to 04 February 1978. Author's collection.

McGee, Francis J. *Analysis of Police Combat Situations (1970-1979)*. Firearms & Tactics Section, NYC Police Department (NYPD Unpublished Report).

Rivers, David, *Homicide Case Number: 153261-G*. Metro Dade PD, Miami, Florida.

Tinney, Roy S. *Letter to the author*. 26 April 1956. Author's collection.

NONPRINT SOURCES

Cooper, Jeff. "Armed Defense, Cooper's Way." Colonel Jeff Cooper's Personal Defense Course on Video, Tape 4 (Quad Productions, Reno, Nevada, 1995).

"Deadly Weapons." Video (ANITE Productions, Pinole, California, 1985).

"Deadly Effects – Wound Ballistics." Video (ANITE Productions, Pinole, California, 1987).

* * * * *

While all of the works listed in the bibliography provided the author with varying amounts (some or much) of useful information; the titles listed in **BOLD** are recommended for additional reading for those individuals who would increase their knowledge and understanding beyond that of the basic material presented in this opuscule.

The Colt Model 1905 Automatic Pistol (Appendix A, pages 121 through 164) by John Potocki is especially recommended for those who would like to peruse the complete (less photographs and skiagrams) "*Thompson-LaGarde Report*" that was submitted to General William Crozier on March 18, 1904. A copy or copies of this book may be ordered by calling 1.800.999.4697.

George B. Bredsten

Handgun Bullet Stopping Power

About the Author

Mr. Bredsten retired from the Federal Law Enforcement Training Center/Firearms Division (FLETC/FAD). With FLETC/FAD he performed duties as a firearms instructor and he also taught ballistics to the FLETC/FAD staff and to students in the Law Enforcement Rifle Training Program and in the Precision Rifle (Sniper) and Observer Program. Subjects covered included the ballistic coefficient, barrel time, the coefficient of reduction (form), Greenhill formula (rate of rifling twist), firearm recoil, bullet time-of-flight, bullet drop, bullet midrange, wind deflection, bullet penetration potential and bullet terminal (wounding) efficacy.

At the request of various local, state and federal law enforcement agencies (e.g., Glynn County (Georgia) Sheriff's Department, the U.S. Bureau of Prisons, the U.S. Capitol Police, the BLM-NLE, the GSA-FPS and the U.S. Marshals Service) technical ballistics data was provided and/or numerous ballistics tests were conducted. Since retiring he has provided ballistics consultation service for the FLETC/FAD, the Transportation Security Agency, the Orange County (Florida) Sheriff's Department and Exxon Mobil Corporation.

Mr. Bredsten attended and completed various classes/courses relating to *firearms* (e.g., H&K MP5, Steyr Aug, Uzi, Tactical Speed Shooting and advanced shotgun) and *ballistics* (e.g., the first and second International Wound Ballistics Conferences, a Federal Law Enforcement Ammunition and Ballistics Seminar and Oehler's Ballistic Instrumentation).

Mr. Bredsten has an AA degree from Chaffey Jr. College and a BA degree from Sacramento State College and currently resides in Georgia.